The American Assembly, *Columbia University*

THE FUTURE OF
AMERICAN TRANSPORTATION

Prentice-Hall, Inc., *Englewood Cliffs, N.J.*  A SPECTRUM BOOK

PRENTICE-HALL INTERNATIONAL, INC. (*London*)
PRENTICE-HALL OF AUSTRALIA, PTY. LTD. (*Sydney*)
PRENTICE-HALL OF CANADA, LTD. (*Toronto*)
PRENTICE-HALL OF INDIA PRIVATE LIMITED (*New Delhi*)
PRENTICE-HALL OF JAPAN, INC. (*Tokyo*)

Preface

After discussing in depth many of the problems of United States surface and air carriers, sixty-five persons from twenty-one states and the District of Columbia, meeting at Arden House, Harriman, N.Y., April 15–18, 1971, in the Thirty-ninth American Assembly, concluded that our "transportation system shows increasing weakness and diminished ability to cope with near-term requirements." Pointing out that much of the railroad system is in precarious financial posture, that the airlines are under stress and the motor carriers having investment problems, they called for major changes in existing policies and asked that these changes be made quickly. The pamphlet report of the meeting may be had from The American Assembly.

This volume, designed by its editor, Ernest W. Williams, Jr., as advance reading for the Thirty-ninth American Assembly, will be used as background reading at regional Assemblies on transportation across the nation. It is also intended for the student of transportation problems in the public at large.

The opinions in the chapters which follow belong to the authors themselves and not to The American Assembly, which takes no official stand on public matters. Nor should The Jonsson Foundation, which contributed generous support to this American Assembly program, be associated with the views herein.

Clifford C. Nelson
President
The American Assembly

 Table of Contents

Ernest W. Williams, Jr., Editor
Introduction   1

1   *George W. Wilson*
    The Goals of Transportation Policy   9

2   *A. Scheffer Lang*
    Demand and Supply: The Technology of
    Transportation   41

3   *Dudley F. Pegrum*
    Restructuring the Transport System   59

4   *John L. Weller*
    Access to Capital Markets   83

5   *James C. Nelson*
    Toward Rational Price Policies   115

6   *Ernest W. Williams, Jr.*
    The Urban-Intercity Interface   155

7   *Lyle C. Fitch*
    Improving Urban Transportation   169

    Editor's Postscript   197

    Index   207

    The American Assembly   213

THE FUTURE OF
AMERICAN TRANSPORTATION

Ernest W. Williams, Jr., Editor

Introduction

The future of American transportation, hopefully, will not be an extrapolation of its recent past. If it is to be different, showing improvement rather than retrogression, then transportation must operate within a changed environment of government policy with the benefit of altered priorities. Technological improvement has continued at a rapid pace, but the application of improved technology has lagged badly in some of the major sectors of transport. Productivity in freight transport has increased more rapidly than that of industry at large, yet the financial health and physical condition of facilities of significant groups of carriers have declined badly.

The Penn Central disaster, the poor showing of the airline industry, the failure of Hennis (a large well-established motor common carrier), and the worsening emergency faced by local bus and transit operations the country over, brought the nation to a realization in 1970 that all

ERNEST W. WILLIAMS, JR., *is professor of transportation at the Graduate School of Business, Columbia University. During World War II he was chief of the Transport Division of the United States Strategic Bombing Survey. Since then he has been fiscal analyst in the United States Bureau of the Budget (1945–46), member of the New York–New Jersey Metropolitan Rapid Transit Commission, and member of the task force of the President's Advisory Commission on Transportation Policy. Professor Williams was also a member of the first Hoover Commission (task force on regulatory agencies) and Visitor to the United States Army Transportation School. He has written many books and articles on transportation policy, including (with Marvin Fair) the well-known* Economics of Transportation.

was not well in transport. These were but episodes, however, in a little noticed gradual deterioration in the earning power of rail and motor transport and a more rapid decline of urban public passenger transportation.

The railroads, still carrying 41 percent of the nation's intercity ton miles of freight, found their earnings (when adjusted for inflation) generally lower at each postwar cyclical trough with the following recovery weaker than its predecessor. The motor carrier industry, despite rapidly growing gross revenues, has seen its aggregate net income shrink. Both industries have limited access to the capital markets and must rely heavily upon reinvestment to keep their facilities abreast of technological improvement and traffic requirements. The railroads, particularly, have been compelled to accumulate deferred maintenance and to forego improvements to basic plant. Car shortages have become more severe and shortages of greater or less severity have been recorded in every year since 1939. Urban bus operations have been abandoned in increasing numbers, leaving many communities wholly without mass public transportation. Elsewhere operating subsidy has had to be added on top of long-standing subsidy of capital requirements for many such systems.

There is growing realization that the nation for a long period of time has indulged in unbalanced development of its transport systems: overemphasis of highways, marginal waterways improvement, relative neglect of airports and of urban transport facilities of all kinds, failure to use the rail technology to advantage. In less than a decade environmental features, hitherto ignored, have been brought into high visibility. Highway, airport, and some waterway construction are suddenly seen as destructive of environmental values. The auto is identified as the greatest source of air pollution. The ugliness of much development along the highways and in the urban sprawl is finally perceived. Not only the principles upon which government investment decisions in transport are made, but the structure of organization through which they are made require reexamination and reform.

The commercial transport industries, thus far, do not appear to have impeded economic growth although the expansion of their capacity may not have paced such growth. The anemia now visible in major sectors of those industries, however, gives pause to any contention that the base is sound for a resumption of national economic growth. Greater earning power is essential, especially in the regulated industries (other than pipe lines) and in local cartage operations which have experienced the same severe pressures on productivity as have intercity transport firms in their urban terminal operations.

The responsibility that public policy should bear is obscured by the fact that, as in Penn Central, there is room for criticism of a long-term history of indifferent management performance. Neither severely depressed earnings nor a business in which major functional decisions are not within the control of management, however, will prove attractive to a high order of managerial talent. The profitability of individual carriers depends heavily upon their location and route pattern and the rate of growth of the territory served. That some of the more profitable appear to be among the better managed may reflect less cause and effect than a natural conjunction of circumstances.

The transport industries, except pipe lines and most water services, are labor intensive. Railroads as a whole find 59 percent of their operating expenses to represent payments to labor. The Penn Central trustees, operating a property with inordinate proportions of passenger and terminal services, report a ratio of 66 percent. Motor carriers generally operate at 60 percent or above.

Labor in the railroad and airline industries is covered by the Railway Labor Act, a separate and different plan of national labor policy than that under which the rest of industry operates. Experience under the Act has been less than satisfactory. The railroads and the deep-sea water carriers, more than other forms of transport, are affected by the craft form of union organization and the attendant sharp demarcation of classes of work which belong to particular employee groups. Railroads, in addition, face the problem that train service employees have their rights confined to divisional bounds and to either yard or road service. Crewing standards and work rules have compelled emphasis upon the long heavy train which depreciates the quality of rail service and have inhibited adequate and flexible service in terminals and across divisional lines. Work rules, which often had excellent justification in historic conditions, have proved remarkably resistant to change. It is an anomaly that the railroad, which is the most promising candidate for operational automation next to the pipe line, is largely barred from movement in that direction. Both automated industrial railroads and transit operations exist where the systems were created *de novo*.

In an inflationary period the regulated industries are caught in a squeeze between the upward thrust of wages, characteristically without helpful change of working rules, and the control of their maximum rates. Wage settlements are frequently retroactive; rate increases cannot be sought until the wage settlement has been reached. They then encounter delay, sometimes of major proportions with respect, at least, to the full measure of price increase sought. The fault is very little with the regulatory body. The law requires justification of increases, and shippers in their thousands will insist upon "due process." Not infrequently, too, it takes longer for the carriers to agree upon the plan of price increases to be sought than it does for the regulatory agency to dispose of the applications.

Subsequent chapters will suggest that transport operates under conditions different from those of other industry; that it requires separate statutory treatment. Certain aspects of the present regulatory system, where change is thought to be appropriate, will be described. Here a brief sketch of the present regulatory plan may be appropriate as background since a large part of the book deals with issues that arise out of regulation.

TRANSPORT REGULATION

Most regulation of business is retrospective—that is, businesses are free to change their prices, undertake mergers, and execute other policies subject to possible challenge after the event. Transport regulation, for the most part, is prospective. Common carriers must publish, file, and post their rates and may charge no other rate than that lawfully on file and in effect on the date when the movement commenced. Rates may be changed only by tariff reissue or supplement on statutory notice—that is, filing and posting 30 days in advance of effective date unless special permission is secured for shorter notice. Tariff filings naming changes in rates, rules, or regulations may be suspended, generally for seven months, for investigation of their lawfulness. Meanwhile the former rates remain in effect. Rates must be just and reasonable and not unjustly discriminatory, and just and reasonable classifications of freight must be maintained. The commission may prescribe the minimum, the maximum, or the actual rate in the place of any found unlawful, and such orders may remain in effect indefinitely. In the case of rates that have gone into effect without suspension, reparations may be awarded if a rate is subsequently found, on complaint, to be in excess of a lawful rate. Carriers are entitled, under section 5a of the Interstate Commerce Act, to make rates by group agreement without risk of antitrust prosecution. They do this through rate bureaus in which representatives of the member carriers vote upon rate changes and through which the great bulk of rates are published. The regulatory plan propositions that rates will be made for territorial groups of carriers, i.e., that they will tend to reflect average conditions and revenue needs.

Carriers may not issue securities, either debt or equity, without prior approval of the appropriate regulatory body which may prescribe the terms and conditions of an offering. New carriers, except pipe lines, may not enter the regulated transport business nor existing carriers expand the area of their service in interstate commerce, nor in intrastate commerce in many of the states, without first applying for and receiving a certificate of public convenience and necessity as a common carrier or a permit as a contract carrier. The burden of proof is on the applicant carrier and existing carriers generally oppose. Those documents will specify the routes and points that may be served, the radius around a point in which pick-up and delivery operation may be conducted, the commodities that may be carried, and whether the authority granted may be "tacked" onto existing authority to provide through service. Railroad applicants for motor carrier authority will ordinarily be held to the performance by highway of service ancillary to the rail operation—traffic which has a prior or subsequent haul by rail—and will be denied authority to handle traffic by highway through specified key points. Rail carriers will generally be denied authority to conduct water-carrier operations. Surface carriers of any type will be denied entry into air transport except as indirect carriers (forwarders). No carrier will ordinarily be permitted to hold both common and contract authority except in air and bus transport where charter operations are normally authorized.

As entry is regulated, so also is merger with or acquisition of control of other carriers. In general, prior to acquisition of 10 percent or more of the stock of another carrier, application must be filed and approval sought. The statutory standards for approval of such applications are vague, but if approval is obtained, the merger may be consummated, the laws of any state to the contrary notwithstanding and with benefit of exemption from antitrust prosecution. In rail merger proceedings, however, labor protective provisions must be prescribed. Despite the provisions of the applicable statutes, many mergers will be opposed by the Department of Justice right up to the Supreme Court. Final approval of a railroad merger within five years from the date of filing an application is a good performance and the cost of the administrative and judicial proceedings may sometimes approach the annual anticipated savings from merger.

Service abandonment in air, motor, or water carriage may provoke the revoking of certificates after a show-cause order has been issued. Railroads, however, may not abandon lines or service over them without prior approval evidenced by a certificate. In effect it must be shown that the public interest no longer requires the service or line in question. Passenger service and agency station abandonment have, in general, been under the jurisdiction of state authorities. Not until the 1958 amendment was the Interstate Commerce Commission given what amounted to appellate authority. By then the drain of passenger service deficits, which reached a maximum of $750 million per annum in the early 1950s, had taken its toll.

Common carriers by land are generally insurers of the goods entrusted to their care, responsible for the full actual value of such goods unless the proximate cause of loss or damage falls within a very limited set of causes beyond the control of the carriers. By contrast air and water carriers have limited liability, and the minimum liability of air carriers, alone, is not covered by federal statute. Rail carriers are required to join in through routes with other rail carriers and with certain domestic water carriers. Other carriers have no like obligation, although they are permitted to make through routes with carriers of any mode. The Interstate Commerce Commission may, in the absence of agreement among the rail carriers, determine how joint rates should be divided among connecting carriers.

Nowhere has so comprehensive a plan of regulation been devised and applied to a group of industries. Yet, in the United States, roughly 50 percent of all freight transportation based on revenue and revenue equivalents is exempt from all but safety regulation. This follows from the fact that private transportation performed by industrial or commercial firms on their own behalf may not, constitutionally, be subjected to economic regulation. In addition, there are major areas of exemption in water transport, embracing both liquid and dry bulk commodities, and in motor transport in respect of unprocessed and unmanufactured agricultural commodities of all kinds, live stock, fish, and shell fish. The point has often been made that an industry half regulated and half unregulated cannot indefinitely survive in so mixed a condition. The regulatory task is rendered not difficult, but well-nigh impossible.

The drift of all major proposals for transportation policy originated in the executive branch of the government over a period of nearly 30 years has been toward some measure of regulatory relaxation. The National Resources Planning Board in 1942 called for a critical reexamination of regulation. The Board of Research and Investigation under the 1940 Act critized the regulatory plan severely, especially as concerns control of entry in the motor carrier business. The Sawyer Report a few years later recommended cost-based rates. The Weeks Report of 1955 sought deregulation on a wide front, but especially in competitive rate-making. President Kennedy's special message on transportation to the Congress in 1962 recommended major deregulation. The philosophy of the Johnson and Nixon administrations has clearly been in the same direction. Yet almost nothing has resulted in the way of effective statutory revision.

The public statements issuing from prominent members of the Congress in recent months evidence a disgust with the regulatory agencies and process. They show scant understanding of the fact that most of what is complained about is imbedded in the law itself, hence is the responsibility of Congress. The sink-hole of Penn Central poses the possibility of government ownership of at least a part of the rail system more seriously than at any time since Walker D. Hines urged continuance of federal control after the end of World War I and the rail unions came up with the Plumb Plan. The danger of precipitate action is great. The future health of the American transportation system depends most largely on constructive action by the Congress in the months immediately ahead. It is toward stimulating fruitful discussion of the issues related to the future of transport that the following chapters are addressed.

THE LOOK AHEAD

These chapters were not designed as a comprehensive treatment of the status, problems, and prospects of transportation. Instead they have been designed to focus upon the more significant issues relating to domestic transportation. International movement is left out of account. They are not designed, either, to afford a balanced treatment of pros and cons, but rather to express the viewpoints of their authors upon the issues assigned to each. While the general drift of the authors' views is consistent, there are important differences in detail among them. They have not been asked to develop, nor have they developed, an agreed program of action. The suggestions in the *Editor's Postscript* which draw upon materials presented in the body of the book do not, in any sense, constitute an agreed set of proposals to which the various authors would be prepared to subscribe.

The book begins with an examination of possible and appropriate goals for transport policy which is linked with a discussion of the relevance of present policy to such goals. The kinds of policy change which would seem appropriate to redirect events toward the goals are also discussed. Many of the matters touched upon here are dealt with in greater detail in subsequent chapters. The argument found there can be fitted back into the pattern provided in chapter 1. The possibility that our current problems in transport may be swept away or even substantially alleviated by technological development within the decade is discounted in chapter 2. The large increments expected in traffic volume will, it appears, have to be coped with principally by continued development of existing technological forms. In particular only a whittling away of our automotive orientation can be anticipated. Chapters 3-5 deal largely with the institutional framework within which transport functions, especially the regulating and promotional schemes. Differences in the economic characteristics of the several modes, their comparative ability to function in a competitive environment, and their respective capital requirements and prospective availabilities are discussed. Special emphasis is placed upon public policy in respect of entry and merger, financial assistance, subsidy and rate regulation. As chapter 1 indicates, these several areas of policy, while they can be separately discussed, are nevertheless inextricably linked. The final two chapters connect intercity transport performance with the urban transport problem, expose the complexity of the latter, and emphasize the necessity to link urban transport development closely into urban planning at large.

George W. Wilson

1

The Goals of Transportation Policy

Transportation is not desired for its own sake, except for some passenger travel. Thus desirable goals for transport policy cannot be separated from national goals. Yet the goals of any society are not spelled out with sufficient precision that the relationship of any industry, or set of industries, to them can be very clearly discerned. For example, some of the general goals of the United States include freedom, equality, democracy, peace, security and growth, among others. Not only are these both difficult to define clearly and partially inconsistent, but the relationship of any one of them, even to the economic system as a whole, is unclear. While certain economic goals such as high employment, rapid growth, and price stability can be viewed as proxies for more fundamental social objectives, the relationship remains tenuous especially since the whole question of the distribution of the benefits and costs from improved economic performance in each of these dimensions remains unanswered.

If we cannot be sure of the nature of the relationship between general economic improvements and other social goals, how much more difficult it is to deduce the relationship between a single aspect of the economy (transportation) and such goals. While it is easy, nay facile,

GEORGE W. WILSON *is dean of the College of Arts and Sciences, Indiana University. Author of numerous articles and several books on transportation, economist Wilson was chairman of the Transportation Research Forum (1969) and a member of the Nixon Task Force on Transportation. He has also directed a study of transportation and economic development for the Brookings Institution.*

to define an efficient transport system as one that facilitates achievement of national goals at least economic cost, this is not very helpful when it comes to specifying particular policies with respect to transportation. Indeed, it begs the whole question. Although many have itemized the desirable effects of improvements in transportation, these have not been unambiguously beneficial to all regions or all segments of the population; nor have they, in any direct and obvious way, contributed to realization of general social goals.

Thus I will construe efficiency in transportation somewhat more narrowly than in terms of its contribution to general economic and social well-being and basic national goals. But even looking at transportation in such a fashion and defining efficiency in terms of least economic cost within transportation, difficulties remain in specifying appropriate policies.

EFFICIENCY WITHIN TRANSPORTATION AS A GOAL

As a general rule, the goals of policy with regard to any industry are the efficient production and distribution of its product in a static sense and continuous improvement in its technology (i.e., quality improvement and cost reduction) in a dynamic sense: the price of such a product should reflect its marginal cost[1] and such marginal cost should include all social as well as private costs in connection with its production and distribution.

The amount of output produced under such circumstances is governed by the present and changing demands for it at prices reflecting long-run marginal cost. This is the familiar textbook statement regarding what a market-oriented society can or should expect from any industry, although the argument is usually couched in terms of efficiency and optimal resource allocation and how these tend to be achieved automatically and impersonally in competitive markets.

Such a statement is usually qualified by four main caveats: (1) since the pattern of demands for goods and services depends upon the overall distribution of income, if this is not in some sense "efficient" or desirable, the resulting production and resource allocation in response to it will not be efficient either; (2) the external costs and/or benefits

---

[1] Marginal cost is defined as the extra cost of producing an extra unit or set of units of output. Clearly if any firm can correctly ascertain the added cost of additional units of production, it would not willingly sell these at prices below such marginal cost.

from a particular industry may be so substantial and diffuse that they cannot be correctly encompassed in the cost-price structure of the industry; (3) in cases where there are large economies of scale[2] or sharply decreasing unit costs of production, the competitive outcome breaks down as does the general rule for efficient pricing; (4) if there are large deviations from efficient pricing throughout the economy, insistence upon basing prices on marginal cost in any particular industry *may* cause more inefficiency—the so-called "second-best" situation.

All of these qualifications are or are believed to be applicable to transportation. Indeed, it is largely because of these "exceptional circumstances" that transportation was early subject to regulation in the United States and nationalization elsewhere. For example, in the nineteenth century the pattern of personal income redistribution caused by the discriminatory pricing of the railroads was felt to be socially undesirable. On the other hand, by subsidizing canal and railway construction it was felt that a "better" or more equal income distribution among regions along with more rapid general economic growth could be achieved. By virtue of real or assumed externalities, transportation investment has often been viewed as *the* or at least *a* significant contributor to economic growth, political cohesion, and social intercourse. Thus, public assistance stimulated transportation investments in the nineteenth century beyond what was economically necessary at the time and in some cases even beyond current needs. (Note the present excess capacity in rail transportation.) While the past tended to overestimate the external benefits of transportation through a belief in what I have referred to as the "grand transportation mystique," at present the stress is on the external costs in the form of urban congestion, pollution from the emissions of automobiles and aircraft, noise pollution of modern transport technologies, and the like. Thus, the adverse environmental impact of improved transportation is now receiving the attention previously devoted mainly to the actual or assumed positive developmental impact.

In transport, the ability to imbed large externalities into the industries' price and cost structures is impeded not only by the vast diffu-

---

[2] Scale economies refer to the behavior of unit costs of production as the size of the firm or plant changes. Thus, if unit costs decline as the plant size expands there are said to be economies of scale. If there are large scale economies, the cheapest way to produce any given output is to have one firm or plant. It is for this reason that the competitive solution breaks down when economies of scale are substantial. Diseconomies of scale occur when unit costs rise, usually after some relatively small production level has been attained, in response to increases in firm or plant size.

sion of benefits and costs, especially evident in urban transportation, but also by the public provision of rights of way for some modes for which inadequate user charges are imposed. Thus, the gap between private and social costs in transport is believed to be particularly wide, thereby "justifying" less reliance upon market forces than would otherwise be warranted. This tendency is reinforced by "second-best" considerations.

For these reasons, public authorities have attempted to restrain certain aspects of monopoly-like behavior through special regulation and have used public transport investments as well as control over freight rates and passenger fares as instruments to achieve other social objectives.

It is now fairly widely believed that achieving social objectives by manipulating freight charges is no longer appropriate or necessary. Indeed, present economic regulation of intercity freight transportation contributes to misallocation among the transportation industries themselves and between transportation and other segments of the economy. In the past, when the size and influence of the public sector was much smaller, there was little alternative but to use transportation as a means of influencing regional equality and development, income distribution, and, to some extent, competitive equality among firms in industries heavily reliant upon transportation. At present there are more direct ways to achieve these and other social objectives than deliberate manipulation of the transportation industries, either in the form of nonoptimal investments or in requiring rates that do not correctly reflect the economic costs of providing the particular transportation service. In fact, it is generally believed that greater reliance on market forces, especially in *intercity freight transportation,* will be more conducive to achieving social objectives than the existing regulatory machinery.

The same view is not so widely held when it comes to *intercity passenger transportation* where issues of safety and increased availability of service often requiring subsidy generally take precedence over market forces. In terms of *intracity passenger and freight transport,* the goals of transport policy coincide closely with the goals of the city itself. That is, transport capacity within a city is so much a part of the complex set of urban relationships that it is relatively meaningless to refer to efficient transit systems and pricing thereof without specifying the impact upon the whole urban environment—i.e., efficiency for what purpose? Passenger fares, for example, are often kept below cost to enable the poor to have access to job opportunities despite the economic cost involved.

In discussing goals of transport policy, it is therefore essential to distinguish among these three major categories of transportation service which differ not only in the relative importance accorded prices, costs and quality of service, but also in the extent to which improved transportation itself can be expected to alter patterns of movement or behavior. At one extreme is intercity freight transportation, where the overall network has been pretty much established. Improvements in transport alone will not sharply alter existing trading patterns. The basic plant is there and the general pattern of industrial location established. The question is mainly one of utilizing the plant more efficiently by reallocating traffic, mainly among road, rail and water, so that it is moved at least economic cost, bearing in mind the cost and service characteristics of each mode and the evolving technologies. At the other extreme is urban transit where major alterations in capacity can change the whole pattern of urban relationships and influence the entire environment. Urban transit planning therefore becomes part and parcel of urban planning and the achievement of urban goals to an extent that is simply not true anymore in intercity freight transportation. Internal efficiency is therefore a more appropriate goal in the latter case than in the former.

The present relative pattern of goals, emphasizing internal efficiency and external (noneconomic) effects in varying degrees depending upon the type of transportation service, seems to reflect general historical trends. In the early stages of development of either a new technology or rapid expansion of the right of way and related facilities, concern for internal efficiency plays a lesser role than concern for noneconomic factors. In these stages the role of public policy is generally to accelerate growth by some form of subsidy, direct or indirect. Thus, we have the land grants to the railroads in the nineteenth century, highway and airline subsidies (both direct and indirect through inadequate user charges) in the late 1920s and 1930s for intercity passenger transport and, more recently, proposed subsidies and direct federal support for urban transit facilities.

The pattern in transportation has been that as a need is perceived to expand facilities to accomplish some social goal (e.g., development of the West via rail subsidies in the nineteenth century, accommodation of the new auto and air technologies in the 1920s and 1930s, and now a move to make cities less polluted and more mobile), massive public support is provided. When the facilities have been put in place, usually in excessive amounts, the further social gains relative to costs or returns to be reaped elsewhere, diminish: the basic pattern by then is largely complete and social and economic activities have more or less adjusted and fully responded to the new accessibility as both cause and consequence. When this point is reached, concern then shifts to more efficient use of available facilities: hence there exists a lag in relative emphasis which at the present time manifests itself in the differing emphasis upon internal efficiency vis-à-vis external social goals, as noted above. In time we can be sure, if past patterns prevail, that the social benefits of greater intercity passenger mobility will take second place to emphasis upon the total costs of providing such service and, much later on, that urban transit will be viewed more in terms of narrow efficiency criteria than as a contributor to urban mobility, clean air, and aesthetic surroundings.

The balance of this chapter will treat each of the three areas of transportation separately. For each, I will designate what appear to be appropriate goals and examine the changes in present policies that seem essential to achieve them.

Intercity Freight Transportation

The goals in this area of transportation have increasingly become oriented to improvements in economic efficiency and greater degrees of innovation, flexibility, and experimentation within transportation itself. As such, the role and impact of economic regulation have come under critical scrutiny as barriers to enhanced efficiency. The central issue, therefore, boils down to the question of what changes in present regulatory policy would enhance the efficiency and improve the overall performance of intercity freight transportation.

There are several aspects of present regulatory policy that merit separate discussion.

THE NECESSITY OF COMMON CARRIAGE

The present regulatory policies originated from an attempt to prevent abuses of monopoly power and to require certain transport firms to provide service to whomever requested it at nondiscriminatory and publicly disclosed rates. The necessity for imposing restraints upon firms' behavior and requiring service to all was rooted in the absence of competition and a serious limitation of shipper options in transportation. To prevent abuses and ensure fairness, especially as far as pricing is concerned, a regulatory body (initially the Interstate Commerce Commission [ICC] in 1887) was established. Effective regulation, however, required authority of the Commission well beyond the area of rates. Discrimination could be, and was, practiced in terms of quality of service, availability of equipment, and in many other ways. Thus the ICC, after being shorn of most of its powers by Supreme Court interpretation, gradually obtained from Congress between 1903 and 1910 the authority commensurate with the goals of regulation as then specified. By the beginning of the First World War it could be said that the Commission's ability to regulate effectively was assured. Its authority furthermore encompassed the overwhelming share of intercity ton-miles. Ironically, not long after having acquired the requisite authority for effective and pervasive regulation, the Commission's *raison d'être* was progressively eroded by the advent of the truck and the increasing share of total intercity freight traffic, especially after 1926, generated not only by truck, but also by oil pipe lines and inland water transport. Despite further extensions of Commission authority over water and truck transport, designed less to prevent abuses than to preserve common carriage, the proportion of traffic moved by regulated carriers diminished sharply after the Second World War and now amounts to barely half of total intercity ton-miles.

The role of the ICC was thus transformed from protecting the shipper to protecting the common carriers subject to its jurisdiction— the latter, of course, also affords protection to those shippers whose transportation options are restricted to one or two firms or modes. But the steady relative erosion of common carriage and the impossibility of complete regulation of all freight transportation create pressures for changing the approach to regulation. Furthermore, it is now questionable whether regulated common carriage is essential anymore or at least whether the costs occasioned by regulation are more than covered by the benefits reaped from maintaining common carriage.

While it is difficult to find a clear-cut statement concerning the present significance of common carriage in terms of the benefits allegedly flowing therefrom, it is even more difficult to derive a quantitative measure of such value that could be compared with the social costs of preserving the common carrier obligation. The latter have been estimated to be as high as $5 billion annually. This figure is the sum of several types of costs all of which are believed to be caused by economic regulation as presently practiced. These costs are: (1) the direct regulatory costs including the costs associated with regulatory proceedings, preparation for them, and subsequent litigation and appeal; (2) excess capacity costs associated with regulation; (3) misallocation due to failure of the rate structure to reflect marginal costs; and (4) the costs to society related to the effects of regulation on technological change. Estimates in the first three categories are extremely fragile while no one has yet attempted a numerical calculation of number (4) although some of the costs of dynamic inefficiency are inevitably included in estimates of (2) and (3). Nor could the above "costs" be entirely avoided if economic regulation were to be removed, because much of the present litigation would simply be transferred to the courts under the antitrust laws. Nevertheless, all recent computations of the real costs of present transport regulation suggest substantial sums in the order of magnitude of $5 billion at present levels of GNP. The inability to indicate benefits whose value is anywhere near this amount suggests that it may not be worth attempting to preserve common carriage anymore, at least using present techniques.

Historically, the nature and apparent severity of the common carriage obligation have been closely linked with monopoly power of an industry deemed to be of substantial importance. From a strictly economic point of view, such a correlation implies that the obligation should change as competitive relationships themselves alter. That is, the closer particular markets approach the competitive ideal, the less the need for requiring specific firms to perform particular functions or to refrain from certain practices (e.g., discrimination, refusal to serve, etc.) that while privately profitable may be judged socially harmful. The assumption is that adequate service will be provided to all at minimum social cost wherever markets are highly or even workably competitive—that is to say, when buyers have a sufficient number of alternatives at reasonable prices that abuses of whatever degree of monopoly power exists cannot seriously damage any buyer.

This viewpoint, linking common carriage to competitive circumstances, implies that with the greater degree of competition in an ever increasing number of transportation markets there is little relevance to the imposition of certain obligations to serve, except in those markets where competition does not provide either an adequate incentive to offer good service at fair prices or suitable protection to shippers against monopolistic abuses. The fact that regulated common carriage in the United States has steadily declined as a proportion of total transportation indicates that such carriage does not provide the kind of service that appears to be essential to a growing number of shippers. The upshot of this view is that the common carrier concept in transportation has become obsolete and more costly to preserve in direct proportion as the degree of competitiveness has increased.

If, therefore, one views competition in transportation as sufficiently intense to provide the appropriate checks to monopolistic abuses and incentives to efficiency subject only to those legal constraints applicable to other industries (e.g., antitrust laws), then imposition of the common carrier obligation on carriers conducting a decreasing proportion of total transport service can only serve to increase the competitive disadvantage of the common carriers—both by requiring them to perform tasks, and hence incur costs that their rivals do not, and by enforcing a set of procedures that prevents rapid response to changing circumstances.

Where transport firms have or had substantial economic power in a large number of markets involving many important commodities, the imposition of regulation both to curb abuses and to enforce certain levels and patterns of service and rates seemed to represent a not unreasonable *quid pro quo*. But the growth of alternative modes of transport circumscribed the ability of firms to recoup the amounts required to finance the common carrier obligations, while at the same time it encouraged private and contract carriers to offer tailor-made service at special rates to an ever greater range of shippers. The so-called "plight of the common carrier" is, in part, related to the failure to alter the obligations in the light of present-day needs.

This requires a new set of standards to apply to two aspects of the obligation to carry, namely, (1) adequacy of service (e.g., frequency, regularity) and (2) pricing policy. As noted earlier, the economic analysis pertinent to these suggests that transportation, being a derived demand, should respond to shippers' needs at prices that, in the aggregate, cover the total costs and that, for particular services, cover the "marginal" costs incurred in their production.

Indeed, it is now old hat to argue that for an efficient transport system relative freight rates should reflect cost differences. Only in this way will shippers be given appropriate incentives to utilize those forms of transport that minimize the direct transport costs as well as the indirect costs of production, inventory, warehousing, and so on that are related to the qualitative service differences among the several modes.

The fact that regulated common carriers are losing out relatively to other forms of transport arises largely from the failure to base their rates more fully on costs in addition to the extra costs occasioned by the obligation to carry and the procedures under regulation, themselves designed to bolster and enforce common carriage. In the past, these features of the transportation system caused less harm mainly because a more effective system of price discrimination was supportable. However, the growing feasibility of private and contract trucking undercut much of the effectiveness of the previous pricing pattern. At the same time, the availability of private trucking and an extensive highway system have reduced the seriousness of failure to fulfill all the common carrier obligations.

What this means is that presently regulated common carriers need to be given more flexibility both in responding to changing situations and in providing more tailor-made service to particular shippers so long as such service (1) covers the costs of its provision and (2) is available to all. Furthermore, there must be a more rapid readjustment of freight rates to reflect costs. If we wish to maintain publicly available transportation for reasons of defense, the post office, small business, equity, and so on, changes along these lines are essenial and have often been proposed.

THE ISSUE OF MERGERS IN TRANSPORTATION

There are two aspects of mergers that have frequently been discussed. The first involves intramodal merger; the second, merger among several modes—the so-called integrated transport firm. Since the most important aspect of the former involves railroads, I will concentrate on that mode before turning to the problem of the integrated transport firm.

Toward a Rational Policy for Railway Mergers—The primary purpose usually stipulated for railway mergers is to reduce the degree of excess capacity in the railway system and to concentrate traffic over fewer routes involving fewer yard or interchange operations. The consequences of such a pruning of capacity are alleged to be lower unit operating costs achievable either through increased density, heavier loading, longer average hauls, and/or lower terminal expenses per unit of freight shipped or through achieving greater scale economies where such exist. In addition to this, proponents of mergers also argue that service will be improved and, in some cases, lower rates will be permitted because of lower costs, both of which will stimulate additional volume, thereby contributing even greater utilization of plant and equipment. In one form or another these constitute the essential ingredients of the case for mergers with primary emphasis upon the reduction in excess capacity when parallel lines are involved and primary emphasis upon service improvements where end-to-end lines are involved.

There is little doubt that these socially desirable and privately profitable results can be obtained from carefully worked-out mergers. However, the fact of the matter is that most large mergers consummated in the last decade have not conspicuously contributed much either to efficiency or profitability. There is no reason to expect that the present set of merger proposals will produce any significantly different results.

If this is the case, and fully acknowledging the need to eliminate excess capacity and improve efficiency in rail transportation, there are alternatives to merger that do not have the kind of irreversibility that is a major drawback of the merger device. That is, since there is no overall plan for what may be deemed an optimal pattern of rail ownership for the nation as a whole, a particular merger may make subsequent rationalization more difficult. The problems of unscrambling the corporate eggs following merger are well known. Thus, without a clear idea of an optimal—or even desirable—pattern of rail ownership, no basis exists for adequately appraising each merger except on a case by case basis, which may be inconsistent with an ultimately desirable pattern.

In addition to the problems created by lack of a comprehensive plan to which individual mergers should conform, many of the recent and proposed mergers have an anticompetitive effect as far as intra-railroad rivalry is concerned. As such, they are inconsistent with the now widespread belief that a major relaxation of regulatory constraints and increasing reliance upon competitive forces in transportation is the most appropriate policy for the future. Any large-scale elimination of rail service options at major points clearly renders further progress in this direction infeasible, or, at least, undesirable.

There is a further consideration. Large mergers may not create a profitable situation, as past evidence amply indicates. In such instances, recourse to bankruptcy has a particularly severe impact upon financial markets and other railroads to whom money is owed by the bankrupt firm. This also creates pressures to have public funds made available. Should mergers continue with the same degree of economic success as evidenced by Penn Central, a repetition of that unhappy event can be expected.

The implications of the foregoing are that mergers should be viewed as a last resort after existing railroad companies have had an opportunity (1) to divest themselves of excess capacity, (2) to reorganize capital structures, and (3) to experiment with rate incentives and service improvements. These in turn require that the ICC make abandonments easier to obtain. Certain types of service could continue at public expense, as is proposed by the Congress with respect to some passenger service under Railpax, along with provisions for emergency loans. (Emergency loan provisions should however be viewed with far more caution and skepticism than Congress has thus far shown. Bailing out bankrupt firms often prevents the kinds of adjustments needed to make the enterprise viable in the future.) Finally, the Commission would have to enforce more vigorously its authority over through routes and joint rates to determine whether voluntary cooperation could achieve many of the alleged advantages of merger.

In short, there are many possible changes in public policy that could create conditions for more successful mergers in the future and thereby leave more options open. Premature mergers foreclose alternatives, and there is no guarantee of their economic success. It would be particularly unwise to accelerate mergers in rail transportation because of the current financial difficulties which are more related to the general state of the economy and forced continuation of large amounts of unprofitable rail service. Both of these conditions can and doubtless will be changed. If, after a trial period of say five years, when unprofitable service and capacity have been reduced or partly subsidized and after some experience with greater rate freedom and experimentation has been gained, the major railroads are still in poor financial condition, that is the time to contemplate what patterns of ownership of a trimmed-down railroad system would be expected to lead to economic viability. Premature rail consolidations can thwart desirable trends in public policy and impede the determination of an efficient pattern of rail ownership. A five-year moratorium on pending and future mergers, combined with a relaxation of ICC and state restrictions on abandonment, greater rate freedom, and some public loan provisions in emergency situations, may prepare the way for a merger policy more consistent with economic efficiency, adequate service, and a large reduction in the amount of detailed economic regulation of the transportation industries. It may even eliminate the trend toward massive rail systems under single management and preserve those smaller, efficient railroads whose prime concern is the development of the region they serve. Much of the evidence suggests that the economies of scale argument for mergers has been grossly overstated and that the anticompetitive nature of large mergers has been given inadequate consideration. In view of the great uncertainty in these matters, the course of prudent public policy would be to explore first those options that are not irreversible and whose consequences are more predictable. Merger is not one of these.

Inter-Modal Mergers—Historically, United States transport policy has sought to keep the modes separate. Except for "special" circumstances, a railroad, for example, is not permitted to provide trucking service or own a trucking enterprise. The purpose of such a policy is to maintain as much competition as possible between modes and to ensure a variety of shipper options. At the same time, it is necessary to have joint rates and through service involving shipments using different modes such as rail-truck, rail-water, and so on. Thus, regulation seeks to retain modal separation while encouraging coordination of service. The difficulties of the latter, especially, where joint service would deprive an originating carrier of some revenue have induced some to advocate abandonment of the policy of modal separation. The apparent, though not well documented, success of transport companies in Canada reinforces the attack upon the policy of modal separation.

Yet there are very real problems as well as potential economies of the integrated transport firm. In the first place, it would limit shipper options and, unless there were a large number of such firms in a given market, this would be inconsistent with a policy of increasing reliance upon competition. Again, such firms would tend to have assets rather heavily concentrated in rail facilities; hence management would be expected to use non-rail facilities in a manner less conducive to their development than as a device to protect the heavy rail investment. Problems of cost-finding, rate-making, and management would be more difficult in a firm selling all forms of transport than in a more specialized firm. There is, however, no denying the fact that greater coordination among modes *could* be achieved by this technique. Yet substantial integration is already occurring in the realm of piggy-back and fishy-back service, the fastest growing area of transportation at present. A further acceleration along these lines will occur as containerization gains momentum. Thus, without greater assurance that real economies would in fact be realized by abandoning the policy of modal separation, I see little purpose at the present time in altering policy in this respect especially in view of the anticipated adverse effect upon competition.

THE PROBLEM OF FREIGHT RATES

There is little doubt that existing regulation leads to generally higher rates and perpetuates a system of pricing that leads to economic waste since particular rates deviate from marginal costs. Even though marginal costs are notoriously difficult to determine, especially in rail transportation, various studies have noted significant departures from efficient pricing. In fact, one of the purposes of economic regulation was to preserve a structure of freight rates based more on the value of a particular service than on its costs. While a substantial reduction in economic regulation would not eliminate all vestiges of value of service pricing, if competition in transportation is as pervasive as frequently believed, a far greater coincidence of rates with marginal costs can be expected, and with this a more efficient allocation of traffic among the several modes.

Yet, we should not overemphasize the significance of freight rates. In terms of total distribution costs, freight charges in fact are relatively minor. Some studies estimate that the freight bill is only 20–25 percent of the total distribution costs in many industries. The freight charge as a proportion of delivered value of commodities is estimated to be less than 10 percent for the nation as a whole. Thus, many shippers worry less about the level of the freight rate than they do about quality of the service (in terms of speed, dependability, and safety) and whether their competitors are paying the same rates.

To be sure, deviation from marginal or even average cost pricing induces shippers to use transportation facilities inefficiently, and one should attempt to prevent waste wherever possible. However, despite acknowledged inefficiencies arising from the present rate structure, these appear to be far less significant than the costs associated with excess capacity and the inability of regulated carriers to respond quickly to change or new technological opportunities. Indeed, it is in this area that the case against present regulatory practices of the ICC is strongest.

REGULATION, EFFICIENCY, AND INNOVATION

Economic regulation of transportation cannot possibly guarantee or compel the kinds of rate, service, or technical innovations that regularly occur even under noncompetitive conditions. Any regulatory agency is and must be concerned with questions of equity and must give all affected parties their day in court. This inevitably leads to far longer delays than would be the case without such restraint where two or more firms are concerned. No regulatory agency can have the intimate knowledge of particular problems facing individual enterprises in given markets that the firms themselves possess. Adam Smith long ago argued that each man in his own local situation is a better judge of his own best interest than others could be, and, so long as competition existed, each would be led, as by an invisible hand, to promote an end that was no part of his intention, namely the public interest. Thus, the role of public policy was seen as creating conditions in which private self-seeking would coalesce with public benefits. No *detailed* regulation of specific industries or firms could be expected to accomplish this as effectively as competitive pressures. Competitive-like responses to changing situations must therefore inevitably be more delayed and protracted under regulation even where considerations of equity are not involved. In short, economic regulation cannot be nearly as effective in stimulating improvements or in speeding their introduction as interfirm rivalry even where the latter refers only to a few enterprises. Regulation is more geared to and effective in the negative role of prevention of monopoly-like abuses of economic power than in the positive role of stimulating changes leading to cheapness and plenty.

Even where significant gains in economic efficiency may be expected to occur through creation of monopoly, these would not necessarily accrue to the public unless there were some pressure guaranteeing that they be passed on in the form of lower prices and/or better quality. The possibility of a regulatory commission finding out about the magnitude and nature of the potential efficiency gains, even with full access to the company's files, is problematical. Prices are far more certain to be reduced and/or quality of service improved if there exists one rival firm, always assuming, of course, no collusion between or among them.

There are some who argue that competition between or among railroads in particular is not possible because of economies of scale. Thus, regardless of the problem of regulation, society has no alternative but to abandon reliance on competitive forces. One can readily accept the fact that all major transport markets are structurally oligopolistic (or concentrated) in terms of railroad alternatives and that freedom of entry is not to be expected. It is obvious that such a situation naturally discourages price competition. Yet many, if not most, large manufacturing industries are similarly situated (e.g., steel, automobiles), and public policy has been content to rely on market forces and general antitrust policy. Furthermore, the whole theory of oligopoly really argues that there will be little in the way of persistent and pervasive *price* competition, which then focuses rivalry upon innovation, quality, sales effort, and so on. As far as innovative rivalry is concerned, it was long ago argued that this was the most powerful force breaking down islands of monopoly and that small price jiggles were of insignificant impact compared to new products, new ways of doing business, and so forth. If then oligopoly fosters non-price competition and does not lead firms to seek the real monopoly profit (the "quiet life"), one could argue convincingly that in the long run this may be most important. And railroads as well as other forms of transportation have innovated or at least adopted the innovations of the supplying industries. For example, various estimates indicate that productivity in rail, air, inland waterways, and petroleum pipe lines has increased some three to five times the national average since 1947. Longer-run estimates for railroad productivity gains indicate better performance than in mining, manufacturing, and the total domestic private economy in general as far as annual rates of improvement are concerned. Thus, even under regulated oligopoly, "progress" may be a firm's most important product. If so, then the fact of innovative rivalry may be worth whatever short-run misallocation arises due to failure to compete on a price basis and to equate price with an elusive, and in my view, subjective notion of marginal cost. It may even justify in the long run the existence of more firms than would be necessary on strictly technical grounds. The same reasoning applies to service quality.

Furthermore, since transportation firms serve other producers, who do a better job in assessing the value to them of particular products or services than consumers in general, the dangers of wasteful sales effort, or inferior product quality, which emerge as potential features of non-price competition and account for the general economic disparagement of oligopoly, are scarcely relevant here. It is most valid for consumer products but far less so for producer services like freight transport. Much of the alleged economic waste of oligopoly really emerges from thinking about advertising excesses and trivial product and packaging adjustments in cigarettes, soap, and other consumer goods. Few people criticize freight transportation firms for excessive and persuasive sales effort—the criticism is more often the reverse.

At present, intramodal rivalry exists, though in varying degrees among the several modes. It is far from perfect and one can cite evidence that its effects do not appear to be dramatic. Yet such rivalry has probably kept rates lower, made service better, and contributed more to innovation than would have been the case had there existed a monopoly of transportation facilities in every major transport market even under pervasive regulation. Indeed, intramodal competition is the most effective form of competition as far as ensuring that rates reflect the lowest economic cost and that normal profits prevail. The reasons for this are fairly obvious. Firms in the same industry or mode have similar cost structures and products; hence each firm can approximately match a rival's price and service, whereas competition between different modes provides the opportunity for excessive prices where one mode has a large cost advantage.

For example, if rail costs are considerably below truck costs, then even the existence of truck competition will not prevent a high degree of monopoly profits on particular traffic by a railroad whose rates need not be reduced to rail marginal cost to meet truck rivalry.

Intermodal competition on the other hand may be viewed as being more effective in inducing those radical, dramatic changes in techniques that occur from time to time. Indeed, new forms of transportation are themselves significant innovations. Good examples include the various piggy-back plans in operation today and, of course, the development of trucking in the 1920s. These changes are no less important than the constant pressure to keep prices in line with costs. In general, intermodal competition creates constant pressure for longer-run and more revolutionary improvements in techniques which may explain the relatively high rates of productivity growth among the modes noted earlier. Both forms of rivalry are more pervasive, compelling, powerful, and unrelenting than even the most comprehensive form of economic regulation could possibly be. It is therefore highly desirable to have and retain both kinds of rivalry and, at the same time, to prevent gross abuses of monopoly power by antitrust enforcement. The former provides positive inducements to improve efficiency and advance technology, while the latter is a negative constraint on activities inconsistent with the public interest.

Economic regulation should thus rely mainly on competitive market forces and this presupposes legitimate concern for the maintenance of competition. This is largely because even under a situation of structural oligopoly, incentives to be efficient and progressive are more effective than the coercive power of any regulatory commission conceivable. This means that any reduction in the number of buyer or shipper options should not be lightly regarded, even where a persuasive case for economies of scale can be made.

The role that regulation plays in innovation is rather difficult to untangle. Certainly the past productivity gains of the transportation industries compare favorably with large segments of the economy. However, even if this evidence could be deemed accurate (a large assumption!), it does not denote achievable performance. Since freight rates have not mirrored efficiency gains and transport firms have performed very little research and development, both of which are related to economic regulation, society may still be paying too much for transportation. In fact, the major transportation innovations have come not from the transportation firms themselves but from the equipment suppliers who naturally view the transport function from a narrower perspective than the transport firms as far as their own or shippers' needs are concerned. More directly, economic regulation has served to discourage innovation by attempting to preserve historical rate relationships, by delaying for long periods of time certain major technological improvements (e.g., the unit train), and by moderating competitive forces thereby reducing incentives to innovate. These "costs" of regulation combined with the failure to permit abandonment of excess capacity are responsible for the bulk of the costs to society noted earlier. A recent study indicates that the short-run loss to society from misallocation of traffic caused by the failure of rates to reflect marginal costs in transportation is barely 12 percent of the "costs" attributable to excess capacity in rail transportation in 1969.

PUBLIC INVESTMENT IN TRANSPORTATION

One serious additional source of inefficiency and excess capacity in the transportation industries is the uncoordinated nature of public investments in highway, waterway, and airline facilities. The amounts involved are substantial. For example, in 1969 the federal government spent about $6.1 billion for transportation systems and facilities, $4.5 billion of which was for highways, $343 million for waterways and $1.1 billion for airways, airports, and airline subsidy. State and local governments spent $15 billion of which almost $14 billion was for highways. Although the concentration upon highways is expected to decrease, the total amounts to be spent on transportation facilities during the 1970s will grow substantially. Despite such large amounts, there is no device at present and none officially proposed for the future for determining an efficient set of priorities. Investment decisions in rail and pipe-line rights of way are largely private, which further complicates rational overall investment programs in transportation.

Finally, direct subsidies to some forms of transportation and failure to implement a system of user charges, either at all (e.g., inland waterways) or in adequate amounts for specific users, distort perceived costs and thus ensure an inefficient rate structure even under competitive conditions.

At the very least, therefore, there is needed something like a "Transportation Investment Review Board" which would assess the relative net social benefits from public investments in highways, waterways, airways, and other modes when federal funding is proposed. Such a board could rank all new capital projects in terms of social benefits and costs (or internal rate of return) and determine not only which projects to undertake compared with anticipated rates of return outside of transportation but also could evaluate the systems effects of new investment regardless of mode. Unlike the present divided authority with respect to federally financed transportation investments, such an approach provides a comprehensive overview that would be acutely conscious of excess capacity in general. It is, however, noteworthy that such a proposal was conspicuously excluded from the act creating the Department of Transportation, which provides some indication of the strength of existing vested interests.

CONCLUSION

Although many more evidences of practices inhibiting more efficient and responsive provision of intercity freight transportation could be given (such as differential state and local taxation of common carriers and rail transport compared to truck and water; the varying pattern and nature of collective bargaining arrangements among the modes; entry controls in truck transportation as well as route, back-haul, and commodity restrictions), enough has been said to suggest that President

Kennedy's assertion in 1962 that the present policy with respect to transportation is a "chaotic patchwork of inconsistent and often obsolete legislation and regulations" is substantially correct. There is, indeed, great need for a less segmented approach and a more comprehensive overview combined with a substantial reduction in the extent of economic regulation. These are pious and oft-repeated phrases. Yet the potential gains are enormous.

However, not all regulation should or could be removed at once. The experiment in deregulation should begin by eliminating minimum rate control, since such control is the major device for attempting to protect common carriers from competitive pressures and for preventing rates from reflecting more accurately present marginal costs or new lower costs possible through technological change. The experiment in minimum rate decontrol is clearly worth trying. It would, of course, have to be phased initially perhaps along the lines of allowing all presently regulated carriers to reduce any rate by, say, a maximum of 20 percent per year for two or three years without prior ICC approval, such rates to remain in effect for a specified period of time (say twelve months) to reduce the chance of predatory behavior. Combined with this should go (1) a more economically rational scheme of public investment and user charges, (2) a moratorium on all rail mergers in order to keep as many shipper options open as possible, and, in effect, to allow "competitive forces" maximum opportunity to work, (3) some attempt to equalize tax burdens both among the various modes and between presently regulated and nonregulated carriers and (4) maintenance of the policy of modal separation of ownership.

Such a package of proposals would maximize the probability that an experiment in minimum rate decontrol would improve static and dynamic efficiency in transportation. It would also be more politically realistic since it obviously gives no special advantage to any particular mode. That is, unless we block the wave of proposed railway mergers and forestall the so-called "integrated transportation firm," the package of proposals will appear so pro-railroad that it will fall easy prey to political objections from the other modes.

But I am not sanguine enough to believe that there is much chance of passage of such a set of proposals even purged of pro-railroad bias. The transportation industries comprise a set of vested interests any one of which can block major legislative change. Indeed, they have consistently done so since World War II. The only possibility of major changes in the direction of economic rationality in transportation requires a degree of crisis in intercity freight transportation and a presidential commitment supporting the changes that do not exist at present. Urban problems, extrication from Indochina, and the civil rights movement each deserve far higher priority in terms of presidential concern and activity than intercity freight transportation. In fact, aside from the quibbling regarding the small shipment problem, the intercity freight transportation industry is tranquil compared to the problems of urban transit and intercity passenger transportation which will be examined next.

But in the final analysis, economic regulation of intercity freight transportation is a relative failure largely because of administrative infeasibility which has become progressively worse since the late 1920s with the sharp growth of the motor carrier. Economic and even social regulation of monopoly or oligopoly is possible and can be effective. However, the attempt to regulate, perhaps as many as twenty thousand firms operating in an environment of probably more than one hundred thousand providers of transportation service in one form or another, poses administrative problems of the first magnitude. It is mainly for this reason that some alternatives in the direction of simplification and reduction of regulation seem long overdue. The prime candidate would be gradual abolition of minimum rate control which would contribute to the goal of greater internal efficiency in freight transportation.

It must, however, be acknowledged that the consequences of substantial deregulation are not fully understood. Furthermore, the adjustment process will be painful for many shippers, communities, regions, and modes of transport themselves. These uncertainties cause far more fear and misapprehension than is doubtless realistic, but they cannot be ignored as major barriers to widespread acceptance of deregulation and support for it. Yet, despite an inability to predict in detail the consequences of such a policy, continuation of present policies will become increasingly costly. Nor does the alternative of extending regulation appear either feasible or desirable. The experiment, and it should be viewed as such, in at least rate decontrol thus appears to be the best of available options.

Intercity Passenger Transportation

The goals of policy in this area, though not clearly articulated, have changed from heavy emphasis upon sheer physical accessibility to concerns for safety, quality of service, and more recently, environmental problems. The early goals, following completion of the railway network, were to provide technological alternatives to rail transportation. This involved heavy public outlays for highways and, later, airports and airways. Furthermore, the policy appeared to be one of providing such passenger alternatives to as many places as possible regardless of their traffic-generating capabilities. As a result the nation acquired an extensive network of intercity passenger facilities clearly beyond any reasonable assessment of economic need. This has required continuing public subsidy in one form or another to ensure maintenance of commercial passenger service. The objective is presumably to create and maintain travel options available to all on reasonable, often below cost, terms. Such a policy related as it is to the more fundamental goal of promoting national consciousness, cohesion, and regional interchange has fostered several distinct trends leading to what some have termed "crisis" situations in the three dominant modes —auto, air, and rail. The crisis relates primarily to issues of safety on the one hand and pollution on the other. In fact, economic regulation in conjunction with uncoordinated federal promotional policies especially with respect to air and automotive travel have compromised several other desirable national objectives.

As is well known, the intercity passenger market is dominated by the private passenger car which accounts for 85–90 percent of total intercity passenger travel. The trends with respect to the three commercial options show continued declines in rail service matched by a rise in airline travel which now far exceeds that of rail, and rough constancy of the bus share. In large part this reflects past public policy which deliberately sought to promote airline travel through direct subsidy and provision of airway and airport facilities at less than full cost to users. Highway facilities were also expanded in advance of demand. The superior quality of both auto and airline service in response to the above policies virtually ensured the sharp decline in the rail share of the passenger market. This was further augmented by economic regulation of air transport that prevented price competition among carriers. Airline rivalry was thus channelled in the direction of improved quality, chronic excess capacity, too frequent scheduling, as well as an abundance of frills.

Rapid technological development of air transport, largely stimulated by federal research and development efforts associated with military needs, further increased the relative quality and capacity of air travel vis-à-vis rail. Indeed, as rail patronage dwindled, the refusal of the

ICC and Congress to permit equivalent service abandonment led the railroads to permit service quality to deteriorate in preference to the more profitable freight service.

There is little doubt that public policy deserves much credit or blame for accelerating trends, some of which would doubtless have occurred anyway but at a far slower pace. The alarm recently shown over further rail passenger abandonment and deteriorating rail safety (the latter related to undermaintenance of right of way, which reflects in part the rail response to dwindling profits) indicates that the goal of having as many commercial passenger options for intercity travel as technically possible cannot be fulfilled. Indeed, the subsidization of local feeder airline services, the proliferation of local airports, and continued highway improvements proved to be inconsistent with maintenance of adequate rail service even between major cities. The consequences, however, were mainly to reduce the intercity travel options at the expense of low-income families since the bulk of air travel is undertaken by a minority of the relatively more affluent.

THE ISSUE OF SAFETY

The most serious problem in terms of number of deaths and injuries is of course related to highway traffic. Over fifty-five thousand people were killed last year on the nation's highways and many times this number injured. Property damage amounted to about $16 billion. Attacks on this problem involve efforts to improve the right-of-way, make the equipment (cars and trucks) safer, and improve driver skills and care. This requires substantial and growing outlays. From an economic point of view, however, there appears to be little coordination of efforts either in the area of safety generally—with respect not only to highways but to air, water, and rail—or among the categories of right of way, vehicle, and operator for each mode. The truth of the matter is that the economics of safety is not well developed. Politically and emotionally society reacts sharply to air crashes which have a kind of instant drama in contrast to the regular occurrence of automobile accidents and drownings from pleasure boating. As a consequence large sums are spent to promote airline safety but, despite a much larger number of deaths annually from even boating accidents, little is devoted to water safety and in terms of vehicle miles, less is devoted to highway or railway safety. The tendency is to view with alarm accidents in the air but to accept as inevitable regularly recurring accidents on land and water. Thus some rather serious imbalances occur among the modes when it comes to allocating resources to improve transportation safety. Indeed, throughout society in general there appear to be severe misallocations with respect to the resources devoted to death prevention or prolonging life from particular causes. Since so little is known in this realm, I can do no more here than raise the issue.

However, within transportation, certain contemporary practices appear to contribute to the probability of accidents. Since a major goal of transportation policy is an increase in transportation safety, several changes in present practices immediately come to mind.

Forced continuation of unprofitable rail service provides incentives for the railways to reduce or skimp upon such safety-enhancing expenditures as those for right-of-way or equipment maintenance. In fact, there is a close inverse correlation between expenditures on railway right-of-way and rail accidents. Thus, allowing firms to abandon unprofitable service, as previously argued, would not only promote efficiency in freight transportation but would positively influence safety as well.

Similarly, airline rate regulation induces carriers to stress "service" and, in particular, increases schedules at popular hours. This has contributed to congestion and delays especially at major terminals at peak hours. The direct rationing of the number of landings and take-offs at especially congested airports like O'Hare and Kennedy partly reflects the failure to allow varying combinations of rates and service available at less preferred hours during the day and days during the week. It is difficult to know how effective more rate-service options would be in reducing congestion and thus improving safety, since a large portion of airline travel may not be especially sensitive to fare discounts. However, the growing acceptance of low-priced group charter flights suggests that more promotional pricing and service options would find a responsive market presumably among the middle- and lower-income groups. Thus, prevention of greater fare differentiation by regulation for domestic service and the cartelization and price-fixing schemes for international aviation not only contribute to overscheduling and congestion but prevent greater accessibility of air travel to the lower-income groups.

One of the key problems of the airline industry is the rapidity of technological change which increases the capacity and efficiency of individual aircraft. Failure to tap a broader market and restrictions on price competition thus combine with growing capacity to produce load factors that regularly inhibit profitable operations. The carrier's response is to blame the Civil Aeronautics Board (CAB) for permitting too many firms to enter particular markets, whereas most economists would argue that restricting price competition and raising costs through duplicated and excessive advertising and other promotional expenditures (or gimmicks) are to blame. At the very least, sensible policy would suggest greater experimentation with fare-service options. This could contribute both to improved safety and accessibility to a broader and more representative consumer market, which would further the goal of greater equality of income distribution insofar as federal support for air transportation is concerned.

Part of the safety problem will require improvements in ground control equipment and personnel as well as in the aircraft and for pilot training. The difficulty here, however, is one of relative emphasis. Much can be accomplished by using existing capacity more effectively throughout the day, either by more competitive pricing policies or by limiting the number of landings and takeoffs per hour. Levying heavier user charges at major airports upon private air operations especially at peak hours, or even a total embargo, would reduce congestion sometimes significantly. While some additional outlays can be justified to promote airline safety, the more serious problem relates to highway safety. Indeed, it is becoming increasingly true that the trip to and from the airport is the most dangerous and often time-consuming part of the intercity passenger transportation.

Quantitatively, of course, highway safety is most significant. Better highways, better equipment, driver education, more rigorous enforcement of traffic laws, and specification of safety features on vehicles, plus public campaigns stressing safety, may have been responsible for the first decrease in highway fatalities (1970 over 1969) in twelve years. A key problem is, however, the behavior of individual drivers and particularly the excessive use of alcohol which is involved in half of all highway deaths. A program of alcohol countermeasures would appear to promise significant payoffs, since some countries have reduced the incidence of alcohol involvement in highway fatalities to about one-fifth that of the United States. I cite this mainly to stress the point that massive expenditures on new equipment or facilities may be less effective than rather straightforward policies using existing assets in the promotion of safety. This applies to all forms of transportation. As previously noted, however, we have been notoriously lax in applying efficiency criteria to the issue of safety and are doubtless not devoting the appropriate amount of resources to this goal nor allocating them effectively.

THE ISSUE OF ENVIRONMENTAL DAMAGE

Transportation has contributed to a reduction in the quality of the environment in several ways. First, rights of way and terminals have in the past been constructed without much reference to anything beyond least cost principles. Other things being equal, this is an appropriate criterion, but too often other things were not equal. Much land was therefore used for transportation purposes whose value in alternative uses was and is much greater. Industries were permitted to develop along the rights of way in a haphazard fashion, the cumulative effects of which not only have little aesthetic appeal, but also have damaged forests and rivers and jeopardized safety and accessibility. This is not, of course, solely the fault of transportation, but rather the whole complex of values and goals that precluded much in the way of advance planning or concern for environmental effects. The recent cessation of work on the Cross-Florida canal indicates, by contrast, the previous environmental neglect. It is now a goal of policy for all future investments in right-of-way and terminal facilities explicitly to consider such consequences and thereby increase the net social benefits of transport infrastructure. As indicated in a later chapter, however, there are serious difficulties in effectively quantifying external effects (mostly costs) that in the past were ignored. One suspects, however, that the real problem here is that, like Christianity, it has never been tried. The quest for new social indicators to supplement the far easier calculation of market costs and prices has barely begun and perhaps none too soon.

The most dramatic form of damage recently stressed is air pollution —especially from cars, trucks, and aircraft. To a lesser extent, noise pollution has become of some concern as well. The goal of policy has now broadened the definition of efficiency to include such side effects and to attempt to reduce them, even if this will require higher explicit costs of producing the service. New standards providing for maximum permitted emission and noise levels are being established which, if properly enforced, will generate incentives to develop engines and fuels permitting a reduction of pollution to "tolerable" levels. However, little is known about such tolerable levels and the costs of achieving them, partly because they occur in conjunction with a wide variety of non-transportation pollutants and partly because research into and enforcement of such standards are in their infancy. Despite all the recent rhetoric, barely 12 percent of the total cost of federal-aid highway projects was devoted to environmental considerations in fiscal 1969. Thus, although the goals of transportation policy have changed and have come to encompass more than internal efficiency within transport companies, the resources needed to implement the expanded goals have not yet been committed.

The issues of pollution and quality of the environment, including aesthetics, are more critical in urban areas to which we now turn.

Intra-Urban Transportation

The creation of excess capacity and greater efficiency in intercity transportation for both freight and passenger service made possible ever increasing concentrations of people in urban areas. However, while public policy attempted to make available to all every option technically feasible *between* cities (whether or not economically feasible), there was little comparable concern for providing options for travel within the city. It is thus often easier today to get *to* any given city than it is to move within it. Until recently, public policy was content to allow the private automobile to take over progressively more of the intra-urban travel function. The responses to growing congestion since World War II mainly involved building more right-of-way capacity to accommodate greater numbers of automobiles. As a consequence, not only do city streets account for slightly over half of total national travel (in vehicle miles) although representing only 14 percent of total mileage, but within urban areas upwards of 90 percent of all travel is by private passenger car and almost one-third of urban land areas is devoted to the car. Transit patronage has accordingly declined by over 50 percent since 1950. There are, of course, significant variations among cities, but the general picture is one of domination of the cities by the car. This has progressed to such an extent that there may be a conflict in goals between the city and the car or, as Wilfred Owen puts it, "between the desire for mobility and the side effects of achieving it."

It is now the side effects that are receiving most attention. These include air and noise pollution, traffic congestion (especially in the morning and evening rush hours), and the lack of aesthetic appeal of much transport infrastructure. In fact, these side effects are closely interrelated—slow-moving traffic increases pollutant emissions; such emissions damage physical assets; new construction of transport facilities may destroy other assets deemed to have eye appeal, disrupt neighborhoods, and so on. Furthermore, all of these interact with other urban trends, including housing, jobs, population density, recreation, taxes, and property values, which are themselves closely interrelated. It is in this sense that the goals of urban transport policy are more intimately connected with general urban goals than is the case with respect to intercity freight and passenger service. What is done with respect to transportation arrangements within a city can importantly influence the location of jobs and housing and thus the entire spatial distribution of productive, leisure, recreational, and educational activity. Within the limited urban space, decisions to expand or contract the areas devoted to mobility directly impinge upon alternative land uses. The tradeoffs here are more compelling and significant than is the case for intercity transport. Thus, what should be the goals of transport policy depends critically upon the goals of each urban community. Since such goals tend to be no more specific than national goals, it is clear that far more knowledge of the relationship of alternative transportation policies to the total urban environment and structure is needed.

However, there are certain trends in urban development that have contributed to the urban transportation problem. Assuming the goal of transport policy is to alleviate this problem, we need to examine briefly the causes and indicate the role of transportation in their alleviation. Essentially the needed policy changes can be viewed as those required to permit a more effective use of existing facilities and those involving additional facilities—i.e., short-run compared to long-run solutions.

The dominant trends in the location of urban and suburban economic activity are now well known and need not be repeated here. These trends, combined with population movements to the suburbs, have resulted in a separation of residential areas from job and recreation areas. In general, the majority of residents of the central business district do not possess the skills or educational levels needed for the commercial, banking, and other service industries located there; whereas, those more affluent residents of the outlying suburbs have their major employment opportunities in the central business district (CBD). There is therefore a large-scale movement from the suburbs to the CBD and back at the peak hours during weekdays only partially matched by an opposite and more diffuse movement to and from the suburbs. The former movement, except in the larger cities, is primarily by private auto, while the latter movement relies mostly on public transportation. These general movements are rendered more complex by a large proportion of cross-town-journey-to-work movements.

This increasing separation of jobs from housing, exacerbated as it is by racial discrimination in both, causes longer average journey-to-work trips, fosters cross hauling, and thus contributes to peak hour traffic from relatively light density areas in the suburbs to heavy density areas downtown—i.e., too many people trying to get to a single area at the same time.

But the inward pattern of movement is dominated by automobiles which prove to be high cost and contribute to congestion and pollution when peak hour traffic exeeds five to ten thousand passengers per hour per corridor. At the other extreme rail transit tends to be the most efficient mode of transportation only when traffic volumes exceed forty thousand. Most urban corridors lie between these two extremes when it comes to maximum peak hour traffic. The least costly form of transit for this range of traffic is bus. In short, given present urban highway and rail capacity, the predominance of the private auto in large-scale movement of people, and the continual decline in public transit by bus, subway or rail commuter, implies inefficient use of existing facilities at the peak hours.

Several obvious solutions to reduce this inefficiency are available and have often been recommended. In any peak-off-peak situation there is a need for price differentials. Higher prices should prevail at the peak period, lower at the off-peak, to reduce traffic at the former and increase it during the latter periods. There is much evidence to suggest that the total costs of using the private car are not only ill-perceived by the user but are not adequate in amount. Thus, higher tolls for use of city streets during peak periods could provide incentives for increasing the number of passengers per car and/or could shift some patronage to lower-cost public transit or to off-peak periods. If this were combined with improved quality of public transit and fare reductions or possibly even free transit, a more efficient use of existing capacity should result despite the real and apparent preferences for using one's own car.

Supplementing a more rational pricing scheme are certain physical options designed to speed up peak hour movement such as automatic traffic signals, reservation of lanes for buses, restriction of access to high performance facilities, or banning the automobile from various portions of the central business district altogether.

In addition, efforts to stagger hours of work among different industries could reduce the hourly rate of passenger movement. Although little progress has been made along these lines, the future possibilities implicit in the progressive reduction in hours of work per week and the four-day workweek make this a more feasible option than in the past, assuming some concerted effort is made. Furthermore, there is some evidence that peak hour traffic may be diminishing along presently congested corridors due to the decline in employment opportunities in the core of the city. This suggests that the future problem is less one of making large new investments in capacity than one of better use of presently available rights of way.

All of the above assumes that a major goal of urban transportation policy is reduced dependence upon the private automobile and the desirability of maintaining or expanding public transit options including taxis and jitneys. This would be true even in the absence of the pollution problem inherent in the present internal combustion engine. The latter simply makes it more compelling. An expanded, and more flexible, public transit and taxi system is necessary to provide access to employment opportunities for the carless poor and to urban amenities for the elderly and the young, as well as the low-income groups and other nondrivers. Reduced reliance upon private automobiles will also permit a reduction in the amount of space required for access and this in turn will provide opportunities for improving the aesthetic quality of urban life through use of the added space for parks, shopping malls, recreation facilities, and so on.

In the longer run, it may be necessary and desirable to bring jobs and housing closer together. The creation of satellite cities has often been suggested. Travel to traditional urban centers could then be confined mainly to purposes other than journeys to and from work. Part of the present separation of jobs and housing, however, is due to racial discrimination. Job discrimination reduces access to the kinds of employment opportunities increasingly concentrated in the urban core while housing discrimination forces greater numbers of nonwhites to live near or within the core. While improved transit flexibility can ensure that the poor and the nonwhite are at least able to move about in the modern city and reach employment opportunities open to them in the suburbs, it will not contribute much to the goal of eliminating discrimination.

However, in this, as in other areas, cities are changing. Job and housing patterns of the future may be quite different from the present. If so, the travel patterns will be different. Thus, massive investments in new rights of way for urban highways or rail and subway facilities represent extremely high-cost and often socially and aesthetically disruptive solutions to what may turn out to be a short-run problem. Improved use and selective upgrading of existing capacity seem to be a more sensible first approach than devoting even more of the increasingly scarce urban space to transportation facilities.

The difficulties of implementing comprehensive urban planning and the specific changes suggested above are formidable. Such difficulties include the multiple political boundaries and jurisdictions into which urban areas are divided, the lack of information concerning intracity *freight* movements and terminal operations which probably aggravate congestion, and the problem of making sensible investments where externalities and systems effects are large and where evaluation techniques are possibly misleading (e.g., valuation of travel time, the issue of aesthetics, and other noneconomic considerations). The last two have only recently been acknowledged.

These and other impediments to alteration of past trends are discussed in chapter 7. Yet if urban goals, whatever they may be, are to be achieved, the almost complete domination of the city by the private automobile must be altered. How extensively it needs to be altered will vary from city to city depending upon size, density, and industrial structure. But in virtually all medium and large cities the use of public facilities (including taxis and jitneys) will necessarily rise relative to the private car if the city is to become a safer, cleaner, and more attractive place to live. Fortunately recent public policy has recognized this need. Whether the response is adequate remains to be seen. It is already late in the day.

Summary and Conclusion

I have emphasized that the primary goal of transportation policy is efficiency but that "efficiency" is to be viewed somewhat differently as among intercity freight transportation, intercity passenger transportation, and urban transportation. For the former, it is now appropriate to view efficiency mainly in terms of economic criteria stressing "cheapness and plenty" largely because the relationship of improved freight transport to other social objectives is unclear and because changes in present facilities cannot be expected to have major external effects. If this is so, it is fairly easy for an economist to suggest specific policy changes that would improve efficiency in this sense. It is largely for this reason that the section on intercity freight transport is lengthy compared to the other two. Such relative length should not be construed as indicating greater importance—merely greater ability to be more specific. In the other two areas, noneconomic concerns and external impacts tend to be more significant; hence "efficiency" needs to be interpreted more broadly. Yet, we know so little about the external effects of improved transportation and even less about the issues of safety and the environment pertaining to transportation, that it is difficult to be more specific. The discussion of desirable or rational policy changes thus emphasized various actions mainly designed to encourage better use of existing capacities. To be sure, much new investment will be needed, especially for equipment; but the possibilities of serious waste are so great, the proponents of massive rebuilding so persuasive, and the immediate needs so compelling, that less grandiose and less time-consuming solutions deserve to be emphasized and tried first.

At the same time, in all areas, certain obvious longer-run needs and approaches are becoming evident: first, the need for comprehensive planning and coordination of transport with general economic and social planning, especially in urban areas; second, the need not only for simplification and reduction of economic regulation but for more general and comprehensive coordination covering all modes; third, the need for research and experimentation especially in the areas of safety and urban transit to prevent a repetition of past mistakes.

It is no accident that policies toward transportation are now turning in these directions. If this continues, it may well be that the decade of the 1970s will witness a large increase in price-service alternatives for shippers and passengers, a significant reduction in deaths, accidents and pollution, the end of the virtually complete auto domination of most cities, and the elimination of indirectly subsidized common carriage.

These and other possibilities will result in a transportation system that is flexible, versatile, and more accessible to all with far fewer adverse external effects than exist today. In the final analysis, these define "efficiency"—*the* goal of transportation policy.

A. Scheffer Lang

2

Demand and Supply: The Technology of Transportation

Our intention in this chapter is to look first at the aggregate demand for transportation as it can be expected to develop over the years immediately ahead and second at the technology we will have available for meeting that demand. This will then form the basis for a discussion of the directions which the development of new technology might most usefully take.

For purposes of discussing both the demand and the supply (technology) side of this demand-supply equation, we can usefully disaggregate transportation into four major sectors: intercity passenger, urban passenger, intercity freight, and urban freight. We must break these sectors down further into commercial and private transportation for estimating transportation expenditures; but to the traveller or shipper many of these distinctions are actually somewhat blurred.

Transportation Demand to 1980

The most reliable source for estimates of aggregate national transportation demand is the economic sector input-output studies which

A. SCHEFFER LANG *is professor of civil engineering and head of the Transportation Systems Division at Massachusetts Institute of Technology. His most recent prior assignment was as the first federal railroad administrator in the United States Department of Transportation. He has also been deputy undersecretary of commerce for transportation research. In addition to his direct experience in transportation companies, Professor Lang has written books and articles on transport problems.*

are done for the United States Department of Transportation. These studies project total demand and revenues for each of the four transportation sectors on the basis of several possible growth rates of the gross national product (GNP). Tables 1 and 2, abstracted from these studies, show projections for 1980 based on a 4.3 percent annual growth rate in GNP, a rate which seems generally accepted as reasonable. These projections pose several problems, however, because to get them one must make a number of questionable assumptions about pricing, regulation, public investment, and technological change in the transportation industries.

First, the input-output model used to generate such projections must assume fixed ratios of factor inputs to transport (and other industrial) outputs. An analysis of the transportation sector itself, for instance, shows that the ratio of output to investment in equipment has varied widely during the 1960s. (There were signs that the utilization of capital equipment was improving up through the middle of the decade, but it has since gone down—perhaps due to excess capacity.)

Second, the projections assume that relative price and service characteristics will remain the same for each mode of transportation. In reality, existing trends can be affected by managerial changes, regulatory changes, changes in public investment policy, and technological progress. For example, the small share of the intercity passenger market attributed to rail necessarily (in the model) assumes that passenger trains will continue to be slower than air and more expensive than bus. Arguments have been made, however, that a properly designed, higher speed, short-haul service could actually be the low-cost mode and could reverse the competitive shift away from air.[1]

Of course, the advent of a more suitable vertical takeoff and landing aircraft could not only affect the competitive balance with rail and bus; it could have a significant impact on the total intercity travel market.

The intercity freight transportation sector poses problems similar to those cited above. As discussed elsewhere in this work, rate regulation forces an allocation of traffic between modes (if not between regions of the country) which would shift—perhaps drastically in some cases—if this regulatory constraint were removed. The institutional constraints on the use of labor (particularly in the railroad

[1] See T. E. Keeler, "The Economics of Passenger Trains," *Journal of Business* (April 1971).

TABLE I. *The Nation's Transportation Bill, 1970*[a]
(in millions of 1965 dollars)

Mode of Transportation	Passenger	Freight
Commercial Transportation	12872.0	34595.0
Railroads	358.0	11230.0
Airlines—domestic	6993.0	835.0
Airlines—international	1742.0	441.0
Intercity buses	657.0	—
Local transit	1296.0	—
Taxicabs	1594.0	—
Domestic water	11.0	1636.0
Overseas water	221.0	2460.0
Trucking	—	16735.0
Pipe lines	—	1258.0
Private Transportation	44605.0	48673.0
Personal auto [b]	29851.0	—
Business auto	9596.0	—
Government auto [b]	1117.0	—
Personal aircraft [b]	172.0	—
Business aircraft	948.0	—
Government civil aircraft	56.0	—
Other general aviation aircraft	305.0	—
Private trucking—freight	—	19447.0
Private trucking—nonfreight	—	25999.0
Government trucking	—	3032.0
School buses [c]	647.0	—
Other private buses	165.0	—
Recreational boating [b]	1748.0	—
Commercial fishing	—	195.0
Equipment Purchases [d] (not included above)	20265.1	293.5
Personal auto	18730.6	—
Government auto	700.9	—
Personal aircraft	72.0	—
Government civil aircraft	21.2	—
Government trucks	—	293.5
School buses (government)	87.8	—
Recreation boats	652.6	—
Total Transportation Bill	77742.1	83561.5

[a] Based on the current projections of GNP as distinguished from the trend projections. Figures represent revenues for commercial transportation and costs of operations for private transportation.

[b] Depreciation not included.

[c] Depreciation not included (except for commercially-operated school buses). See Note [d].

[d] Expenditures for equipment purchases by households and government for which depreciation accounts are not kept and therefore not included in operating costs.

43

TABLE II. *The Nation's Transportation Bill, 1980* [a]
(in millions of 1965 dollars)

Mode of Transportation	Passenger	Freight
Commercial Transportation	26468.0	56483.0
Railroads	300.0	14860.0
Airlines—domestic	16457.0	3090.0
Airlines—international	5469.0	1858.0
Intercity buses	699.0	—
Local transit	1587.0	—
Taxicabs	1739.0	—
Domestic water	9.0	2386.0
Overseas water	208.0	4161.0
Trucking	—	28241.0
Pipe lines	—	1887.0
Private Transportation	69647.0	77314.0
Personal auto [b]	43156.0	—
Business auto	15843.0	—
Government auto [b]	1739.0	—
Personal aircraft [b]	430.0	—
Business aircraft	2912.0	—
Government civil aircraft [b]	122.0	—
Other general aviation aircraft	660.0	—
Private trucking—freight	—	30815.0
Private trucking—nonfreight	—	41563.0
Government trucking [b]	—	4799.0
School buses [c]	618.0	—
Other private buses	266.0	—
Recreational boating	3901.0	—
Commercial fishing	—	137.0
Equipment Purchases [d] (not included above)	29873.0	464.5
Personal auto	27079.0	—
Government auto	1091.2	—
Personal aircraft	125.8	—
Government civil aircraft	36.6	—
Government trucks	—	464.5
School buses (government)	83.9	—
Recreation boats	1456.5	—
Total Transportation Bill	125988.0	134261.5

[a] Based on the 4.3 percent annual growth projection of GNP. Figures represent revenues for commercial transportation and costs of operation for private transportation.

[b] Depreciation not included.

[c] Depreciation not included (except for commercially-operated school buses). See Note [d].

[d] Expenditures for equipment purchases by households and government for which depreciation accounts are not kept and therefore not included in operating costs.

44

industry) constitutes a different sort of problem, but one again which distorts these forecasts from what *might* actually take place at some future time.

Other problems with the ratios used to generate these forecasts derive from such anomalies in our present transportation system as over-investment in fixed facilities for railroads and perhaps for highways. Certainly there is widespread agreement that our railroad plant is overbuilt; so that the costs associated with increased rail output should (in theory) be lower than for present traffic. Similar arguments can be made for intercity (but not urban) highways.

Despite these and other problems, input-output techniques are probably the best thing available to use today for generating forecasts of our gross transportation demands. The results shown here point up the significant trends, in any case. (Refer to Tables 1 and 2.)

First, it is clear that a sustained growth in the demand for intercity (and overseas) air travel is likely. The estimate here is for an increase of 150 percent from 1970 to 1980. Second, there will be a large increase in expenditures on automobile transportation, the estimate being that they will increase 50 percent from 1970 to 1980. Third, there will be a large increase in both commercial and private trucking, the estimate being that they will increase by 60 percent from 1970 to 1980. (The significant growth in "non-freight" trucking is also of interest, because this involves vehicles which contribute much to street congestion in our central cities.) Projected growth in the remaining transportation sectors is more modest, if not stagnant.

Translating these growth estimates into investment requirements poses still another difficult set of problems for many of the same reasons that the demand forecasts themselves pose problems. The most critical issue in this regard, though, is probably that of technology; that is, of the "supply" side of transportation, to which we shall now turn.

The Supply Side of Transportation

The most important fact we must confront on the supply side of the transportation demand-supply equation is that our transportation technology is not standing still any more than the demand is. Not only has it changed in some ways rather dramatically in recent years (e.g., through the introduction of jet aircraft); it will predictably continue to change in the years immediately ahead. What those future changes could mean to us if we pushed them in one direction or another is of critical importance to us as a nation. Let us look at what seems probable and at what seems possible.

First, it is important to understand what probably will *not* change in the next decade and even beyond; namely, our substantial reliance on highway transportation and, more especially, our use of the personal automobile. More than 90 percent of our passenger dollars are spent for auto and bus transportation, and all but about 3 percent of that for autos. In addition, nearly 75 percent of our national freight dollars are spent for truck transportation. We cannot give up such an overwhelming commitment to highway transportation very quickly, regardless of what new technology might appear. In the next ten years, the most we can do is nibble at the edges; but that it seems we inevitably must do.

The automobile has given us the world's finest transportation system, but it has brought a host of problems with it. These problems in one way or another derive from two developments. The first is that our highway vehicle fleet has reached a critical size. Where it was about 49 million in 1950, it was 72 million in 1960 and an estimated 112 million in 1970! Quite aside from this mechanical population having grown at a faster rate than our human population, there are now simply too many automobiles in the Los Angeles basin for the atmospheric system and too many in the center of our cities for the "people system."

Problems of congestion we thought just a few years ago we could lick by building more and better highways, we know now may never go away. Problems of air pollution we scarcely recognized a few years ago, we know now we *have* to lick, despite the enormous number of vehicles already on the road. And the attendant problems of noise and aesthetic pollution are almost as critical and almost as intractable as those of congestion and air pollution because of these same numbers.

These same problems also derive in part from a second and perhaps more significant development of the last decade; namely, a major shift in the values of our society. When automobiles, expressways, and jet airplanes were fewer—and when the unmet needs for mobility were greater—we were generally willing to vote for transportation "progress." Now, most of us are beginning to wonder whether the quality of our environment is not in the long run more important than how fast we can get out of or around in our cities! People have learned, moreover, how to use their political power in pursuing objectives consistent with these new values and blocking transportation "progress" in the bargain.

Doing less damage to the environment is, thus, going to be a major thrust in transportation development over the next ten years. So is solving another major problem; that of providing adequate mobility for the old, the infirm, and the poor. As the mobility of the rest of the population has improved, these groups have been put relatively at an increasing disadvantage. Again, this problem has come to the fore as our sense of values has changed.

Along with these problems, we must also rank the general problem of what appears, at least, to be steadily increasing congestion, both in our urban and interurban transportation systems. So far, the facts do not bear out the appearances; but, again, what was acceptable even a decade ago is less so today when our aspirations for quality of life have risen.

The facts of present-day congestion notwithstanding, it is predictable that with a continuing growth in population and economic activity, congestion levels will increase in many areas over the next decade unless present trends are altered. We cannot, as an example, halt urban expressway construction on environmental grounds, raise the level of urbanization and automobile ownership, provide only spotty improvements in public transportation, *and* keep street congestion at present levels, too. Something has to give!

These problems cited above are ones inherent primarily in our passenger transport systems, urban and intercity; but they touch our freight movement system, too. In particular, our truck transport system contributes importantly to air, noise, and visual pollution along with its passenger-carrying counterparts, the automobile and the bus. And in our cities, where virtually all freight movements are by truck, congestion is very much a by-product of freight as well as passenger transport.

What can be done about these problems and what will be done about them depends very much upon the technological options available to us. Let us look first at those and then go on to look at the contribution that each might make to solving our transportation and transportation-related problems.

Intercity Passenger Transportation Technology

Our intercity passenger transport system seems inevitably the "glamour-girl" of transportation to the man in the street. Jet airplanes, ocean liners, and streamlined trains are what many think of when one speaks of transportation—even though such commercial systems account for less than 15 percent of our intercity passenger-miles and well under 10 percent of our total expenditures on passenger transportation. These systems are important to us, nonetheless, because they literally and figuratively extend the range of our society and our economy.

The jet airliner has, of course, been the greatest recent advance in intercity passenger transportation technology. It provided a quantum jump in speed and a substantial increase in passenger comfort over its propeller-driven forerunners of only a few years ago. The next generation of these subsonic aircraft, the "widebody" 747, DC-10, and 1011s, does not promise any such dramatic advances for the air traveller. These aircraft will provide roomier accommodations, but no significant increase in speed or ride quality. Their important contributions will be to lower costs—and thus to lower fares slightly—and to increase the passenger-carrying capacity of our limited resources in airspace and airport landing facilities.

In fact, the steady increase in the size of commercial aircraft, coupled with a slowdown in the dramatic air travel growth rates of the 1960s, should provide some temporary respite from the capacity crisis which seemingly confronted our major airports in the latter years of that decade. These developments are particularly welcome at a time when community opposition to airport expansion and building plans has reached such proportions that many predict we will not be able to build any new airports anywhere in the United States anymore!

This cannot be taken to mean that the growth in air travel will stop altogether. The Department of Transportation figures cited earlier show a dramatic growth through the decade of the 1970s. Though recent trends suggest these forecasts may be too high, even the most bearish observers agree that air travel still has a long way to go. The most important answer to how it will get there, however, probably lies in short takeoff and landing (STOL) and vertical takeoff and landing (VTOL) aircraft. Though both types of vehicles are with us today—in the form of the Twin Otter and other STOL aircraft and in the form of helicopter VTOL machines—neither has yet reached a level of development necessary to trigger the kind of widespread commercial adoption enjoyed by conventional takeoff and landing (CTOL) machines.

Given a clear federal policy of support and encouragement, that development could come for both types of vehicles by the end of the 1970s. If and when it does come, a significantly different mix of intercity air services will come with it. We are seeing this in a preliminary way with STOL today. Small airline operators are offering service from small cities and towns to big-city airports where, in some cases, special STOL runways have been provided to accommodate these aircraft outside the regular, congested airspace and runway system. Major cities such as New York, moreover, are planning "STOL-ports" in or near the central city to make faster door-to-door trips possible for many travellers now bogged down in highway traffic going to and from the airport. In general, enthusiasm for expanded STOL service runs high, though larger, lower-cost aircraft that could handle large numbers of travellers were still very much in the development stage at the beginning of the decade.

Most transportation planners and agencies have been betting heavily on STOL to provide major help in solving both our airport capacity and our airport access problems. While it can help both, it is probably less promising than its near-cousin, VTOL. Up to this time, the more exotic VTOL machines have been largely discounted because of their noise and high operating costs. The technology for quiet VTOL machines, however, is nearly at hand; and operating costs, which are coming down for VTOL, have in the overall become steadily less important for commercial air transport service. These two factors make it possible to think of a relatively ubiquitous intercity "air-bus" type of service operating out of small and inexpensive ground facilities spotted in a number of easily accessible locations throughout each metropolitan area.[2]

Our technological aspirations for improved intercity passenger service are not, of course, confined to improved air travel. The hopes of many travellers have, in fact, been riding on high-speed ground transportation, including improved railroad systems. These hopes are

[2] This type of system was first outlined in detail by Professors Rene Miller and Robert Simpson of Massachusetts Institute of Technology in a study done in 1965 for the United States Department of Commerce. A more recent study, "Short Haul Inter-Urban Air Systems," done by the MITRE Corporation in 1971 for the United States Department of Transportation, offers some additional encouragement regarding the feasibility of such systems.

not without foundation. Early results show that the improved (100-plus mph) "Metroliner" rail service between New York and Washington has met with generally favorable market response; and further improvements in this service are possible. The development of ultra high-speed (200–300 mph) tracked air-cushion vehicles (TACV) is also proceeding satisfactorily, and their availability in the late 1970s seems increasingly likely.

Possible improvements in conventional intercity railroad passenger transportation have been foretold, of course, by the widely-renowned New Tokaido Line of the Japanese National Railways and, more recently, by the high-speed, electrified London-Manchester service in Great Britain. Both of these have demonstrated that in dense-traffic corridors over trip lengths of perhaps 100–400 miles, higher speed rail is a formidable competitor. The technology, moreover, has yet to be pushed to its limits. The second section of the Japanese line involves cruising speeds in the 150 mph range, and research here and abroad looks to eventual rail speeds of close to 200 mph. The problem with such higher speeds is the cost of the straight and level track alignments which they require—$2.5 billion plus, for example, for a line through the Northeast Corridor from Boston to Washington.

These high construction costs, and higher, would also be characteristic of the ultra high-speed TACV systems. Because of these costs, it is not clear whether such systems can compete economically with either improved existing rail or VTOL systems. In particular, VTOL has the advantage both of lower initial cost *and* an ability to serve more directly the widely dispersed trip origins and destinations now typical of our metropolitan areas.

Urban Passenger Transportation Technology

The technology of future urban (intracity) passenger transportation is at once less glamorous and more intriguing than that of intercity systems. Tracked air cushion vehicles and vertical takeoff and landing aircraft have no important part in that future; but the evolution of new technology and service systems that can help articulate the intricate social and physical fabric of our metropolitan areas is actually a more challenging task for planners, engineers, and public administrators.

Again, this is a scene dominated today and still-to-be dominated tomorrow by the automobile. The automobile provides *the* ultimate mode of intra-urban movement—door-to-door, completely flexible, completely private, and competitive in cost with the best of public transportation. The problem is that automobiles get in each other's way and in the way of pleasant urban living!

Some improvement in the conventional auto-highway system is possible, but the gains in themselves will not be dramatic. The air pollution problem will be largely licked before the end of the 1970s—not by electric automobiles, but by redesigned internal combustion engines. (The technical shortcomings of electric propulsion for automobiles are apparently not going to be overcome at any reasonable cost.) The noise problem may take a bit longer, but it too will be improved.

The aesthetic problems associated with streets and, in particular, expressways are less susceptible to correction, if only because most of the facilities in use at the end of the decade will be those in place at the beginning. Nonetheless, improved designs intended to harmonize more with their surroundings are under development, and their effect will increasingly be felt as new construction replaces old.

The equally visible problem of traffic congestion will also yield only marginally to improved technology. Engineers will continue the development of better traffic control devices and will continue improvements designed to make better use of our existing investment in surface streets. Priority systems and dedicated lanes or rights of way for buses will also raise the passenger- (as opposed to vehicle-) carrying capacity of our urban systems. *All* of this will whittle away at the edges of our present problems; but the most important breakthroughs will probably have to come in other ways.

One of these is demand-activated transit, a class of new services (as opposed to new technology) which is most prominently represented by the "dial-a-ride" concept. This concept involves the use of small buses, dispatched by a computer in response to telephone requests for service, taking people on door-to-door trips in a shared mode (several passengers making different trips in the vehicle at any one time). The result is public transportation somewhere between the taxi and the conventional bus in *both* quality of service and price. The idea is important, not because it will sweep automobiles from the streets, but because it will offer service to many who live in our smaller cities and the less-dense parts of our larger ones and cannot afford conventional taxis. Thus, demand-activated transit will help fill out our spectrum of urban transportation services.

More dramatic gains can be made in our larger cities through the

use of automated vehicle systems for public transportation. These will
be systems operating on guideways or tracks, without drivers, but otherwise providing a service similar—at least in its initial phases—to that
offered by rail rapid transit systems. The most significant difference
between these new systems and conventional ones will be in the size
of the vehicles. More specifically, they will use single vehicles of from
four to perhaps twenty passengers versus trains of vehicles which each
have a capacity of upwards of a hundred passengers. This single difference in turn makes the automated systems attractive in several important respects. First, the small vehicles can be mass produced; and
because of this and their relatively light weight, they will be much
cheaper to build (per passenger of carrying capacity) than conventional rail vehicles. Second, because they will be light (and small), they
will use light, and thus small, guideway structures, ones more capable
of integration with their environment and much cheaper to build.
They will also use smaller and thus cheaper tunnels. Third, the small
vehicles will depart on much shorter headways, thus significantly improving the quality of service available to users. Additionally, these
systems will be much cheaper to operate, because they will not employ
drivers.

These automated vehicle systems when adequately tested out will
probably displace all further rail rapid transit construction other than
a few additions to existing systems. Their use will not be restricted
to operation on guideways, however, since some and eventually most
of these systems will be built to use vehicles that can also operate on
surface streets under driver control like a conventional automobile.
That is, they will be so-called "dual mode" or "mixed-mode" systems.
It is important to recognize, though, that in the early years of these
systems the vehicles will all operate as public transportation vehicles
both on and off the guideway. This will distinguish such systems from
the "automated highway" designed to move the user's own personal
vehicle under automated control on a guideway. That will come, if at
all, at a later stage of development.

These dual-mode public transportation systems will substitute in
most major metropolitan areas for the additional expressways that will
not be built. They will provide significantly better service than rail
transit systems at much lower total cost. In their smaller scale versions,
they will be captive-vehicle "people-movers" substituting for pedestrian movement in large activity centers, such as shopping centers.
In their larger, higher-speed versions they will provide fast city-to-

suburb line-haul movement and door-to-door off-guideway collection and distribution at the suburban end of trips.

Unfortunately, no corresponding technology is in sight to provide enhanced transportation for the less fortunate residents of the inner city. Dial-a-ride and other demand-activated services will help, but it is unlikely that automated systems will offer adequate internal circulation for such medium-density areas as are found immediately adjacent to the central business districts.

Intercity Freight Transportation Technology

The technology of intercity freight transportation can be expected to undergo steady evolution throughout the 1970s, but there are probably no revolutions in sight for that decade. This evolution will be the result of the continuing drive to improve efficiency and quality of service, rather than the result of any pressing problems in available capacity. Capacity is simply not a significant problem in this sector.

Intercity freight transportation is, like the other three sectors discussed here, dominated by highway operations. While trucks account for a bit less than one-quarter of our intercity freight ton-miles, they take in about three-quarters of the money spent on intercity freight transportation. That is, in terms of the value of service rendered, the highway mode is dominant.

With the steady improvement in both trucks and highways which we can look forward to over the years immediately ahead, there is no reason to expect that trucks will not continue to dominate this transportation market. At the same time, such marginal improvements as the addition of double and triple trailers will not produce any dramatic improvements in the truck's ability to compete for this market. On the contrary, the prospects are that rail piggyback service will take over a larger share of the line-haul, but not the terminal, job.

The future prospects for railroad freight transportation technology are less clear. Progress in improving this technology has been steady, but generally unexciting. Many observers feel that a gap has been opening up between what is now available and what should be possible and that if that gap were closed it would produce a dramatic improvement in rail freight service. These hopes are based on suggestions for further automation of train operations, for the introduction of more reliable and cost-effective freight equipment (cars and locomotives), and for the application of modern computers and control techniques to the operation of trains and the movement of individual cars. These kinds of improvements might not reduce costs significantly below their present levels, but they might increase the quality of service offered shippers to levels that would make rail transportation a much stronger competitor for the more remunerative markets now being served by trucks.

The further development of rail piggyback and container service is, perhaps, the most important of the potential improvements in rail transportation. The cost economics of rail line-haul (perhaps one-fifth the cost of truck line-haul) are attractive; but some of these are sacrificed in the transfer to and from truck, and service quality remains a difficult problem to solve. All in all, the problems here do not seem to be those of technology but ones of management, marketing, and institutional integration.

Intermodal service of all kinds seems destined to grow in importance despite the problems cited here. The technology of marine container operations, largely perfected during the 1960s, will continue to move inland as more extensive arrangements are made with both railroads and truck lines to provide service to more shippers. Except for improvements in the control of container movements (through such devices as automatic container identification), however, the major breakthroughs in technology seem already to have been made.

In water transportation per se, the container development seems to have been *the* breakthrough. Novel shipforms, such as the submerged hull, and the development of more economical reactor power plants can produce important further improvements in overall system performance; but now that the container has broken the back of port costs and delays, the more important improvements may come on the land leg of sea journeys.

Air cargo operations pose a slightly equivocal prospect. The very large cargo jets such as the C-5A, not yet in commercial operation at the beginning of the decade, will probably not produce the dramatic savings in cost once forecast for them. Even if they do, the steady improvement in truck transportation (due in large part to the Interstate Highway System) will have narrowed the service gap enough to assure that aircraft will capture only the very top premium traffic. In terms of cargo volume, the diversion to air will not be noticed by the trucking industry.

This brings us, finally, to the "sleeper" in freight transportation technology—solids pipe lines. These take two forms: "slurry" lines which pump finely divided solids, such as pulverized coal or sulphur, in a liquid suspension; and lines which push capsules containing solids, such as wheat, with a liquid (which may be oil or water). A number of slurry lines were already in operation in the United States and Canada by the end of the 1960s and more were being planned. A continuing program of research was underway on capsule lines.

Where a large, guaranteed, long-term movement is available, and especially where reasonably direct rail lines do not connect the origin and destination of the movement, slurry lines may move a commodity at as little as one-half the cost of the cheapest rail operations. The prospect is, moreover, that many commodities will be added to the small list of those already found suitable for handling this way. Capsule lines will, of course, widen these possibilities even further; and where capsules can be moved with oil that must be pumped anyway, the resulting costs may be equally as attractive as those forecast for slurry lines.

Urban Freight Transportation Technology

Of all the areas of transportation, this is the one about which we know the least. That is, we know it consumes over one-third of the total dollars we spend on freight transportation; but we do not know much about where things move or how they move within our urban areas. What is more the point here, we do not have any clear idea of what improvements in technology are feasible.

As pointed out earlier in this chapter, urban freight transportation is accomplished entirely by truck, and these trucks contribute significantly to congestion on our surface streets. Unfortunately, it is to the advantage of those performing this service to conduct their operations during the same business hours that the streets are being used for automobile and bus transportation. Most attempts here and abroad to shift local trucking operations to evening or nighttime hours have seemingly foundered on institutional and cost problems of one sort or another. At the same time, most attempts to consolidate deliveries of more than one carrier have also failed.

Conventional technology thus poses problems that it would seem only unconventional technology or unconventional city forms can solve. Either we must find ways to put automated delivery systems into our central cities, or put our truck roadways underground, or both.

Lacking such steps—and they seem unlikely in the immediate future—
we shall have to live with our urban freight transportation system
much as it is.

What Development Seems in Order

Before discussing where it seems we should go over the next
decade with transportation technology, it should be noted again that
most of our transportation capability in 1980 will be that which was
already in place or available in 1970. That is, ours will be essentially
a highway-oriented society and economy, regardless! Given the problems of our highway-dominated transportation system, however, we
can scarcely settle for the status quo. Our job, thus, is to get the most
improvement out of our available dollars and technology.

Our most important opportunities for improvement in intercity
passenger transportation seem to be (1) some selective upgrading of
short- and medium-haul rail and (2) accelerated development of VTOL
aircraft. (Over a longer term, TACV systems may also have some
place; but their future is less certain.) These changes will not produce
major savings in cost. (For example, our need for improved intercity
highways will continue to grow.) What these changes will do is to
assure continued improvement in the quality of service available. They
will do this by helping to break key bottlenecks in highway and air
transportation around our major cities and by offering a broader
range of service to our expanding population.

In urban passenger transportation, our most important opportunities for progress lie in the development of (1) demand-activated transit
service and (2) automated guideway transit systems using both captive
and dual-mode vehicles. As distinct from the intercity improvements
cited above, these developments will *both* reduce costs and improve
service. In fact, they will save some semblance of public transportation
for our cities! Both conventional bus systems and conventional rail
systems have reached a point where their costs are inexorably increasing and their service just as inexorably deteriorating; and there is no
way out of this spiral *except* with unconventional systems! Both of the
developments cited here can be with us in this decade, however, if we
will only push them as a matter of conscious national policy.

In intercity freight transportation, it seems that little in the way
of explicit technological development is in order, except for across-
the-board improvements in rail technology. The payoff here could be

of some consequence; since significant improvement in rail performance could divert as much as 20 percent of intercity truck ton-miles to box-car and piggyback movement. Removing this percentage of the growing truck volume from our highways has been variously estimated to save perhaps $1 billion a year in operating costs and at least as much more in highway construction and maintenance costs.[3] At the same time, we might do well to encourage development of solids pipe lines since their aggregate cost savings to the economy, even by the end of this decade, could be substantial.

Finally, it seems there is little we can say at this time about urban freight transportation technology except that it is a problem!

[3] See, for instance, Ann F. Friedlaender, *The Dilemma of Freight Transport Regulation* (Washington, 1969), for some analysis of this issue.

Dudley F. Pegrum

3

Restructuring the Transport System

Introduction

Technological developments in transportation in the twentieth century have resulted in a transformation in this area of activity, in services performed and in the means of performing them, that has created a system radically different from anything that obtained theretofore. The structure of transport has undergone drastic modifications, partly unforeseen and partly the result of conscious action. In both cases, however, they have taken place under public policy as expressed in whatever laws or "rules of the game" have been applicable. All industry is, and must be, regulated in some way or another.

ASSUMPTIONS OF PUBLIC POLICY

Public policy for restructuring the transport system, or directing the development of the structure, must be based on certain assumptions regarding the regulation of transport. If it is assumed that the current practice of separate treatment under the direction of the regulatory commission is to be abandoned, then considerations for restructuring would have to be framed in light of present laws as enforced by the Antitrust Division, United States Department of Justice, and the Fed-

DUDLEY F. PEGRUM *is professor emeritus of economics at the University of California (Los Angeles). Consultant to many American and foreign carriers and to governmental agencies, he won the Distinguished Service Award for Transportation of the American Economic Association in 1966. Dr. Pegrum has written numerous books, articles, and reports on transportation.*

eral Trade Commission. This would mean that the restructuring would
have to be voluntary within modes, and among them, subject to the
challenge of the antitrust authorities. It would also entail abandoning
cooperative arrangements on such matters as joint rates, through rates,
etc., at least pending judicial clarification. The complete reorientation
to so completely a foreign environment would present such a welter
of unknown problems that one may be permitted to assume that this
is an unrealistic way to deal with the current issues of transport structure. The appropriate approach seems to be that which assumes separate and distinct regulation of transportation in light of its unique
features, and of the specific issues that have arisen as a result of those
features.

Restructuring of the transport system involves an understanding of
the economic characteristics of the various modes, their functions in
the transport system, their rights and responsibilities with regard to
service, the role and possibilities of competition, and the relation of
transport to non-transport enterprises in the economy. Consideration
must also be given to ownership and organization relationships among
the modes and within them as well as to the role of public investment
in the industry. Public policy has dealt with all these matters in various ways and the present structure is the result of that policy. The
issues today are how that policy has fallen short of achieving tolerably
acceptable results, or to what extent it is responsible for the present
transportation "crisis," and what seem to be necessary and acceptable
changes designed to bring about a resolution of current difficulties.

The Economic Structure of the Modes of Transport

TRANSPORT—A GROUP OF INDUSTRIES

Proposals for restructuring transportation must first of all give clear
recognition to the economic characteristics of the different modes.
If one were to discuss the restructuring of the steel or aluminum industries or automobile manufacture, he would in each instance be dealing
with an area of production in which the firms have the same basic
economic characteristics. Therefore they can be dealt with by rules of
public policy that apply equally to all.

Transport, however, does not fit into such a convenient mold. Instead, it consists of a group of industries both in terms of economic
structure and in terms of substitutability of services. It is an industry
only in the sense that it provides the means of moving people or com-

modities from one place to another. Railroads and pipe lines have economic characteristics arising from their technological structure that make them "natural" or technological monopolies. Motor, water, and air carriers have the economic characteristics of competitive undertakings and exhibit them more completely even than steel, cement, automobile manufacturing, or oil refining.

Railroads have relatively large fixed costs, resulting in a capital turnover of about once every three years. These carriers are confined to the market areas tapped by their fixed physical facilities, and once these are installed they cannot readily be changed. Customers who seek their services must go to them or be connected directly with them. For example, in the Chicago Milwaukee and North Western merger application (ICC Finance Docket No. 24182, December 18, 1968), Examiner Darmstadter, after careful evaluation of the testimony of the witnesses, concluded that the carrier serving a shipper's plant is in a dominant position in competing with other carriers which can gain access to the plant only by cooperation such as reciprocal switching or otherwise. This is undoubtedly a significant reason why railroads seek to develop industrial sites on land which they own or can acquire. Motor, water, and air carriers have lower fixed costs than many heavy industries and have the cost attributes of competitive industry. Furthermore, they possess the mobility that makes it possible for them to seek traffic wherever it is available if they are permitted to do so legally. As a result of this not all of the services supplied by these modes are subject to transport regulation and there is little prospect that such control can ever embrace all of them.

MONOPOLY THEORY OF PUBLIC REGULATION

Present public policy in the field of transport commenced with the railroads approximately a century ago. The approach to the problems was based on the theory that the railroads were monopolies to which competition alone afforded inadequate protection to the consuming or shipping public. The idea soon developed that the railroads were public utilities in both the technical and legal senses, that overall competition among them was ruinous and had to be curtailed. The complete public utility approach was embodied in the Transportation Act of 1920, which unfortunately, however, did not resolve the inconsistent provisions regarding monopoly and competition that it contained.

The basic theory of the Act of 1920—that transportation had to be regulated as a public utility—was extended to common carriers of the other modes by legislative enactments down to and including the Act of 1940. No significant modifications have been made since then.

That these other modes fitted uncomfortably into the public utility mold was recognized by the exceptions and exemptions in the various legislative acts which have sanctioned the growth of a very large amount of traffic that is completely outside commission control. The newer modes of motor and air transport do not conform to the pattern and, of course, water never did. One may hazard the guess that if there had been no railroads, regulation of transport based on the monopoly theory never would have emerged. We have the railroads, however, and as a consequence transport services are supplied by both "natural" monopolies and thoroughly competitive modes. This is the reason for the dual problem of intramodal and intermodal competition. If it were not for the railroads this distinction would have no significance because they would both amount to the same thing. On the other hand, if each mode offered only unique services, that is if there were no appreciable intermodal competition or substitutability, each could be dealt with separately. This is obviously not the situation.

THE UNIQUENESS OF TRANSPORT

The theory of monopoly that underlies present transport regulation is wrong; it flies in the face of facts. Unfortunately, the industry throughout its entirety does not conform to the competitive model either. Herein lies the complexity of the problem. The railroads still possess the same economic characteristics they had before the other modes emerged. The fact that they are now subject to severe competition does not alter their structure but it does complicate the problems of public policy. A single pattern of regulation to be applied to the various issues that arise in connection with each of the modes cannot bring satisfactory results. Furthermore, cognizance must be taken of the inescapable presence of available transport facilities that fall outside any conceivable scope of regulation and which present major competitive challenges to the regulated carriers.

Restructuring therefore must be undertaken in light of the different economic features of the modes. It must also recognize that this requires, over a considerable range at least, a public policy of control that cannot be afforded under antitrust, at least as the latter is interpreted today. In addition the services supplied by transport require cooperation within and among the modes on pricing, routes, carrier obligations, etc. that would receive inhospitable treatment under present antitrust administration. We have had no experience in developing public policy for transport under antitrust. Any development of public policy that fails to recognize the uniqueness of the transport industry in its economic structure and the types of service it must offer will have little chance of acceptance or success.

The Common Carrier

THE NATURE OF THE COMMON CARRIER

A common carrier in transportation is an enterprise that holds itself ready to serve the general public for hire at reasonable rates up to the limit of the facilities of the carrier for the particular services which it is prepared to offer. The idea of the common carrier arose under the common law in England from the guild system wherein certain activities could be undertaken only by a special grant of privilege which excluded the competition of others. With the breakdown of the guild system and the rise of competitive enterprise to take its place, the special grants of privilege disappeared, but common carrier obligations continued to be imposed upon those who held themselves out, either expressly or by a course of conduct, to transport for hire all goods or persons seeking the service which was proffered. The obligation to provide common carriage was voluntarily assumed but did not apply either to all the business of the enterprise or to others who did not seek general public patronage.

Common carriage has never been an attribute of all transport for hire, nor have all carriers assuming common carrier obligations been confined solely to that activity. The restrictions imposed upon common carriers and the control of entry into this line of business are the result of legislative enactments. This has led to the identification of common carriage with rate regulation and control of entry, based on the premise that common carrier transportation is offered under a monopolistic grant of privilege that precludes, or should preclude, the discipline of the market and competitive forces, except in a very limited way.

The requirement that common carriers meet certain specified obligations to those who demand services from them did not result in direct price regulation until railroads (and water carriers controlled by them) were brought under the Act to Regulate Commerce in 1887. It was not until 1906 that rate regulation was effectively instituted, and even then it was applied only to maximum rates. Precise rate-fixing by public authority was finally inaugurated in 1920 but it was confined to the railroads and oil pipe lines. Common carriage, however, was supplied by other agencies. In other words, common carriage and price regulation are not two sides of the same coin. One can exist without the other. A common carrier, if statute does not prohibit it, can serve in a competitive atmosphere without the necessity of rate regulation if there is a demand for that type of service. It is legislative enactment that has superimposed price regulation on previously existing transport. This has been done on the theory that a monopoly grant was given, or that monopoly prevailed. Legislative control of rates has even been extended, in a somewhat limited way, to contract carriage, clearly for the purpose of protecting the common carrier price structure and traffic.

PUBLIC POLICY AND THE COMMON CARRIER

Down to 1920 intercity transport was supplied primarily by the railroads. Federal legislation from 1887 to 1920 converted the railroads totally into common carriers and, with the Transportation Act of 1920, subjected all of them to thoroughgoing regulation in the public utility mold that had been developed in a number of states to deal with local utilities. Oil pipe lines, other than those of a strictly private nature, were also included. There was no demand at that time to extend this regulation to common carriers by water or the other emerging modes. Certificates of public convenience and necessity were required for railroad extensions, but these were not required for entry by other common carriers. Regulation was for the purpose of controlling monopoly and restricting competition among the railroads, but was not applied to the other modes of transport, common carriage or otherwise.

Technological developments, particularly in motor and air transport, brought about a drastic change in the transport structure in a short period of fifteen years. Transportation ceased to be a monopoly of the railroads or of the common carrier. The impact of these changes would have called for a thoroughgoing reevaluation of public policy even under the best of circumstances. Unfortunately, the situation was complicated by the onset of the Great Depression. Competition came under a cloud and in every area of economic activity restriction of competition and protection against it became the basis of public policy. The Motor Carrier Act of 1935, the Civil Aeronautics Act of 1938, and the Act of 1940 as applied to common carriers by water embodied this philosophy. That these other modes did not fit very comfortably into it was clearly recognized by the exemptions and exceptions contained in the legislative enactments. The Interstate Commerce Commission (ICC) has used every means at its disposal to limit these exemptions and the exceptions, which has led to continuous litigation over private carriers, contract carriers, and farm cooperatives, together with legislative controversy over agricultural exemptions and the "mixing" rule. There can be little wonder that the so-called "gray" area of transport operations has been a matter of grave concern to the regulatory authorities.

THE NEED FOR COMMON CARRIAGE

That there is a need for common carrier service can scarcely be argued. The statistics of transport in this country demonstrate this decisively. At the present time approximately 62 percent of the total intercity freight traffic is federally regulated and about 50 percent of the total is moved by common carrier. This represents a drastic decline in the position of the common carrier in the last 50 years. However, it should be noted that the total traffic by common carriers is at an all time high for all of the modes and for each of them separately. Furthermore, it continues to increase in total. Even in the passenger field, where only about 10 percent of the traffic is by public carrier, the intercity passenger mileage by that means has continued to grow to the point that it is now almost 2.5 times greater than in 1920. With such a development, subsidy and public aid to the different modes to compete with each other embody a curious concept of efficient resource allocation. Why there should be such concern over the percentage decline is difficult to understand; there seems to be plenty of business for all. The problem apparently arises from the impact of the changes on the different modes and the implications of this for public policy. Common carriage as such still occupies a secure position in transport.

The demand for common carrier services arises from the need of the shipping and traveling public for reliability and regularity of service, as well as the assumption of common carrier obligations, the latter being the most important. Reliability and regularity of performance are of particular significance in intercity passenger transport, but they also play an important role in the movement of goods. Transport of bulk commodities and agricultural products to primary markets can be provided by individualized contracts; unit coal trains, for example, may operate as common carriers, although in effect they are really in the contract category. At least half of the intercity freight movement is under common carriage and much of this is by shippers who cannot undertake the task of individual negotiations and enforcement of contractual obligations. Public regulation with compulsory adherence to the responsibilities voluntarily assumed seems to be the only feasible alternative. The uniform bill of lading and responsibility of the carrier as bailee with published rates that must be adhered to are necessary conditions for the movement of such traffic. How this, or comparable results, could be obtained, at least for interstate commerce, without federal legislation and enforcement is difficult to see. It does not follow, however, that transport for hire should be the sole preserve of the common carrier by public edict. If the shipping and traveling public demands common carrier service it should pay for it, and at the same time be protected from abuses arising from violation of the obligations. The shipping public, on the other hand, should not be compelled, by the exclusion of non-common carriage, to rely solely on the services offered by common carriage. Consumer interests and privileges deserve some consideration to say the least.

CURRENT ISSUES OF PUBLIC POLICY

The relative decline of the role of the common carrier in transport, together with the development of "pervasive" competition particularly among the modes and with non-common carriage, has created three main issues with regard to the preservation of the common carrier. The *first* of these relates to the degree of protection that should be afforded common carriers against each other, regardless of the mode. Certificates of public convenience and necessity are required of all common carriers except pipe lines. When application is made to expand the authority of the certificate or to establish new operations, the applicant must contend with a public policy that is designed to limit competition. Vigorous opposition from existing common carriers is seldom lacking. Certification results in strict delineation of operating authority, as well as rate regulation even though the rates themselves may be arrived at by private price-fixing agreements.

The *second* issue is that of the protection to be afforded common carriers from those that cannot be forced into this category. Permits to contract carriers are severely limited in scope and not easy to obtain. Present policy imposes the strictest possible limitation on the operation of private carriers. Similar remarks apply to the application of the law on exempt commodities, where distinctions are made between exempt and nonexempt ones that would defy identification by even the most fastidious dietitian. Current controversies over the "mixing" rule and cooperative activities merely add to the list.

The *third* issue concerns the question of whether common carriers should be confined to common carrier transport. Public policy has adopted the position that they should be restricted entirely, or almost entirely, to common carriage. This seems to be the result of the interpretation of the law by the regulatory agencies on the basis of legislation originally developed for the railroads. The argument supporting this policy is that to permit common carriers to engage in other transport would lead to discriminatory rate-making in favor of the nonregulated transport to the disadvantage of those relying on common carrier service.

Current regulatory policy for common carriers is designed therefore: (1) to protect them against outside competition; (2) to protect them against competition within each mode; and (3) to limit them to that type of transport. These restrictions make rate regulation inescapable. Whether they are necessary for the preservation of the common carrier or of the public interest must be evaluated in terms of the costs to the shipping public which this entails, the probability of success of preserving at least the relative position of the common carrier, and justification for the costs of the protection that is now provided.

PROTECTION OF COMPETITION VERSUS PROTECTION OF COMPETITORS

The need for common carrier services is manifest by the volume of traffic that moves in this category and by the fact that the shippers are willing to pay for it. Where this is not the case they avail themselves of other sources of supply. This utilization of other services indicates that shippers are willing to purchase other transportation because the price-obligation combination is preferable to that which is offered by the common carriers. Moreover, non-common carriage for hire is obviously profitable or it would not be available. In other words there is a definite place for service of this type in the transport system. The issue therefore is the role that common carriage should be required to play, or to put it another way, the extent of the restriction that should be imposed on the competitors of the common carrier.

The economical allocation of resources in any system must use competitive guidelines as far as they are available. In a private enterprise economy, at least, the market place is the obvious testing ground. If it is to play this role, rules of the game must be established that will give the fullest play to competitive forces. Common carriage needs protection but not the common carrier. If an enterprise undertakes to offer common carrier transport it should be compelled to accept the attendant obligations. To prevent traffic from moving under other circumstances is to prevent shippers from availing themselves of other opportunities which they prefer. If this is done to preserve common carriage then it means "subsidizing" the customers of common carriers by other shippers. This is a policy of preserving competitors by restricting competition. The cries for protection of the consumer are not all without foundation.

In a similar vein, preventing common carriers from engaging in non-common carrier transport encourages the growth of that kind of traffic through the restriction of competition. The alleged danger of discrimination against the buyers of common carrier services in favor of those who do not fails to recognize that the latter will go to other means of transport if the common carrier is denied the privilege of meeting the competition. This is the surest way to undermine the common carrier; it cannot be preserved by an attempt to reserve all traffic to it. We should have learned that lesson long before now. The alternative is to permit common carriers to undertake the movement of other traffic. They cannot very well meet nonregulated competition with their hands tied behind their backs.

Control of Entry

THEORY OF CONTROL OF ENTRY

Control of entry into economic activity may be undertaken through various means set up for different purposes. It may be set up for the purpose of establishing standards of competence, as, for example, in the professions of medicine, law, and accounting, to assure initial levels of competence of those offering the services. It is not, theoretically at least, designed to limit the numbers of those desiring to enter these professions. Control of entry may also be imposed in order to avoid ruinous competition in natural monopolies where the ultimate outcome will result in only one supplier of a given market in any case. Finally, it may be used as a means of preserving competitors by restricting patronage to them which competitors would otherwise seek.

Control of entry as a means of controlling or restricting competition among transport enterprises is effected by requiring certificates of public convenience and necessity of permits from those seeking to offer specified services. The presumed need for the control of entry arose from the development of the regulation of "natural" or technological monopolies to prevent the duplication of facilities that would lead to ruinous competition among public utilities of the same type. Federal regulation of transportation adopted the idea for railroads in 1920 and expanded it to common carriers by motor, air, and water agencies in subsequent legislation. All common carriers must receive certificates, permits being confined to contract carriers. The Interstate Commerce Commission in particular has been very restrictive in its grants of certificates, has confined permits to the limit provided by the law, and has restrained nonregulated carriage to the narrowest scope possible under the statutes.

Control of entry is administered in two ways: (1) by specific authorization of routes and places to be served; and (2) by designation of the particular service or services that the carrier may offer, together with the schedule of service offerings of common carriers and the rates that may be charged for them.

CONTROL OF ENTRY FOR THE DIFFERENT MODES

The rationale of control of entry in transport requires separate consideration for each of the modes because of their different economic characteristics and also because of differences in public policy adopted for them.

Railroads—Entry through new construction of railroad facilities has been only a minor consideration since 1920, but such extensions as have been requested have come under close scrutiny. In some cases the ICC has even required the construction of new facilities as illustrated by the Union Passenger Depot in Los Angeles. Extension into other railroad territory, however, has not presented a matter of serious importance. The nature of railroad economics indicates that steps to do so require close public scrutiny.

Motor Carriers—Certification of motor carriers has occupied most of the attention of the ICC. Here the policy has been highly restrictive. When application is made by a common carrier to expand the authority of its certificate or to establish new operations it must contend with a public policy that is designed to limit the expansion of existing firms and the entry of new ones. The applicant must prove that public convenience and necessity require that the certificate be granted. This usually is onerous and expensive. The ICC has held that existing carriers will normally be given the privilege of handling all the traffic in the territory served by them if they insist that they can do so efficiently and economically. Only positive proof to the contrary, without benefit of experiment, will result in permitting new entry. Even the showing that rates would be reduced as the result of the introduction of competition is not a determinative factor in demonstrating public convenience and necessity, because this might result in rates that are too low for the occupant, at least according to his standards. This is a contention invariably advanced by all of the competitors. Presumably, permits for contract carriers are less difficult to secure, but the ICC strives to restrict these to the limit of the law, and all of the competitors lend their vigorous support. The Commission also employs all resources at its disposal to limit the sphere of operations of private carriers and agricultural cooperatives.

Air Carriers—Control of entry in air transport follows a parallel course, but is complicated by the promotional responsibilities of the Civil Aeronautics Board (CAB) and the subsidy provisions contained in the Federal Aviation Act. Freedom of entry cannot be extended without limit as long as present subsidy provisions exist. The CAB has restricted entry where subsidy is not immediately involved on the grounds that it must preserve the carrier's financial integrity. This seems to have a hollow ring in light of CAB resistance to rate increases, the success of the unregulated Pacific Southwest Airways in California, and the present desire of trunk lines to limit their offerings. One might also question the logic of refusal to permit Pan American Airways to offer domestic service when some domestic carriers are permitted to serve foreign markets. One can only conclude that the CAB wants to prevent the market from allocating traffic. The success of this approach faces a severe challenge in the immediate future as a result of the current financial plight of the airlines. The entire policy toward air transport is in dire need of a thoroughgoing reexamination and overhauling.

Water Carriers—Control of entry into water carriage can be explained only on the theory that transportation is a public utility and must be regulated accordingly. Application of this theory can serve only the purpose of reducing competition. Fortunately it has had little scope in water transport.

Pipe Lines—Entry to pipe-line transport is not restricted and has no place in the present system. Whether, in light of the economic characteristics of this mode, it would be necessary if the pipe lines were divorced from the oil industry does not need to be discussed here. If the issue should arise it would be because of restructuring the latter.

Control of entry, then, is a public utility approach to regulation based on the theory of natural monopoly. Motor, water, and air transport do not fit into this category. Their economic and cost characteristics are those of competitive industry. Their physical facilities are highly mobile and they can readily tap available markets if they are permitted to do so. Moreover, the extensive exemptions that apply, particularly to motor and water carriers, indicate how uneasily they fit into the mold of regulated monopoly. Competitive pressures in these modes are not likely to find a very workable restraint through a policy aimed at confining all commercial transport, or even transport for hire, to the common carrier and by control of entry.

ABANDONMENTS

The issue of abandonments is related primarily to the railroads. For the other modes ready substitutes for shippers are available if the traffic warrants it and public policy permits it. Railroad abandonment represents a more drastic change, but even here substitutes over a considerable range are usually at hand. Public policy which requires continuance of unprofitable services or lines places a burden on other traffic which it should not be expected to bear. Continuance of such a policy can well spell disaster for particular railroads. Shippers may contend that abandonment of service may put them out of business, but they cannot be compelled to carry on their activities by the carriers nor can they be compelled to continue their patronage of a particular firm or mode. Community insistence on retention of passenger service illustrates this, and restriction on requests for abandonment of service has done nothing to resolve the problem either. If the public does not wish abandonment it should be prepared to pay for the cost of continuance directly through public payments for the services. Perhaps Railpax is a recognition of this, but one may be permitted to be skeptical of a successful outcome.

CONCLUSION

Control of entry in transportation today has very limited application in achieving an economical and viable transport system. It is oriented to the protection of common carriers, not the consuming public. Furthermore, it imposes and will continue to impose severe handicaps on the survival of the common carrier. This is not to suggest that elimination of present restrictions should be of a catastrophic nature. It does mean, however, that positive and significant steps aimed at much greater freedom of opportunity to provide transport services need to be instituted at once.

Consolidation and Merger

RAILROAD CONSOLIDATION

Consolidation as a unique problem for transport economics is largely confined to the railroads. This is because they possess most of the economic characteristics of public utilities, even though at the same time they afford limited opportunity to shippers to select the firm to render service where the railroads come in close contact with each other.

Railroad development in the nineteenth century took place under the assumptions of competition and was also fostered by public aid. This led to duplication of facilities and excess capacity. When the railroads attempted to resolve the resulting problems they were met first by public regulation of rates and then, after the Sherman Act, by antitrust action on rate agreements and consolidation. It is instructive to note that the Northern Securities case of 1904 prevented a merger that took 48 years to achieve after the Transportation Act of 1920 was passed. Recognition of the need for a consolidation policy for railroads that could not be carried out under antitrust led to the consolidation provisions of this legislation. These provisions, however, did not reconcile the problems of the monopoly features of rail transport and competition. Subsequent modifications of the law have led to no improvement in the situation; indeed they seem to have made it worse. The ICC has failed to develop any guidelines or principles upon which a rational program could be developed, nor has Congress or the executive branch of the government come to its rescue or taken the initiative.

The only contribution to date in regulatory circles to a recognition of the unique economic features of railroads for consolidation policy was set forth at some length by Examiner Darmstadter in his report on the proposed Chicago and North Western-Chicago, Milwaukee, St. Paul, and Pacific merger application. In a careful analysis of the evidence presented at the hearings he concluded that the monopoly features of railroads must be a matter of prime consideration in consolidation proceedings:

The isolation of intra-rail competition as a separate factor indicates that the geographic limitations of roads and yard, with minor exceptions, inhibit service to industries located off line without the cooperation of other roads. In many respects, railroads possess the characteristics of a natural monopoly, and analysis of their market actions must be made on models of monopoly or oligopoly. (Finance Docket 24182, p. 95)

In other words, regional monopoly is the appropriate pattern. This would not preclude more than one railroad from serving the key transport centers; in fact it would be unavoidable on a regional basis, but a program based on this approach would eliminate the unnecessary and uneconomical direct competition over much of the area served by a particular system. Mr. Darmstadter did not discuss the issues presented by economies of scale because he was able to deal only with the application before him and not the structure of the whole western region. A comprehensive program for regional consolidation would need to give serious consideration to this matter because of the question of number of railroad companies that should be permitted to serve in the area. The same remarks apply to the eastern and southern regions. Had they been given careful evaluation the Penn-Central blunder might well have been avoided. What the ICC thinks of Mr. Darmstadter's analysis is a deep secret.

A completely fresh start on railroad consolidation policy is clearly needed at the present time. Unfortunately, this is likely to be severely encumbered by recent developments, particularly in the eastern territory. A completely fresh start would seem to call for some new body specifically set up by Congress to study consolidations in keeping with the economics of the railroad industry, with power to approve acceptable merger proposals or to propose and carry through its own plans. This requires a moratorium on mergers until a coherent policy has been developed.

MOTOR AND WATER CONSOLIDATION

If it were not for policies regarding control of entry, consolidation in the motor carrier field would call for application only of the antitrust laws and no modification of the standards developed for them would be required. The tests of section 7 of the Clayton Act are equally valid for motor carriers as for industry in general and should be applied. The same criteria apply to water carriers. This can be administered by the ICC by appropriate application of the tests.

AIR TRANSPORT

Air transport presents a somewhat different problem from that of the water and motor carriers because of current policy on promotion and subsidy. Approval of consolidations, particularly of the trunklines, should await clarification of the issues of promotion, subsidy, and control of entry. Application of the tests of section 7 of the Clayton Act would seem to be more appropriate to an industry possessing the economic characteristics of air transport than a public utility approach. Current regulatory policies, however, are based on the latter concept. Reconciliation of the contradictions should be worked out before consolidation plans are developed; today we seem to have the worst of both viewpoints.

Diversification and Intermodal Ownership

MEANING AND OBJECTIVES OF DIVERSIFICATION

Diversification in transportation usually refers to common ownership of different modes by unification into transportation companies prepared to offer the services of any of them to the shipping or traveling public. This may entail the supplying of only ancillary or supplemental transport, or it may embrace competing carriers of the different modes. The principal problem concerned with restructuring relates to the provision of line-haul carriage either separately or by coordination under single ownership.

Proposals for common ownership have emanated largely from the railroads who seek equal freedom with others to secure entry or to acquire existing operators. At present, the other carriers evidence no great enthusiasm for acquisition of the railroads and they probably do not possess the necessary resources even if they received sanction to do so. The railroads advance the argument that the shipper today is confronted with the necessity of determining the most economical and efficient means of moving his goods. This quite commonly involves using more than one agency, especially motor carriers. Formation of transportation companies, it is contended, would afford the shipper complete transportation service under one management, and would result in more efficient and more economical use of all transport facilities and equipment. The point is also made that integration of the different modes would add to the financial strength and stability of the carriers by reducing the chance of failure of the entire enterprise if any one of the types of service being offered should fail—that is, if any one of the modes in the combined undertaking should turn out to be unsuccessful. It should be noted that the same contentions are applicable to passenger transport, and that the steamship companies pressed this position vigorously in the years immediately following World War II.

ECONOMIES OF SCALE

If lower cost and more efficient traffic movements are to result from the formation of integrated companies, they must be derived from economies of scale. The economies of scale which may be realized from common ownership are dubious to say the least. As already noted, this is a critical matter for railroad consolidation. The competitive nature of motor, water, and air transport make it impossible to use them as a means for "spreading the overhead." In addition, there are clearly economical limits to which these undertakings can grow in their respective areas. Common ownership by railroads would not assist the railroads as such unless it resulted in reducing competition among the different modes of the same company. If this were the outcome it would result in transport monopolies. Furthermore, if a competitive environment is to be retained, the railroads would have to offer the same types of privileges and facilities to the competitors of the other modes which they owned.

TRANSPORTATION COMPANIES

Coordination of Traffic Movements—One argument for the formation of transportation companies is that they would provide more effective coordination for shipments that require the use of different modes. Apart from strictly ancillary services the reasons for this are not at all clear. Unless one assumes a single transport system for the entire country, traffic interchange within modes, and among them, would still be necessary. These would have to be undertaken between transport companies and with the operators of particular modes. How this would differ from the present situation remains to be described, but preservation of intermodal competition would necessitate equal treatment of those not controlled by the transportation companies. This would present a more difficult problem for public supervision than separate ownership and operation of the modes. If one assumes that competition among the companies would serve as the counteractive, he must predicate this on overall competition among the railroads also.

Relation to Railroad Consolidation—The formation of transportation companies is directly related to the problem of railroad consolidation. As has already been noted this might take the form of competitive regional or national systems. The last two seem to offer the only workable possibilities. If the regional plan is adopted, then it would seem to be logical to confine the transport companies to the same areas unless they were allowed to penetrate each other's territories at will with the other modes. How this would be of any assistance to the railroads in the resolution of their problems is difficult to see. On the other hand, if the companies were to be confined to the territory of a particular railroad, it would not necessarily be economical to confine motor transport to the same territory and it would certainly be undesirable to do this for air. Furthermore, the problems of coordination would be increased, not diminished, as already pointed out. In addition, the threat of regional transport monopoly, or at least dominance of a region by a particular corporation, would be very real because it would be organized around the inescapable monopoly structure of the railroad. If a limited number of national systems were established, the threat to anything resembling healthy competition in transport would be too great to be tolerated. Transport companies with the continued existence of rate-making by agreement would serve to reduce competition and would require more detailed regulation than we have at present. One may be thankful that the Penn-Central system is not a totally integrated transportation company.

Other Agencies—Intermodal ownership among the other agencies possibly does not present issues as critical as those connected with the railroads. The advantages from the standpoint of the shipping public are not at all evident and have not been spelled out. Analysis of the economies of scale would indicate that they are not significant to say the least.

CONCLUSION

The objectives behind the formation of transportation companies seem to be those of empire building, corporate profits, and control of competitive alternatives. It is rather anomalous to seek diversification through transport companies, immunity from antitrust, and reduction in regulation all at the same time, especially if concern for the consumer is a strong motivating factor. The verdict on the desirability of diversification as a means of restructuring the industry is a negative one at the present time. There are too many other more basic issues which need to be dealt with first. When this has been done the question of the transportation company can be viewed in a new light. Diversification should be evaluated from the viewpoint of the transport system as a whole, and not merely from that of a particular mode.

The Conglomerate Undertaking

THE CONGLOMERATE IN TRANSPORT

The conglomerate form of business organization is one in which an enterprise undertakes to supply various services or to produce various commodities that are not directly related to each other in the production process, or in fact are quite independent of each other. This is another aspect of diversification, but in the field of transport, at least, it means entry into industries that do not supply transportation services. The rise of the conglomerate in transportation is not directly a problem of restructuring the industry but it is certainly very closely related to it. It presents a serious problem for public policy in transport organization because of the impact on investment, and because of the effect on carriers owned by the conglomerate in the event that the latter encounters financial problems.

The reasons for conglomerate entry into the field of transportation are many and varied and not all of them have been clearly exposed to date. Tax considerations that may have saved some firms from immediate insolvency have played a role; an exuberant stock market that capitalizes on book profits resulting from currently permissible accounting practices has given ample scope for speculation in an inflationary atmosphere; the mania for new management techniques that allegedly do not require specialized contact or information has created a new era for the promoter; and the idea that giant enterprises with a broadly diversified base alone could survive in today's world has played its part. Perhaps the desire for empire building should be accorded first place. In any case transportation does not seem to have been the most important consideration in most of the holding company development in this field.

The most prominent activity of conglomerates in transport has taken place in the railroad field. Here, the inverted holding company, under which a corporation is formed by the railroad to own it, is set up, the new enterprise really being the old one under a new name.

The Interstate Commerce Commission reports that 15 of the 70 major railroads were controlled by holding companies in 1970. Disclosure of the ramifications of this development must await public investigation because strict secrecy has enshrouded much that has taken place. A cursory examination of these holding companies by the present writer indicates, however, that the financial structures of the enterprises have not been improved by the holding company acquisitions, trading on the equity playing a prominent role in the exchange of stock. This does not augur well for the transport companies that have been involved.

DANGERS OF THE CONGLOMERATES FOR TRANSPORT

The danger of undermining the financial integrity of the owned transport company is obvious, especially when the earnings of the latter are limited by regulation or by other factors. If lack of earnings is a reason for employing the holding company device then the prospects of reinvesting capital in the transport company are minimal because the funds can be used more profitably by the holding company in other areas. Similar remarks apply to new capital which the holding company may be able to raise. It is not likely to put it into transport. The new corporate arrangements may help the railroad stockholders, but this is a corporate and not a transport advantage and does not help to solve the problems of the transportation undertaking. Furthermore, if the holding company encounters difficulties it will use the resources of the subsidiaries as much as possible to save itself.

One prominent argument to support the conglomerate growth is that an enterprise can spread the risk of investment over different industries so that if some suffer a decline they can be supported by others. This pap, or pablum to use a more current word, was dispensed with amazing success during the heyday of the public utility holding company. Nothing new has been added to the justification and nothing new has been added to the nature of the developments to warrant any more confidence in the outcome now than in the 1920s. The Penn-Central fiasco promises to be a fit rival to the Van Sweringen, Foshay, Associated Gas and Electric, and Insull debacles.

The collapse of the public utility empires demonstrated conclusively that when the top goes the whole structure topples because management will tap every resource at its disposal in order to survive. It will not hesitate to let a subsidiary go under if it constitutes a heavy drag, and it will not hesitate to drain it dry if this can be done for the benefit of the parent. This might not be too serious in a competitive structure like motor transport because ready substitutes can be obtained, but in the railroad field the results can be thoroughly disastrous.

The problem of the conglomerate presents a major issue in the field of industrial organization in general and we do not have an answer to it as yet. The issues involved in this development are more than those connected with competition and monopoly. A comprehensive analysis will require a thorough examination of the role of the corporation in modern industrial organization, the appropriate scope of its power, and the responsibilities and obligations of management, including the board of directors. So far the corporation *per se* has remained outside the purview of antitrust. It cannot do so much longer. The growth of conglomerate activity in transportation should be prevented until some answers are obtained for antitrust. Meanwhile, a complete investigation of all phases of conglomerate activity and the inverted holding company in transport should be undertaken. Just what can be done about the situation which now obtains may be an open question, but it should be remembered that Congress enacted the "death sentence" clause of the Public Utility Holding Company Act of 1935 and secured its effective enforcement.

Ownership of the Infrastructure

PRESENT OWNERSHIP OF THE INFRASTRUCTURE

The term *infrastructure* as applied to transport refers to investment in the "way" structures such as railroad roadbed and terminals, highways, airways and terminals, and waterways. It encompasses the fixed or sunk investment in transport facilities and therefore does not include operating equipment. In the United States the infrastructure of railroads and pipe lines is privately owned and operated. It is publicly owned for the other modes. There is an inescapably mixed system of ownership for these other modes. If there is to be a single pattern of ownership of the transport infrastructure it must be public; technology makes this unavoidable.

In most countries of the world the infrastructure is publicly owned. In these countries tests for investment, user charges, etc. for the infrastructure have not been developed for the transport system as a whole because of this public ownership. The discussion has consequently centered on policy for the highways. The problem is more complex in the United States because of private ownership and operation of the railroads and pipe lines, the intensity of intermodal competition, and an extensive domestic air transport system. The basic economic issues are the same, however, for all countries, namely: (1) the appropriate criteria for investment in transport as compared with other demands; (2) the appropriate allocation of resources among the modes for an efficient and economical transport system; (3) the appropriate basis for assessing the costs of the infrastructure between users and nonusers; and (4) the appropriate basis for charges among users. The need for facing these questions by those responsible for formulating policy on restructuring must be obvious, but the task is very complex.

PROBLEMS OF THE INFRASTRUCTURE

The issues involved in the ownership of the infrastructures and the bases of pricing for their uses are so numerous and complex that little more can be done in this presentation than to pose a series of questions to which, however, at least a partial answer must be given in any realistic attempt to restructure the transport industry.

Investment Criteria—One of the most fundamental issues relates to the investment criteria for transport as a whole and for each of the modes. In railroads and pipe lines the private investment criterion prevails at the present time, although it is showing signs of erosion. No economic gauges have yet been established for the other modes; public investment proceeds on the basis of alleged needs without any consistent or reliable standard by which those needs may be measured. The Department of Transportation has the responsibility, under section 7 of the law creating it, to deal with this problem, but so far no results have been forthcoming. Even when they do see the light of day they may be quite deficient because of the limitations with regard to waterways that are imposed.

Cost of the Infrastructure—Cost of the infrastructure where it is publicly owned gives rise to some difficult problems of calculation, both practical and theoretical. These costs may be ascertained for rail and pipe lines as for any other private undertaking that uses the market as its primary gauge for raising capital funds. This is not done for air, water, and motor transport. For these modes there are implicit as well as explicit costs. The latter, such as interest on borrowed funds, may be ascertained directly, although whether this represents the true economic cost is debatable because of the tax support for government borrowing. Implicit costs present greater difficulties. Interest on capital raised by taxes or other means is an economic cost that must be included if an economical allocation of resources is to be made. What the rate should be is a matter of controversy, but it certainly should not be less than that on the borrowed funds. Another item of implicit cost that should be included is taxes on the infrastructure. These have to be borne by the users of rail and pipe-line transport while the users of the other modes are not assessed with a corresponding equivalent. They should all be required to carry the same costs. Whether this should be in the form of total tax relief or vice versa cannot be examined here.

Cost-Benefit Analysis—Cost-benefit analysis occupies a primary role in the evaluation of investment proposals for waterways and highways. It is used to compare the costs of constructing projects with the benefits they are supposed to confer, these benefits consisting of those accruing to the users and those derived by nonusers. If the comparison yields a ratio in favor of benefits by some margin the project will be considered economically worthwhile and nonusers will be expected to pay for a share of the benefits through taxation.

The emergence of cost-benefit analysis to its present prominent role started with the appraisal of the economic welfare implications of fixed investment in so-called decreasing cost industries. Its first application was to railroads and public utilities where it was concluded that maximum social welfare from such undertakings would be obtained by public ownership of the infrastructure, the charges for use being based only on the variable costs. The validity of this approach has come under severe challenge, but the idea that those receiving benefits other than those derived from the direct use of the infrastructure should share in the cost still persists. The merits of this approach cannot be examined here, nor the problems presented for calculation nor the implementation of the procedure. Suffice it to say that if cost-benefit analysis is valid for highways, waterways, and air transport then it applies with at least equal force to railroads and pipe lines. The restructuring of transport must give thoroughgoing consideration to this matter. Equalization of competition is meaningless without it.

Ownership of the Infrastructure and Private Enterprise—A private enterprise economy assumes the private ownership and management of the economic resources allocated by the dictates of the market under rules of the game designed to give full recognition to competitive forces. Transportation presents one of the most severe challenges to the viability of this concept. A mixed system of public and private ownership of the infrastructure is inescapable. If we are to have an economical system of transport, however, the tests of competition will have to be used for decision-making in the allocation and utilization of economic resources in this area. There is much greater opportunity for employing these tests than is being used today. The owners of the different modes should recognize this fact if they wish to continue private undertakings.

John L. Weller

4

Access to Capital Markets

Introduction

The evolution of transportation systems depends largely upon the processes of capital allocation and attrition. In the United States, in distinction to most other countries, the decisions by which these processes occur are partly governmental and partly private. Decisions as to investment in highways, improved waterways, airports, and airways are politically reached. In many cases the investment is secured by the general credit of the governmental unit or provided through taxation, although this is not so for revenue bonds sometimes associated with toll roads, airports, and marine terminals. Usually, however, the latter have some advantage of tax exemption.

Investment in trucks, airplanes, barges, ships, buses and railroad equipment, and in most terminal facilities used by practically all forms of transportation, is the result of management decision, backed up by the confidence of private investors in the success of the particular enterprise under the political and economic conditions obtaining.

The purpose of this chapter is to explore the effects of public policy

The career of JOHN L. WELLER *in transportation spans more than forty-five years from his days as a roundhouse laborer for the Great Northern Railroad to his present position as transportation officer for Paine, Webber, Jackson & Curtis. Between times he worked for another railroad (NY, NH & H), for the Bureau of Ships, United States Navy, and for Trans World Airlines. In 1957–64 Mr. Weller was president of Seatrain Lines and the Ship Container Corporation. He has served on many transportation committees, public and private.*

on the capital problems of the railroads. In doing this, it will of course be necessary to compare certain capital and operating characteristics of railroads with those of other transportation.

The Competition for Capital

Growing public awareness of the need for conserving natural and environmental resources must be accompanied by recognition that capital resources also are limited. The capital markets of the nation will be hard pressed in coming decades to meet the total demands, public and private, for funds with which to accomplish the many competing goals of society: adequate housing, medical services, education, the reduction of poverty, global defense obligations, and preservation or restoration of the environment. Industrial expansion throughout the world during the past quarter-century and the costs of restoring the destruction wrought by World War II and succeeding conflicts have soaked up available capital. Meanwhile, the full employment policies followed by most developed nations, accompanied by high rates of inflation and taxation, have tended to inhibit private capital formation. Belated efforts of governments to restrain inflation through monetary policy have squeezed the supply of funds available for investment.

THE DOMESTIC INVESTMENT OUTLOOK

The National Economic Projection series prepared under the auspices of the National Planning Association in March 1970 appear to postulate gross private domestic investment expenditures aggregating $2.2 trillion over the next decade, about 87 percent greater than the total for the previous ten years. Internally-generated corporate funds are expected to supply only about three-fourths of this requirement, so that external borrowings or equity issues must be relied upon for the remainder. With a continuation of present tax policies, personal savings are expected to decline as a share of gross national product and to be insufficient to meet the needs for external investment funds. These projections assume that the "shortfall," approximating $87 billion, will be made up from government budgetary surpluses—in other words, either government or private investment goals as projected, or both, must be modified.

The situation is complicated by the fact that the United States economy entered the decade of the 1970s in an illiquid condition stemming from the Vietnam war and a prolonged investment boom. A study by a New York bond house estimates that interest payments in 1970 consumed 29 percent of total corporate profits before taxes and interest, nearly double the ratio of 1963.

TRANSPORTATION CAPITAL REQUIREMENTS

Estimates of requirements for new private capital investment in transportation vary widely, but they are all very large in comparison with past experience. Government expenditures for transportation, which have been increasing rapidly, are drawn from budgets already overstrained, and private capital must be raised in competition with the capital issues of other industry and of government. The earnings records of investor-owned transportation, particularly the railroads and airlines, in terms of return on investment or of stability, compare unfavorably with those of industrial or utility companies.

Over the ten years 1960 through 1969, for example, *Moody's* tabula-Because of violent earnings and price fluctuations, airline price-earnings ratios lack meaning, but fixed-interest trust bonds for airplanes at mid-December 1970 required a yield of about 11 percent, and high-grade rail equipment trusts upwards of 9 percent.

TRANSPORTATION CRISES

The railroads have experienced repeated capital crises since their run-down condition forced the federal government to take them over in 1918. During the depression of the 1930s about one-third of all railroad mileage was in the control of receivers or trustees. A recession in 1958 caused the Senate Commerce Committee to hold extended hearings on "Problems of the Railroads," resulting in new legislation, including guaranteed railroad loans; and appointment of a special study group (the "Doyle Committee") which rendered a lengthy report and recommendations in December 1960. Labeled *National Transportation Policy,* this group's report focused almost entirely on ralroad capital problems, although at the time airlines were also experiencing difficulties resulting from the introduction of jet aircraft, overduplication of routes, and a slowing down of traffic growth. The coastwise general cargo shipping industry was in extremis, and has since virtually disappeared.

With improving general business conditions and the United States' active intervention in Vietnam, railroad and airline earnings briefly recovered, reaching a peak in 1966. Motor carrier earnings also improved. The airlines, hard-pressed to accommodate an unprecedented traffic boom, and with part of their equipment diverted to military airlift, embarked on heavy capital programs; in the five years 1965–1969 their capital outlays were 156 percent greater than in 1960–1964, and at the end of 1969 outstanding commitments for new equipment and terminal construction exceeded total expenditures for the previous five years. The Civil Aeronautics Board (CAB), concerned at the beginning of the decade about over-expansion of the industry, added to the pressures by extensive grants of new route certificates.

Railroads stepped up their capital expenditures during the last half of the decade by 60.5 percent over the 1960–1964 level. Of the total rail capital expenditures in the latter five years, however, 71.8 percent were for equipment and only 28.2 percent for roadway and structures.

From the 1966 peak, rail net operating income declined 37 percent to 1969, dropping below the "crisis" level of a decade earlier; and net working capital practically disappeared. There is evidence that the railroad plant is deteriorating because of inadequate levels both of maintenance and of investment in roadway and structures, which are subjected to the loads of heavier cars and locomotives. During the five years 1965–1969, train derailments caused by roadway and track defects were 133 percent greater than in the previous five years.

But airline financial results have been even more disappointing to investors. The earnings of the twelve major trunklines declined from $412 million in 1967 to $147 million in 1969, and to an estimated loss of $92 million in 1970. The local service carrier group has reported continuous and mounting losses since 1966, and their financial condition has become desperate. Current liabilities at year-end 1969 exceeded current assets by 39 percent, and long-term debt was 7.5 times equity. Unless earnings can be restored promptly, the ability of the airlines to finance outstanding commitments is in doubt.

In sum, it appears that a capital crisis impends, not only for railroads, but also for airlines. Indeed, a transportation crisis at about the beginning of each decade appears to have become a national habit. The repetition of such crises is not conducive to the securing of private investment capital by either mode on terms comparable to those available to non-transport industries.

Motor carrier financial results also fluctuate, as shown in Table I,

TABLE I. *Motor Carrier Income*

Year	Number of Carriers	Net Income (Millions)	Percent of 1965
1965	3,397	$269.5	100.0
1966	3,469	277.3	102.5
1967	3,615	200.6	74.4
1968	3,235	286.0	106.1
1969	3,260	250.1	92.8
1970 Est.	3,112	228.5	84.8

Source: *Trinc's Blue Book of the Trucking Industry*

on much shorter cycles than those of airlines and railroads, and with less severity because of greater ability to adjust operating costs to current volume. To a substantial degree the earnings cycle is affected by the customary three-year term of national labor agreements.

THE NEED FOR PLANNING

The need for better planning and regulation of transportation, to insure that scarce capital is directed into the most productive channels and to mitigate the severity of recurrent crises, has been urged by one study group after another. But while the need for such planning may be evident, its accomplishment is rendered difficult by the differing proportions of public and private investment in the various transportation modes and by their varying bases of political support. It is complicated also by resistance to change resulting from vast amounts of "sunk" railroad investment, the conflicting interests of managements, employees, users and communities, and by heavy-handed regulation.

The Extent of Planning to Date—The regulated bus, truck, water carrier, and airlines systems existing today may be said to have resulted from federal planning, since these systems for the most part have emerged pursuant to certificates or permits granted by the Interstate Commerce Commisison (ICC) or the Civil Aeronautics Board upon findings that the public convenience and necessity required the services.

The history of the airlines under the Civil Aeronautics Board leads to doubt as to the efficacy of federally-administered planning, since it has been characterized by fractionalization of the industry and by cycles of over-competition, over-capacity, over-investment, and inadequate earnings. Fortunately, rapid expansion of air traffic in the past has permitted over-capacity periods to be outgrown fairly quickly, but as the airlines mature it cannot be certain that this will be the case in the future. As yet there have been no bankruptcies of major airlines, although there have been several failures of specialized non-scheduled and all-cargo carriers.

No federal planning whatever has accompanied the growth of exempt and private highway, air, and water operations. The existing railroad system is completely unplanned, practically all of it having been constructed before 1920, when Congress belatedly enacted section 1(18) of the Interstate Commerce Act, requiring certificates of public convenience and necessity for construction or abandonment of rail lines. The principal effect of this section has been to inhibit adjustment by the railroads to changing economic and social circumstances.

The Department of Transportation—One of the principal reasons put forward for creation of the federal Department of Transportation in 1965 was that planning of the transportation plant had been segmented and incomplete. Too many federal agencies, it was urged, had been involved in promotion and regulation of transportation, and their planning and promotional activities should be collected into a single executive department. This was one of the major recommendations of the "Doyle" report.

Much of the Department's time since its establishment has been consumed in problems of internal organization and staffing, prolonged by the change of administration in 1969. However, it is expected that eventually some sort of outline plan for national transportation needs and goals will be produced. Whether, given the political pressures to which all government agencies are subject, it will be better than plans of the past, and the extent to which it will be implemented, remain to be seen.

Railroad Fixed Investment and Operating Costs

The total net book investment of all Class I railroads[1] at the end of 1969 in operating property used for transportation service, excluding cash, materials and supplies, was $27.1 billion, of which $10 billion represented equipment and $17.1 billion roadway and structures.

[1] Carriers with annual gross revenues exceeding $5 million.

Of the $9.55 billion in external long-term debt, $3.79 billion, or 39.7 percent, consisted of equipment obligations and $5.76 billion, or 60.3 percent, was nonequipment debt. However, these proportions may be somewhat misleading. Had all equipment acquired under lease in recent years instead been purchased, the outstanding equipment debt might have been about doubled, amounting to more than one half of the total.

Shareholders' book equity was $17.8 billion, resulting in a ratio of debt to equity of 37:63.

COMPARATIVE RIGHT-OF-WAY COSTS

Costs associated with private rights of way impose a greater degree of rigidity in rail operating costs, and thus greater fluctuation of operating results with volume, than is the case with transportation companies sharing publicly-provided facilities with other users. Some of the railroad fixed investment, of course, is in office buildings, stations, shops, and similar structures which usually must be privately provided through ownership or rental by trucking companies, airlines, and water carriers. Railroad accounting does not facilitate precise analysis, but of total Class I railroad operating expenses in 1969, approximately 18 percent appear to have been associated with maintaining and operating private rights of way.

In addition, railroad companies incur substantial "fixed charges" for interest on nonequipment debt and rental of trackage, the latter being primarily intercorporate charges. It is estimated that Class I railroads in 1969 incurred about $210 million in interest charges related to track and roadway. Thus, right-of-way operating expenses plus interest charges in 1969 accounted for approximately 19 percent of all operating expenses and fixed charges.

Trucking Company Right-of-Way Costs—For 3,260 of the common and contract carrier trucking companies regulated by the Interstate Commerce Commission, the amounts reported as "operating taxes and license" expense in 1969 amounted to 6.5 percent of total operating expenses.

Including excise taxes on new trucks, tires, tubes and parts, and weight charges applicable to heavier vehicles, the total charges paid by private and for-hire trucks, intercity and local, in 1968 amounted to $4.65 billion or 8.7 percent of the estimated $53.7 billion total operating costs.

Airline User Charges—For domestic scheduled airlines, charges for use of publicly-provided facilities other than terminals, hangars, etc. in 1969 amounted to about 5.8 percent of total operating expenses. (This excludes $180.4 million for facilities rentals.)

The federal airport and airways program adopted in 1970 provides for increasing the tax on passenger tickets from 5 percent to 8 percent, a 5 percent tax on air freight waybills, a "head tax" on international passengers, and increased fuel taxes. Airport landing fees and rentals also have been increasing sharply, so that the above figures probably understate the impact of user charges on airlines in the future.

For trucking companies and airlines, charges for the use of shared right of way as a percentage of total operating costs approximate one third to one half the level of costs incurred by railroads in maintaining and operating exclusive rights of way. Similar data are not available for domestic water carriers; these incur wharfage, dockage, and rental charges for the use of publicly-financed terminal facilities, but as yet no use charges are levied on most improved waterways.

Not only are railroad right-of-way costs as a percentage of total costs greater than comparable costs incurred by trucking companies and airlines—they are also less subject to fluctuation with changing traffic volumes.

The Roles of Private and Public Investment

One of the first findings of the "Doyle" report to the Senate on *National Transportation Policy* was that: "We are unique among major nations in that we have avoided nationalization in any form," and that our policy should continue to rely on private ownership so long as that ownership fills our transportation needs.

Although most intercity transportation operations in the United States are privately owned and managed, the rights of way used by water, highway, and air carriers are necessarily publicly provided and are shared with other users. Certain efficiencies stem from this shared use, but an increasing proportion of the capital inflow into transportation in recent decades has involved government-supplied funds.

Total federal, state, and local expenditures for operation, maintenance, and construction of transportation facilities have more than quadrupled since 1950. In 1969 such government expenditures amounted to $19.6 billion, as shown in Table II.

The state and local rivers and harbors expenditures were incurred primarily in connection with operation and construction of port ter-

TABLE II. *Public Expenditures for Transportation Facilities, 1969*
(in millions of dollars)

	Federal	State and Local	Total
Airways	$789	—	$789
Airports	128	$530 (E)	658
Rivers and harbors	350	420 (E)	770
Highways	4,799	12,591	17,390
Total	$6,066	$13,541	$19,607

E = estimated.
Source: Transportation Association of America

minal facilities. It should be noted that all of these figures represent gross expenditures, before offset by fees, charges or taxes collected from users of the facilities.

By way of comparison, expenditures for privately-owned commercial intercity transportation in 1969 (regulated and unregulated) are estimated to have approximated $93 billion, including $6 billion of airline, railroad, and highway carrier capital expenditures. Operators of private automobiles are estimated to have spent an additional $89 billion, including $37 billion for new and used cars. Thus, total private outlays for intercity transportation were more than nine times federal, state and local government expenditures, although the percentage of publicly-furnished funds may be increasing.

The somewhat dichotomous situation, in which railroads and pipeline companies must maintain and pay taxes upon their rights of way, whereas other transportation modes share the use of publicly-provided facilities, has given rise to proposals, particularly from the railroads, that the circumstances be "equalized" by increasing user charges or taxes imposed on other transportation and by government assumption of substantial portions of railroad expenses.

Capital flow into the railroads appears to be inadequate, and some parts of the system may be close to breakdown. Is this because of the burden of privately-owned rights of way, and if so, how may the problem be resolved?

THE ERA OF PRIVATE OWNERSHIP

In approaching this question, it is necessary to recognize that private ownership of the railroad rights of way results from the conscious choice of the early railroad entrepreneurs, who conceived that they were obtaining valuable rights. Although the monopoly sought was short-lived, it is still advantageous for any transportation company to have exclusive control of the routes over which its traffic moves.

Until the 1920s practically all transportation in the United States was privately owned—railroads, urban and interurban transit, coastwise and inland shipping, and oil pipe lines. True, not all the capital had been furnished by private investors, since the railroads in their formative stages were the beneficiaries of extensive federal, state, and local land grants or bond issues, and they and the interurban trolleys acquired properties by exercise of the right of eminent domain.

Rates and fares collected from users were expected to cover the operating costs and yield a return to investors; if they did not, the company might enter bankruptcy and even disappear. In theory, this provided a ready comparative test of the relative efficiencies of capital and management. In practice, it often did not; railroads, for example, are joint-cost enterprises, and the costs of any particular service are not readily identifiable. Thus, shippers of freight might be subsidizing the passengers or vice versa, and the shippers of one commodity might, either through railroad inadvertence or by reason of regulatory pressures, be called upon to bear an undue proportion of the total burden. Moreover, investors might, as a result of inadequate earnings, be carrying burdens that should have been assumed by passengers and shippers.

For example, the breakdown of the railroads leading to their takeover by the federal government in World War I seems to have resulted from overbuilding of the system and from refusal of the Interstate Commerce Commission to permit rate increases between 1910 and 1915, a period when railroad wages and other costs were rising rapidly. The problem of rail capital inflow began at that time, before the roads had been exposed to significant competition from other modes.

Similarly, until the late 1930s most urban transit in New York and other cities was privately owned. By forcing the private companies to maintain a 5-cent fare in the face of rising costs, the New York City administration drove them into bankruptcy and took over the properties. Although the fare has risen under public ownership to 30 cents, this is expected to cover only the operating costs, the capital requirements being met from the public budget. A similar trend is apparent in urban transit elsewhere. In this case, the reason for public ownership was a desire to provide the users (voters) with service at less than full cost.

PUBLIC INVESTMENT IN INTERCITY FACILITIES

The trend toward increasing public investment in intercity transportation facilities since 1920, and particularly since the end of World War II, stems from quite different causes—social and technological change and public demand for better transportation. Nevertheless, the effect has been to further obscure comparisons of capital productivity and management efficiency.

In contrast to the railroads, the airlines and the motor and water carriers simply could not obtain private and exclusive control of the routes their vessels, vehicles, and airplanes traverse. It would be quite impracticable to reserve exclusive rights of way for any of them. This fact may relieve them of certain direct capital burdens, but it imposes competitive disadvantages and costs which, although not precisely measurable, are nevertheless consequential. The airlines, for example, are subject to increasing cost burdens resulting from delays to aircraft seeking airway and airport clearances in competition with other commercial, private, and military planes. Their terminals and repair facilities must be constructed on land owned by municipalities and authorities; although interest rates on the capital may benfit from tax exemption, construction costs often are higher than would obtain on privately-owned land.

Motor trucks and buses frequently are held up and subjected to extra costs as a result of traffic jams caused by private automobiles and trucks or other commercial vehicles. Also, although commercial operators benefit from sharing the highways with passenger automobiles, achievement of economical size and weight limitations for their vehicles is handicapped by the pressure of lobbyists representing private automobile interests—and railroads.

Public Aids to Railroads—Moreover, the argument, sometimes presented, that rail investment has been secured entirely from private sources, unaided by government, is open to contest. Over the past century, railroads have received assistance from federal, state and local governments, the amounts and present values of which may be disputed, further beclouding comparisons of relative capital productivity.

A study submitted by Robert R. Nathan to the Interstate Commerce Commission in Docket 34013 (*Cost Standards in Intermodal Rate Pro-*

ceedings) recapitulates some items of government aid to the railroads, as follows:

	Millions
Federal and state land and right-of-way grants	$954
Government purchases of rail securities	252
Other assistance to rail construction	48
Federal railroad loans—1920	350
Reconstruction Finance Corp. loans 1932–43	840
Public Works Administration loans	265
ICC loan guarantees, Transportation Act of 1958	243
Investment tax credit, 1962–68	364
Accelerated amortization for tax purposes	2,000

It cannot be demonstrated that any of these amounts represented undiluted gifts to the railroads. The 180 million acres of state and federal railroad land grants in the nineteenth century, although they comprised about 10 percent of the public lands at that time, had the effect, through fostering railroad construction in virgin territory, of increasing the value of the remaining public lands.

The Board of Transportation Investigation and Research commissioned by Congress concluded in 1945 that rate reductions by land-grant and nongrant railroads had cancelled out the value of the grants. There was a dissenting opinion, and in any event the land-grant railroads continue to benefit from nonoperating income received from mineral, timber, and grazing rights on these granted lands or other lands purchased with the proceeds of sale. During the five-year period 1965–1969, nonoperating income accounted for nearly 46 percent of Class I railroad net income before income taxes. It is impossible to determine how much of this income was derived directly or indirectly from land grant properties or properties obtained through exercise of eminent domain.

The various railroad loan programs of 1920, of the Reconstruction Finance Corporation and the Public Works Administration in the 1930s, and of the Interstate Commerce Commission under the 1958 law were intended not only to assist the railroads through difficult periods, but also to help the general economy. Still, they did represent extensions of government credit to the recipient railroads, providing them with funds which, if they could have been obtained at all, would have been more costly to raise in the private capital markets.

Accelerated amortization of depreciable assets and the tax benefits of the 7 percent investment credit were not intended exclusively for railroad benefit. The five-year amortization of new rolling stock authorized by the Tax Reform Act of 1969 does convey a special benefit available only to railroads.

Precise evaluation of government aids to railroads as compared with aids to other transportation is impossible, but it certainly cannot be demonstrated that the railroads have been left to shift for themselves. In fact, it is arguable that some government programs, such as the ICC loan program under the Transportation Act of 1958, have had the effect of perpetuating or inducing uneconomic rail investments or preserving inefficient managements.

The Need for Disinvestment

Complicating any study of railroad capital requirements is the apparent need not only for new investment but for substantial disinvestment, to bring the system into consonance with public needs.

Prior to the Transportation Act of 1920, providing the first federal controls over railroad construction, the railroad system of the country had already been substantially overbuilt, before any significant competition from newer means of transport had emerged. To attempt apportionment of the blame for this as between the rivalries of various communities and states, the cupidity of free-wheeling nineteenth century railroad promoters, and the gullibility of investors would be unrewarding. The promoters, unhampered by considerations of public interest or demand, often gave their principal attention to the prospects of profit from inflated construction contracts customarily awarded to themselves. Commonly, little original equity investment was committed, practically the entire cost of the lines being financed through sale of bonds. In the case of the subsidized Pacific roads, the sale of federal bonds produced much of the money. Sometimes, as in the case of the West Shore, new competitive railroad lines were built for the sole purpose of forcing a buy-out by the existing lines. The history of the United States in the latter half of the nineteenth century and the biographies of such entrepreneurs as Thomas Scott, Jay Gould, Collis P. Huntington, the Ames brothers, and Thomas C. Durant are enriched by examples of such activity.

THE CHANGES SINCE 1920

Since 1920 great changes have occurred. A vast network of improved highways has been constructed, reaching into every corner of the nation. Farmers no longer require a railhead nearby in order to reach it once a week over muddy roads by horse and wagon; in fact, farms operated by individuals are rapidly disappearing. Private automobiles account for more than 86 percent of intercity passenger travel, once almost entirely restricted to the rails. Airlines, providing passenger service at much higher speeds and lower cost than railroads, account for 9 percent of total passenger miles, but 71 percent of common-carrier traffic.

Highway trucks, primitive in 1920, are responsible for 21 percent of intercity freight ton miles and more than half of all freight revenues. In 1968 they moved 86 percent of all small shipments tonnage and received 64 percent of the revenues. The railroads no longer offer practically any package freight service, except as this is conducted by freight forwarders or shippers' associations in carload or truckload lots.

Partly because of the "dust bowl," flood control, and public works programs of the Great Depression, a system of improved inland waterways evolved, capable of moving barge tows accommodating more tonnage than the heaviest freight train.

Rail technology also has improved; with powerful diesel locomotives requiring no ash pits or water or coaling stations, high-capacity freight cars, better signaling, centralized traffic control, and the disappearance of conflicting passenger trains, a mile of railroad track has the potential to move much more traffic in a day than was possible in 1920. Considering the magnitude of these changes and the frequent railroad capital crises, the mileage of railroads has declined surprisingly little—about 14 percent in the 40 years 1920 through 1959, and less than 4 percent in the decade 1960–1969.

Despite all the modern devices for expediting traffic movement, the average number of trains moved over a mile of railroad track per day has declined 45 percent in the last 40 years.

Factors Inhibiting Disinvestment—Why has there been so little change in a railroad system inherited from the nineteenth century? Some of the responsibility must be assigned to burdensome and unreasonable procedures and tests required by the Interstate Commerce Commission for abandonments of trackage under the 1920 statute. Since the Commission has been given little opportunity to pass on construction of new lines, apparently it has wanted to make the most of its abandonment powers.

But in most matters the Commission has proved itself amenable to the Congressional and public mood. Abandonments have been few because the public has not been educated to the costs involved in continuing within the railroad system thousands of miles of useless trackage over which little traffic moves. (It has been estimated that 30 percent of the total railroad mileage accounts for but 2 percent of the ton miles, and that 50 percent of the ton miles move over 10 percent of the mileage.)

Rail managements have been dilatory in seeking abandonment of unproductive lines; shipper interests and labor have been obstructive. State, county, and town governments oppose rail abandonments because of the prospective loss of tax revenues. Moreover, the tendency of Congress to come forth with loan guarantee or other assistance programs whenever any railroad company undergoes a capital crisis, whatever the cause, inhibits the natural process of disinvestment which in any other industry would result in adjustment to changed circumstances.

Management sometimes explains that capital attrition in the railroads is slow, and that little maintenance of light-density branch lines is required. In fact, however, it is probable that a good deal of main-line track could be abandoned. A glance at the *Railway Guide* suggests numerous areas for study.

Between St. Louis and Chicago, for example, where the short-line mileage is 284, there are six rail routes with 1,838 miles of main line.

Between Omaha and Chicago, a short-line distance of 485 miles, there are seven routes with 3,268 miles of main line.

Two main lines parallel for more than three hundred miles between Shreveport, Louisiana, and New Orleans.

For 760 miles between Miles City, Montana, and Spokane, Washington, two main lines run side by side; probably one should never have been built.

Pierre R. Bretey, the dean of rail financial analysts, estimates the amount of rail trackage that should be abandoned at sixty thousand miles, or somewhat less than one third of the present total. An in-depth study on a nationwide basis might well reveal this estimate to be low. Such a study should be undertaken by the Department of Transportation as a matter of urgency, since no rational program of rail capital improvement can be produced without it.

Advantages of Disinvestment—Three obvious advantages might be expected to flow from a drastic pruning of rail trackage: (1) reduction of state and local tax payments; (2) concentration of traffic and of capital programs on fewer lines, permitting movement of heavier trains at higher speeds over improved track and roadway structures; (3) improved car and locomotive utilization, reducing the need for new equipment. In some cases, completely new rail lines probably should be constructed and the old trackage abandoned. The capital costs would be high, but might well be justified if traffic movements could be concentrated.

This may have particular application in those limited areas where, because of air and surface congestion or environmental considerations, establishment of high-speed rail passenger services is decided to be warranted. The present lines of the Penn Central between New York, Boston and Washington, for example, do not lend themselves to truly high-speed service, because of numerous sharp curves and drawbridges.

Rates, Rigidities, and Capital Flow

Because a percentage of rail operating costs is relatively independent of traffic volume, and also because of the redundant mileage, the historical tendency of railroad traffic managers has been to seek "volume for the sake of volume." Political pressures operating through the regulatory process also have held many freight rates, such as those applicable to certain agricultural products and export-import traffic, to noncompensatory levels.

As much as 50 percent of rail tonnage is believed to move under rates at or below the level of out-of-pocket costs as defined in Interstate Commerce Commission formulae. Such out-of-pocket costs cover only the short-run operational expenses of moving the traffic, without adequate provision for costs of replacing the equipment used or updating the roadway.

Such rates, for example, are frequently employed to divert traffic from barge lines operating on the inland waterways, although railroads cannot usually transport bulk traffic at costs competitive with barge operators. Further, even if all the inland water traffic, estimated to have yielded 1969 freight revenues of $477 million, could be diverted to the railroads it would have but moderate significance in relation to total freight revenues of $11.3 billion. If carried at rates comparable to barge rates, it could be expected to depress rail earnings.

In many cases out-of-pocket rates are employed by one railroad to divert traffic from another; the second line is forced to meet the reduction, and the result is that both operate at rates including insufficient allowance for return or attraction of capital. Large corporations are able to pressure railroads into noncompensatory rates by threatening to divert their most profitable traffic to private carriage, leaving the railroads with the dregs.

Rates for piggyback service sometimes undercut those for carload service, although the capital requirements of piggyback operations are higher than carload capital costs. The abandonment of rail less-than-carload service has left the carriers at the mercy of large freight forwarders and shippers' associations.

Since the overall level of rates must at least endeavor to cover costs, the effect of these out-of-pocket or below-cost rates is to force increases on profitable traffic, sometimes driving it to other forms of transportation.

No industry can prosper with half of its output priced at out-of-pocket levels or below. Of equal importance with adjustment of railroad mileage to modern conditions is the need for a massive overhaul of the rail rate structure, selectively adjusting upward those rates which contribute little or nothing to return on capital, and avoiding general increases which tend to force the more profitable traffic off the railroads.

The burden of initiating action here must rest with the railroads, although revision of the Interstate Commerce Act may be necessary to facilitate a wholesale revision of the rate structure without the inordinate delays encountered in present procedures.

THE EFFECTS OF LABOR RIGIDITIES

Although adequate statistical proof is not at hand, there can be little doubt that outmoded work rules have a greater effect on railroad competitive capabilities than the fixed costs associated with right-of-way ownership. Rules arbitrarily limiting crew runs, preventing road crews from performing switching and vice versa, requiring extra and unneeded trainmen, preventing shopmen from crossing craft lines, etc., not only increase railroad costs but restrict flexibility in meeting changed competitive conditions.

Other forms of transportation also have labor problems, it is true. However, although there are some restrictive work rules in the airline and trucking industries, the principal problems involve wage and benefit cost levels. The teamsters' union, for example, does not prevent operation of a truck all the way across the country with a single two-man crew, and airline flight crews operate nonstop transcontinental and transoceanic flights. (The ocean shipping industry, unfortunately, does have some problems with restrictive work rules and overcrewing.)

To date, attempts of rail management to reduce the burden of restrictive rules have been relatively unproductive, and it is doubtful that government intervention, given the realities of politics, would be helpful.

A resolution of this problem is vitally necessary if the railroads are to be competitive for capital. Probably the only solution is for management to continue its efforts, offering to share with labor through increased wage levels the benefits flowing from improved operating flexibility.

Railroad Income, Fixed Charges, and Cash Flow

The five-year totals and ratios in Table III summarize the deteriorating railroad investment picture.

DIVIDEND POLICIES

These data suggest that railroad capital problems have not been assisted by increasingly lavish dividend payouts in the face of declining earnings and unfavorable net cash flow. The 73.9 percent of net income paid out in dividends in the five years 1965–1969 compares with ratios of 29.4 percent for twelve major airlines and 35.9 percent for nine large publicly-held trucking companies.

Had railroad dividend ratios been held to approximately 22 percent, slightly higher than the airline ratio, net cash flow over the entire fifteen-year period would have been sufficient to cover all capital expenditures without increasing debt. (In the latest five-year period alone, it would have been insufficient.)

Even if one excludes from the 1969 results of Class I railroads the Penn Central and ten other systems which have suffered chronic financial difficulties, cash dividends paid by the remaining more prosperous lines were 68.3 percent of net income.

The generous dividend distributions are particularly puzzling considering that the industry has made no effort to obtain capital through new stock issues. Apparently railroad directors fear the ghosts of Robert R. Young and Patrick B. McGinnis, who won control of the New York Central and New Haven in 1954. Both of these gentlemen hinged their proxy contests on rosy promises of increased dividends, and both left the properties in worse condition than they found them.

Whether such high dividend payouts enhance the investment value

TABLE III. *Financial Picture of Class I Railroads, 1955–69*

	1955–59	1960–64	1965–69
	Five-Year Totals (in millions)		
Operating revenues	$50,538.3	$47,559.3	$53,533.8
Income before income taxes	5,352.4	3,652.0	3,941.2
Federal income taxes	1,635.2	904.2	589.0
Net income	3,717.2	2,747.8	3,352.2
Interest and equipment rents	2,994.9	3,596.2	4,896.0
Capital expenditures			
Equipment	3,444.5	3,578.6	5,913.4
Road	1,643.6	1,281.0	1,888.3
Total	5,088.1	4,859.6	7,801.7
Cash flow before dividends[1]	6,684.9	6,058.0	7,141.8
Cash dividends	2,081.2	1,947.0	2,477.1
Net cash flow after dividends	4,603.7	4,111.0	4,664.7
Excess of capital expenditure over cash flow	484.4	748.6	3,137.0
Net working capital—end of period[2]	798.4	730.8	58.4
Debt—end of period			
Equipment	2,756.7	2,814.1	4,202.5
Other	6,578.4	6,072.4	5,830.4
	Ratios		
Percent income taxes of pretax income	30.6	24.8	14.9
Percent dividends of net income	56.0	70.9	73.9

[1] Net income plus depreciation and retirements.
[2] Excludes materials and supplies and current portion of long-term debt.

of a stock in the long run is open to question. Particularly in a period of inflation and high tax rates such as the past two decades, many investors would prefer an opportunity for capital appreciation, since capital gains are taxed at lower rates. Such appreciation can best be obtained if a substantial portion of earnings is retained in the business, hopefully leading to growth of future earnings. In particular, stockholders are not advantaged if improvident dividend payments are a prelude to bankruptcy, as in the cases of the New Haven and Penn Central.

Railroad dividend payout ratios appear especially high in relation to earnings which, under Interstate Commerce Commission procedures, are not considered by investment analysts to be of the same "quality" as those of companies in other industries, particularly those adhering to generally accepted accounting principles.

Income Tax Rates—Net income of Class I railroads would have declined much more than the 9.9 percent actually reported in the 1965–1969 period as compared with 1955–1959 had it not been for the 64 percent reduction in federal income tax accruals. Federal tax laws allowing accelerated depreciation and investment tax credits have been especially beneficial to railroads, which accrued only 14.9 percent of income for taxes in the 1965–1969 period as compared to an average of 40 percent for United States airlines and 37.1 percent for trucking companies reporting to the ICC. Had railroads accrued taxes at the same percentage rate as trucking companies their reported net income for the five years would have been reduced by 26 percent.

In their reports to the ICC neither trucking companies nor railroads are permitted to accrue provisions for deferred tax liabilities resulting from accelerated depreciation, as required by generally accepted accounting rules. However, practically all trucking companies and some railroads do so in their reports to stockholders. To the extent that railroads do not provide for deferred taxes, their income is overstated in comparison with most other industry, although current cash flow is not affected. This factor affects the quality of reported earnings in the eyes of investment analysts.

Undermaintenance—The quality of reported railroad earnings also is lessened by the recognition that in recent years many of the properties have been undermaintained and that the deficiencies will have to be made up at the expense of prospective future earnings.

Depreciation charges have been inadequate, especially in the light of the large amount of obsolete and excess plant. Prior to 1943, railroads made no provision for depreciation of roadway and structures, and under present ICC rules no depreciation is permitted for grading or tunnels and subways. The prescribed depreciation rates for other components of roadway and structures investment are totally inadequate in an age of rapidly changing technology. The result is that the railroad book investment on which rate of return is calculated contains a considerable element of fiction, and reported earnings are overstated.

Future Capital Requirements

A study prepared under the auspices of the Association of American Railroads (*The American Railroad Industry, a Prospectus, June*

30, 1970) estimates gross capital expenditures for the decade 1970–1979 at $25.9 billion for equipment and $5.5 billion for roadway and structures exclusive of rail and tie replacements, or a total of $31.3 billion, nearly three times the amounts expended in 1960–1969.

This might prove to be an overestimate if the rail plant were reduced to proportions consonant with current needs, but there is little doubt that requirements over the next decade will exceed those of the recent past, if only because of inflation. Equipment needs customarily have been met through the device of equipment trusts or leases, with internal cash generation depended upon for roadway improvements. No reliance has been placed on new equity issues, and nonequipment debt has been reduced in the last fifteen years by about 13 percent with funds drawn from internal cash. Because of restrictive covenants in old railroad mortgages, securing new capital through roadway debt in some cases may be impracticable.

The capital problems are complicated by the fact that, while about 75 percent of the rail system in terms of either net investment or revenues is in reasonably sound financial condition, the remaining 25 percent is critically weak and lacks cash flow or credit to support either equipment or roadway financing. To the degree that the merger process links weak roads with strong ones this complication may be minimized, but mergers are not a complete solution; for one thing, they have followed regional, rather than national, patterns. Also, since the Penn Central bankruptcy the willingness of strong roads to absorb weak ones may be diminished. What else can be done to improve rail access to capital markets?

MORE SELF-HELP

So long as the roads are privately owned, the principal initiative must rest with management (and railroad labor): more conservative dividend policies; better market analysis and wholesale correction of unprofitable rates; and elimination of archaic work rules. There is need for cooperation and introspection within the industry to determine the functions it is able to perform economically under prospective conditions and to adjust plant, service, rates, and working rules to the task of performing these functions well.

PUBLIC POLICY

The amount and character of railroad service is a matter of public policy which cannot be left entirely to the decisions of private managements or of rail labor; conversely, rail managements, with the best of will and application, cannot find solutions in the absence of intelligent public policy. Within the limitations and imperfections of the American political system, how can public policy be altered to permit the railroads to resolve their capital problems?

Broadly, the changes which have been suggested toward this end come under the following headings:

1. imposition of penalties on other transportation to raise their costs and force traffic onto the railroads (user charges or other special fees) ;
2. limitations on government-provided facilities usable by other transportation;
3. relaxation of rail regulation;
4. government ownership of the railroads or of their rights of way;
5. restructuring of the railroad system, possibly with government assistance or direction;
6. assumption by government of railroad costs, leaving the management in private hands.

User Charges—Over the years, the railroads have concentrated much of their collective effort on seeking imposition of charges or taxes of one kind or another to be paid by airlines, motor carriers, and water carriers in order to bring about "equality of competitive opportunity." The airlines and motor carriers agree in principle that they should pay for use of publicly-provided facilities; the only disagreement between them and the railroads is as to the amounts.

The water carriers reject the principle in its entirety and insist that use of the waterways, improved or unimproved, should be free. (Aside from the principle, a difficulty here is that no one has yet come forward with a *method* for assessing user charges for the waterways which relates the charge to the use. Several successive administrations have proposed assessment of a tax on fuel consumed by shallow-draft vessels. This would merely be a tax, completely unrelated to the government's costs of waterway improvement. For example, a tow-boat drawing 8 feet of water on the Hudson between New York and Albany would pay the tax, although it occasions no dredging costs; an oil tanker requiring a 26-foot dredged channel would not be charged.)

The principle that users of pubicly-provided transportation facilities should pay charges fairly apportioned to their use and the costs they occasion is difficult to contest; in the light of demands on public budgets in the years to come, the principle probably will not escape the attention of the taxing authorities. On the other hand, assessment of charges at penalty levels intended to prevent realization of the economies inherent in shared use of facilities already provided in response to public demand would be self-defeating and occasion waste rather than conservation of public funds.

Moreover, it is doubtful that imposition of user charges at any foreseeable level would contribute significantly to resolution of railroad capital problems. Railroads and airlines, for example, are essentially noncompetitive, and it is difficult to conceive of any benefit which would ensue from railroad-imposed determination of airline landing fees, rentals, or other charges. On the contrary, were the railroad management time and expertise which has been devoted to this subject applied to internal railroad problems, it is quite possible that some benefit would result.

The extent of competition between railroads and general-commodity truckers is less than many suppose; most railroads long ago embargoed less-than-carload traffic, and increasing use charges on the highways would merely add to the costs of package-freight shippers without proportional benefit to the railroads. Fully compensatory tolls on some of the more expensive waterways might, it is true, deter their use and shift some traffic to the rails, but the amount of probable gain, measured against political realities and overall rail capital problems, does not appear consequential.

In any event, the proposition that the level of rents paid by any business should be determined at the behest of its competitors is a perilous one. Privately-owned newspapers, for example, might with equal justice demand the right to determine the license fees paid by broadcasters. In turn, broadcasters could demand a voice in the postal rates charged for newspapers and magazines, and in their advertising rates. The task of legislators and public administrators would become impossible.

Limitations on Public Facilities—The extent to which government funds are expended for transportation facilities used by some others does have an effect on the railroads. Questions could be raised as to the wisdom of some expensive waterway construction, the establishment of subsidized local service airlines, and the location, if not the existence, of some smog-laden highways.

As the airways become more congested, the atmosphere and the rivers more polluted, and the scenery more repulsive, the necessity for cost-benefit analysis of such projects in the future becomes increasingly compelling, not only for ecological reasons but also because of the need to conserve scarce capital. This is easily said, but in a multifaceted political structure such as ours, how is it to be accomplished? In a totalitarian political system the allocation would be dictated by a central bureaucracy, but so would the lives and thoughts of the people.

It was the need for coordinated planning of transportation allocations, more than any other consideration, that led to establishment of the Department of Transportation. It controls, within the executive branch of government, practically all planning for transportation with the major exception of waterway programs; these probably ought also to be brought within its purview. The department does not control, although it may influence, the appropriations by Congress or the state legislatures for transportation purposes.

The department itself is a political body, subjected to the pressures of conflicting interests and lacking a permanent staff at the policy levels. As yet it has had little effect, but with all its limitations it would appear to be the best hope of those who seek rationalization of transportation planning. As earlier stated, one of its most urgent tasks should be to produce an overall plan for the scope of transportation facilities required during the coming decades, including a plan for a rail network adjusted to essential modern requirements.

Relaxation of Regulation—The general question of regulation is not within the scope of this chapter. From the standpoint of capital access, however, the prime necessity is for the regulatory agencies and the legislators who direct them to comprehend the cyclical nature of most transportation operations and the reluctance of investors to commit their savings in enterprises threatened by repetitive crises. Greater freedom is needed for carriers to discontinue uneconomic operations and to adjust rates on unprofitable traffic. The cumbersome restrictions on the marketability of transportation investments should be relaxed. Unfortunately, the trend of recent years has been in the opposite direction: advance CAB approval is required for purchase by anyone of as much as 10 percent ownership in an airline, and the ICC has been soliciting the power to impose similar restrictions on ownership in carriers subject to its jurisdiction. If the airline legislation is taken as a pattern, no investor would know what standards might govern approval or disapproval of his application; three airlines have already, with CAB approval, come under common control with gambling syndicates. The same rule that subjects purchases of transportation securities to undefined scrutiny also applies to their sale, since there cannot be a sale without a purchaser. Under these circumstances, suppliers of capital to transportation enterprises are subjected to risks and uncertainties not applicable to other investments. Why should they choose transportation?

Government Ownership—To the extent that there is a disadvantage in private ownership of rail rights of way, the obvious solution is outright nationalization, in consonance with the practice of most other nations. Some advantages of this approach would be elimination of cutthroat competitive pricing as between railroads, possibly more logical grouping of railroad operations into a national system without regard to the nineteenth century river barriers which still dictate the boundaries of rates and service, and availability of capital to the limit of the public purse. Unfortunately, the capital funds would have to be drawn from the same pool—the savings of private investors.

Whether government management would be less efficient than private management is conjectural. The principal management problem might be sheer size, since bureaucracies, private or public, have a Parkinsonian tendency to generate inefficiency in geometric proportion to scale of the enterprise.

The greatest danger of this approach is that, as a matter of political reality, it would probably ensure preservation in our transportation system of all the redundant mileage as well as the outmoded work rules, thus imposing a disproportionate drain on available capital resources. For this reason, if no other, it is a recourse not to be adopted lightly.

Some argue that if the railroads were nationalized all other intercity transportation would shortly have to be nationalized also, or would be severely handicapped in continuing under private management. This belief stems from the assumption that a nationalized rail system able to draw on the resources of government and to incur huge annual deficits as the postal service has done would be even more disposed than private rail managements to resort to rates yielding less than full cost. It is a legitimate fear, but the conclusion is not inevitable, since the United States, in distinction to most other countries, has in being a flourishing system of privately-owned bus, truck, barge, and airline companies. With private investors in rail securities eliminated as a political class, the collective political strengths of owners, employees, users, and investors whose interests are involved in these enterprises might be more persuasive than they are now. What does seem fairly certain is that the effects of political influence on rail rates, service, and investment would be accentuated.

Government Ownership of Rights of Way—A variation of this proposal is that the federal government acquire only the railroad rights of way, making their use available to a railroad operating corporation or corporations, and perhaps to private shippers. The government would bear the fixed costs and the charges paid by operating companies would vary with their use. Property taxes to states and localities would be eliminated, but income taxes on the holders of federal securities issued to acquire or improve the properties would not be.

Assuming that the federal government acquired *all* the existing rail trackage, regardless of its usefulness, and that charges for its use were fairly apportioned to cover all the government's costs, several major consequences might ensue. Pressure on the rail operating companies to seek volume for the sake of volume might be diminished; most of their costs would become variable, and presumably rates on all traffic would be adjusted to cover these costs and yield a profit. Service probably would tend to be concentrated on the largest traffic flows and over the most economical routes. The rail operating companies might be more favorably disposed toward arrangements for joint movements with barge and truck operators where costs would be reduced or service improved, since the incentive to obtain the "long haul" over owned lines would be diminished.

Under such an ideal concept, service over redundant lines would quickly cease and presumably the federal government would promptly abandon them. Private investors would obtain a windfall, since the capital shrinkage involved in bringing rail fixed plant into line with reality would have been transferred to the taxpayers. This might be a small price for the taxpayers as compared with the alternative of subsidizing, in one way or another, continuance of all the existing plant.

The complexities of setting up and operating such a partly government, partly private system would be considerable. Merely determining a fair price to be paid by the government for the rights of way could be a process requiring many years and much time of our overburdened courts. Probably the easiest and simplest approach would be issuance to railroad security-holders of revenue bonds, principal and interest of which would be backed by the user charges to be assessed railroad operating companies.

The operating companies or shippers, assuming that more than one were permitted to use the tracks, might encounter severe problems in controlling the movement of their traffic, since it is not as easy for trains to meet or pass each other as it is for trucks on a highway or for airplanes operated at different altitudes.

How would the rail labor force be apportioned as between the operating companies and the government? How would the work rules problem be resolved? These are thorny questions for which ready solutions are not at hand.

Moreover, the assumption that use charges for the federally-owned rights of way would be fairly apportioned to cover full costs may be naive. In our system, the pressures from localities or segments of society and from the operating companies or shippers to reduce charges below full-cost levels would be enormous. If the charges were not fully compensatory the capital problems of the railroads would not have been resolved, but merely passed on to the taxpayers. Should competing demands on the federal budget be pressing, as seems likely, funds for rail capital improvements might not be forthcoming, and the competitive position of the operating companies, as well as service to shippers, might suffer.

Restructuring the Rail System—An imaginative suggestion recently put forward is that the railroad system of the country be restructured into three separate types of private corporations:

1. nationwide, competing companies owning track;
2. national companies furnishing freight cars, trailers, and containers;
3. transportation companies whose sole function would be to move freight.

It may be noted that the Rail Passenger Service Act of 1970 is a small step in this direction, except that the corporation established under it will own cars as well as operating passenger services; it will contract with the railroads for use of their tracks and stations, and presumably for operating crews, etc.

Under this concept the private companies owning track would have an incentive to keep these facilities at a high level of maintenance and capital improvement in order to attract business from the rail operating companies. They would make long-term trackage rights agreements containing both fixed and variable elements with some or all of the rail operating companies, and these would form the basis for supporting both existing roadway debt and new financing, much as tollroad bonds or pipe-line debt are serviced.

The car-owning companies would present no novelty except that they would no longer be competing with railroad-owned cars. Their equipment could be financed by traditional equipment trusts and conditional sales agreements. Their revenues and earnings would derive from long-term leases to shippers and from rental of general service equipment to the rail operating companies.

The rail operating companies under this concept would be shorn of the need for financing anything but locomotives, cabooses, freight stations and offices, and working capital.

Use charges above some minimum commitment fees under their throughput or trackage rights agreements with the track-owning companies would be variable, and costs associated with the various components of traffic could be more readily identified. Operating on a nationwide basis, the companies should be able to offer better service than is possible with the present regional grouping of railroad companies. There would be at least two and possibly more such companies, so that a strike against one or financial failure of one would not deprive the public of service.

Some advantages undoubtedly would flow from this approach. Nationwide car-owning pools should present opportunity for more efficient utilization and ameliorate the regional inequalities in the car ownership burden. Rates of the operating companies could be brought into better conformity with identifiable costs. However, the fixed element of right-of-way costs would not be eliminated. The proposal seems worthy of further and more detailed study.

Yet this proposal also is surrounded by complexities at least as great as those for government ownership of rail rights of way. How would the capitalization of the three types of companies be established? How much would the track-owning companies pay for these properties, and how would the properties be allocated between them? How would railroad labor be allocated, and how would the work rules problems be resolved?

As outlined, the proposal assumes that all of the present rail trackage would be divided between four track-owning companies but that as competition between these companies progressed, large amounts of secondary trackage would be abandoned. Somehow, the prospect of this would have to be allowed for in the initial prices paid by the track-owning companies and in their capital structures. How would the relative claims of present railroad bondholders be worked out? It could be a lengthy process.

Although all three types of companies would be privately owned, the participation of government in such a program would be essential. The laws governing mergers, abandonments, levels of service, rates, and many other areas would require to be changed, and it is probable that some government assistance in arranging at least the initial financial structure would be needed.

Government Subsidies—The proposal most recently sponsored by the Association of American Railroads is that the railroads remain under private ownership and management but that the federal government should subsidize a large portion of railroad costs. The program as outlined apparently would involve at least $1.9 billion of subsidies per year, an amount approximating 18 percent of current rail operating costs. It includes:

1. subsidies to pay railroad property taxes—about $300 million annually;
2. additional federal funds for grade crossing improvements—$500 million annually;
3. subsidies for maintenance and improvement of roadway and terminals—$400 million annually, to be extracted from the highway trust fund;
4. guaranteed loans up to $400 million annually for right-of-way improvements;
5. government advance of down payments on rolling stock, and assumption of interest charges exceeding 4 percent—$200 million annually;
6. reinstatement of investment tax credits for freight cars and locomotives—cost not specified;
7. a federally-financed program of railroad research—$100 million annually.

Were the program to be adopted *in toto*, federal expenditures over a ten-year period would exceed by at least $2 billion the present total investment in roadway and structures.

In addition to this huge subsidy program, the railroads propose several changes in regulation of rates, mergers, common ownership, and abandonments. Although greater freedom of abandonments is urged, no specific schedule for adjusting rail plant to traffic requirements is suggested, except that the proposed schedule of rail renewal seems to contemplate a mere 5 percent reduction in track miles over 30 years. The subsidies sought would, in the main, be available to rich roads and poor alike, without regard to relative need.

Discussion and Conclusions

Although railroad capital problems do not appear to be more severe than those of airlines, there will be substantial future requirements for new capital, particularly for rolling stock but also for roadway and track improvement. Considering the advantages to the railroads of controlling their own traffic movements, the substantial governmental assistance bestowed upon them in the past, and the importance to some of income from nontransport uses of their properties, it is not clear that private ownership of their rights of way imposes any particular inequity upon them in competing for capital. Some investors in rail securities, in fact, have been attracted by the prospects of gain through appreciation of the companies' real estate holdings.

To the extent that any such inequity does exist, the only clear means of resolving it appears to be either nationalization or government ownership of the rights of way. Either of these approaches would involve great complexities; the capital requirements would merely have been assumed by the taxpayers; and the prospects for improved railroad efficiency under such arrangements are at best inconclusive.

The prospect of a railroad industry perennially manning a tin-cup brigade in congressional lobbies, seeking larger and larger subsidies to preserve the status quo, also is not attractive. Probably outright nationalization would be preferable.

Despite the emergence of newer transportation modes capable of providing certain services more efficiently than railroads, it is expected that as the economy grows the total demand for rail freight service also will increase. There is no reason to suppose that a modernized railroad plant geared to future prospects rather than to the past—with a profit-oriented rate structure, updated accounting (including realistic depreciation and amortization provisions), prudent dividend policies, and vigorous management—could not be operated profitably and attract the necessary capital. For such an approach to succeed, less dependence by rail management on government, and less paternalism by government toward railroads would be essential. It should be tried.

Although compensatory user charges should be assessed, efforts to deter use of transportation facilities already provided would be wasteful of capital. On the other hand, a greater degree of cost-benefit analysis should be applied to future government expenditures for transportation facilities. There is a danger, for example, that the interstate highway program, excellent in initial concept, will be carried to extremes, as was the railroad-building spree of the latter nineteenth century—and for similar reasons: profit opportunities for contractors. The Department of Transportation, if it survives, must play a key role both in formulating plans and in educating Congress and the public to the need for conserving capital.

Some railroad companies suffer from financial difficulties the easing of which cannot await development of long-range or far-reaching programs. Some of their services may be essential to communities or industries, or the freight traffic they originate or terminate important to more prosperous connecting lines. Part of the solution is to speed up the merger process, absorbing these weak companies into stronger systems. Where commuter passenger services are involved, some are already receiving financial aid from state governments. The resources available to the states, however, are limited.

At least temporarily—until they can be fitted into a national scheme —it may be necessary for the federal government to extend assistance to these companies in the form of loan guarantees or even grants, where it is determined that the service they provide is essential. Appropriate conditions can be inserted in such loans or grants to insure that the funds provided are not dissipated in servicing outmoded nonequipment debt, in paying dividends, in maintaining uneconomic operations, or in perpetuating wasteful management or labor practices.

Good transportation is an essential of any society; it is also an enormous consumer of capital. Hopefully, government attitudes toward transportation in the future will be more enlightened than in the past, so that the capital demands can be met from private sources. There will be plenty of other uses to which public funds can be put.

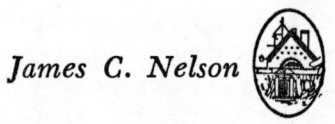

James C. Nelson

5

Toward Rational Price Policies

Abundant evidence exists that present-day pricing policies in transport, particularly in overland freight services, have been far from rational in terms of economics. Close attention should be given to this evidence as it will disclose the best avenues toward rational pricing for transport.

Evidence of Irrational Pricing

Intercity Freight Traffic—One important piece of direct evidence of irrational prices in transport consists of the findings by a number of economists (including Meyer and Associates, James C. Nelson, Williams and Bluestone, Hilton, Harbeson, Friedlaender, and Wilson) that intercity freight traffic has been seriously misallocated among the major modes in close competition for that traffic. Conservatively, the cost of this misallocation amounts to $5 billion per year in added freight costs to the prices for goods, and it might be double that amount or more. Most misallocated freight traffic over medium and long distances has been moved by truck at higher unit costs than it could have been moved by rail, but some was transported by barge

JAMES C. NELSON, *professor of economics at Washington State University, has had extensive experience as economic consultant on highway finance and pricing, railway mergers, and national transportation policy. In addition to serving the Office of Defense Transportation during World War II, he has been chief, Transportation Division of the United States Department of Commerce. He is the author of numerous books and monographs on transportation.*

over marginal waterways at higher real cost than it could have been moved by rail. This is factual evidence that freight services have been priced in an irrational manner, that is, not in close relation to the relative unit costs of the competing modes. This long-standing situation is due both to the pricing policies of the regulated carriers and to the cost standards utilized by the Interstate Commerce Commission (ICC) in regulating competitive rates.

User Fees—Another type of important evidence of irrational pricing of transport services lies in the nonapplicability of user fees to the inland waterways and in the findings of official studies that the intercity trucks in strong competition with the railways pay considerably less than adequate user fees to cover their differential costs for essential highway services. Transport services are distributed among the modes on the basis of shipper and traveler choices expressed in terms of the final market prices for those services. But when the final prices of one major mode include nothing to cover the cost of public facilities and the final prices of another major mode are lower than they would be if the user fees fully covered all differential costs of the public facilities utilized, those final prices for freight services cannot ration traffic efficiently among the competing modes. In other words, the transport pricing system is expected to perform its role of dividing traffic efficiently, but cannot do so because all real resource costs of producing transport have not been included in the final prices of some competitive modes having significant positions in the market.

Differential Tax Policies—A third set of evidence of irrational pricing consists of the differential tax policies with respect to way and terminal facilities that exist in transport. The completely privately-owned modes, the railroads and the oil pipe lines, have to pay property taxes on their private ways and terminal facilities. In 1968, the property taxes of Class I railroads totaled $293 million, including $167 million on their rights of way alone. On the other hand, the modes whose carriers (the truckers, the barge lines, and the airlines) operate over public ways and channels and utilize publicly-owned terminals do not have to bear property taxes on those highly essential facilities toward the general costs of government. This is because no property taxes have been assessed by state and local governments on publicly-owned way and terminal facilities. These have long been treated as "public goods" in spite of their use by carriers competing with the privately-owned railroads and oil pipe lines; and in disregard of the fact that tolerably efficient markets can be established for the services of those publicly-owned facilities as indicated by the tolls charged by the tollroads, the user fees assessed for highway services, and the tolls levied by international canals such as the Panama Canal and the St. Lawrence Seaway. Nor have offsetting increments for property taxes not assessed on public transport facilities been added to the user fees paid for highway services and airway and airport services. So long as these conditions continue for those modes and also for inland waterways, the prices for highway carrier, barge, and airline services cannot fully cover the real resource costs involved in their production. Again, the final prices for the services of carriers using public ways and terminals cannot divide the traffic efficiently.

Social Costs—A fourth kind of evidence of irrational pricing in transport consists of the almost complete failure to assess the social costs of certain modes to the users of their transport services through charges to the carriers to limit those social costs or to compensate for them, or both. In particular, highway carriers contribute a very large part of the smog and noise pollution that occurs from transport, but these social costs are not charged as operating costs to the highway carriers. Thus, those costs are not reflected in the final prices for motor carrier services, or in what amounts to the same thing for private carriers, in the final costs of service to their owners. The same has been increasingly true of airline air and noise pollution, and also of some pollution that arises from barges and tows on the public inland waterway channels. Railroads, too, contribute some social costs in terms of noise and congestion costs, but these are relatively small compared with the social costs associated with motor vehicles and aircraft. In yet another sense, the full public and social costs of highways and airports have not been charged to the motor and airline carriers. For as a general rule, peak-use prices that equate with the social marginal cost of peak-time use of public facilities have not been imposed. It follows that to an unknown but probably significant extent, the final prices for the services of highway, airline, and inland waterway carriers are lower than truly economic prices would be by the amounts of the social and peak-use costs not assessed. Consequently, more traffic has been attracted to those modes than otherwise would occur.

Value-of-Service Rates—Although heavily involved as a factor in the traffic misallocations mentioned above, the continuation of traditional types of pricing for carrier freight services must be accorded an important role in the irrational pricing that has resulted. Specifically, continuance of the historical value-of-service, or discriminating, rate structure by the railroads has been overly long. That rate structure assigned high rates on short-haul services and on high-value goods and low rates, even in considerable disregard of the costs of distance, on long-haul services and low-value commodities. But the high rates under that pricing system have held an umbrella over high-cost modes; have encouraged shippers to select modes on a service basis; and have prevented rates from reflecting the costs of the low-cost mode. The adoption of the rail value-of-service pricing pattern by the regulated truckers, with strong ICC encouragement shortly after the Motor Carrier Act of 1935 was passed, was another irrational pricing policy. This was irrational because that action encouraged the railroads to continue their traditional value-of-service rates and to delay making the competitive rate adjustments that would have brought freight rates more into alignment with costs of service and the relative costs of competing modes.

The continued employment of value-of-service rates on the pattern of the market conditions in past periods was an irrational pricing policy for the railroads and was also an illogical regulatory policy. That policy fundamentally disregarded the strong and pervasive intermodal competitive forces that had emerged in transport, beginning in the 1920s. In highly or workably competitive markets such as have come predominantly to prevail in transport, only competitively-determined prices, or prices closely resembling competitive prices, can divide the traffic efficiently. This is because the process of competition causes the rates of the competing modes to reflect their relevant unit costs whereas under regulated or monopoly conditions carrier rates can, and often do, vary considerably or markedly from those cost limits. Only when rates are closely adjusted to relative costs can the users make fully rational economic choices among the competing modes. Even where the services of the competing modes are not homogeneous as in real-life markets, competitive prices that reflect the real cost differences among the modes are essential to enable shippers to chose rationally between a high-rate service of better quality and a low-rate service of lesser quality.

Thus, there exists abundant evidence that significant misallocations of traffic and resources have occurred in freight transport and that the roots of this uneconomic condition are to be found in carrier pricing policies, regulatory policies affecting carrier prices, and the pricing or nonpricing of public transport facilities. Society relies on prices to bring about an efficient use of resources by allocating them properly among all alternative goods and services. This is also true within the transport sector, but in several respects transport prices have not been designed as efficient allocators of traffic and resources among the competing modes. To a varying but significant degree, transport prices have been irrational and uneconomic. For transport prices to function more efficiently, rational pricing will have to be substituted both for all final transport services and for the infrastructural services of public transport facilities.

Forces in Irrational Transport Prices

A key fact is that most transport firms are privately-owned carriers in the United States. They operate in well developed markets and, to the extent that market forces permit, make their own rates and pricing systems. Even the regulated carriers in each mode at least initially make their own rates, either independently or, more frequently, in rate bureaus where concerted action prevails. In the exempt or nonregulated sectors in several transport modes, the carrier firms entirely make their rates. However, in those cases the forces of free competition severely limit the power of the individual firm over rates, and the going rates that divide the traffic are market-determined prices to which the firm has to adjust as a price taker. Collectively, the regulated carriers organized into rate bureaus have market power to influence their rate levels and rate structures away from competitively-determined prices and toward monopoly prices, or prices with monopoly elements in them. Obviously, then, the regulated carriers, in particular, have been active forces in formation of the price policies that have contributed to irrational results such as misallocations of traffic and resources, high profits in some modes and low profits in others, and to excess capacity and overinvestment in transport facilities.

ICC STANDARDS AND PROCEDURES

The surface carriers regulated by the ICC (all intercity ton-miles by rail, most of the ton-miles by oil pipe lines, somewhat more than a third of the ton-miles by truck, and less than a seventh of the ton-miles by domestic water carriers) are subject, of course, to the rate-filing and rate-changing requirements of the ICC and to the standards of reasonableness and nondiscriminatory rates specified in the Interstate Commerce Act and interpreted by the Commission in rate decisions and orders. To be legal, the rates of the carriers subject to regulation must be filed with the ICC in classifications and tariffs approved as to form by that body. Regulated carriers can change their filed rates only by filing rate changes and waiting 30 days to allow shippers and other parties to learn about, and react to, the changed rates before they become effective—unless permission is granted by the ICC to make rate changes in less time than the statutory notice. Except when carriers elect to file rates independently after failing to obtain agreement for the desired changes by the majority of the carriers with power to vote in the applicable rate bureau or bureaus, common carriers in each regulated mode agree on rates, classifications, and rate changes in rate bureau proceedings under exemptions from the antitrust laws, typically after listening to the positions of shippers and other interested parties in public hearings at regularly docketed intervals. Both the agreed-on rate changes and the independent-notice rate changes are filed with the ICC by the appropriate rate bureau, since rate bureaus are cooperative tariff-publishing agencies as well as organizations for concerted action on rates.

When rates or rate changes are filed with the ICC, they are subject to protest by shippers, other carriers and modes, and by other interested parties whose interests are affected by the modified rates. If a presumption of unreasonableness or undue discrimination can be shown, or if the proposed rate change affects a large number of industries or carriers and a wide area or the entire economy, the Commission can suspend the effective date of the filed rates up to seven months, or longer, if the initiating parties will agree voluntarily to longer suspension periods pending investigation and public hearings as to the lawfulness of the proposed rates under the key rate provisions and standards of the Interstate Commerce Act. In the case of the railroads and the oil pipe lines, their rates must be reasonable as to level under section 1 of part I of the Act; they cannot involve personal discrimination under section 2; they cannot involve undue or unreasonable discrimination against, or undue or unreasonable preference in favor of, particular persons, firms, commodities, localities, ports, regions, or territories under section 3; and they cannot charge higher rates for short hauls than for longer hauls unless special permission by the ICC is granted in advance under section 4. Except that section 4 discrimination prohibitions do not apply to motor carriers under part II of the Act, similar standards of rate discrimination or nondiscrimination and of rate reasonableness are applicable to motor carriers under that part and to domestic water carriers under part III of the Act. In addition, the ICC has the power to prescribe minimum rates, maximum rates, and precise rates for common carriers regulated under those parts and for freight forwarders regulated under part IV of the Act. The minimum rate power is primarily used to limit or to prevent rate competition within a mode or between modes by specifying a rate or rates below which a competing carrier or mode cannot lawfully go in meeting or engaging in competition with other carriers or modes. The maximum rate power is employed to specify a rate or rates above which a carrier or a group of carriers cannot go in seeking greater revenues and profitability. Carrier requests to the ICC for permission to raise the entire rate level usually involve the maximum rate power. A rule of rate-making in section 15a (and comparable rules in parts II, III, and IV) establishes the general standards to be applied by the ICC in regulating the rates of the regulated carriers, particularly with respect to increases in the general level of rates. Section 15a(3) specifies the standards governing changes in competitive rates in intermodal minimum rate cases.

Especially in times of general inflation in prices and costs, regulated carriers have been seriously affected by the delays of months or years required to obtain regulatory permission for rate level increases. This typically requires the ICC's approval to raise established maximum rates and to avoid altering established rate relationships under the discrimination control sections of the Act. Often, common carriers, the railroads in particular, have to bear retroactive wage increases while waiting for authority to increase the rate level, and typically the rate level increases granted have been less than those requested. In recent years, regulated motor carriers have encountered similar difficulties in adjusting to inflation, though they and the regulated water carriers have usually joined the railroads in requesting rate level increases in a follow-the-leader fashion. Railroads, too, have frequently been affected by the minimum rate procedures and decisions of the ICC that result in long delays, expensive proceedings, and limited rate reductions in meeting their intermodal competition. And they have often been prohibited from effectuating the planned rate cuts for that purpose. Similar minimum rate delays and limited competitive rate reductions apply to intermodal competition by the regulated motor and water carriers and to intramodal competition within those fields as well. However, because of the far larger role of the railroads in handling the nation's freight, particularly long distance freight and freight in primary and low-value commodities, the impacts of rate regulatory processes, standards, and decisions have been harshest on the railroads during the past several decades. The Commission's standards and decisions controlling railroad rate levels, discriminatory rate relationships, and competitive rates in intermodal minimum rate cases have exerted powerful forces over railroad rates and pricing policies, some of which have significantly influenced irrational pricing of rail services by the railroads. Additionally, the Commission was influential in the adoption of value-of-service rates by the regulated motor carriers, an irrational rate policy for a naturally competitive mode not subject to chronic excess capacity and economies of scale in size of firm.

MAINTENANCE OF VALUE-OF-SERVICE RATES

Several forces have reinforced maintenance of the traditional value-of-service rate structure long after the monopoly conditions upon which its economic viability rested began to disappear in transport. A major one was the railroads' distinct preference for continuing the discriminating rates that had characterized their rate structure for many decades when the rise of competing modes threatened their high discriminating rates in the 1920s and 1930s. The principal response of the railroads to competition was to urge regulation of competing modes instead of making the full competitive adjustments required effectively to meet their spreading intermodal competition. And when the regulated motor carriers adopted the high rail value-of-service rates for themselves, partly at the urging of the ICC, the railroads accepted rate parity with their principal competitors for the profitable, high-value traffic.

Although the rate parity policy on high value-of-service rates probably yielded higher returns in the short run to both modes, it was an irrational rate policy in the long run because rail freight services were generally inferior to truck services at the time. At the same rates for both rail and regulated truck services, the rational shipper obviously chose the highest quality service, usually the truck service. As entry control limited the number of truckers but not the number and capacity of the trucks operated by the certificated carriers, this pricing policy led to very large transfers of high-value freight and the associated freight revenues to the trucks. The parity pricing policy ultimately led to low profitability for the railroads, although the regulated truckers not heavily limited by certificate restrictions made high returns, even monopoly profits.

From society's standpoint, too, the policy of parity rates on value-of-service factors was irrational in that it shifted traffic from low-cost carriers to high-cost carriers. On the other hand, the low-rated traffic was left largely to the railroads to transport as its movement over long distances depended on very low rates and the truckers' costs were too high to permit them to compete for such traffic profitably. The long-term results were low profits and growth rates for the railroads, high profits and rapid growth rates for the regulated truckers of general commodities having adequate route authority, unnecessarily high freight costs for shippers except when they used private or exempt carriage, and higher-than-necessary consumer prices for society.

Another major force in the continuance of value-of-service rates has been the ICC regulatory policies. First, the ICC advocated regulation of motor and water carriers rather than deregulation of the railroads as measures for dealing with intermodal competition. Second, the ICC encouraged formation of motor carrier rate bureaus and the adoption of the rail value-of-service rate structure by the regulated truckers, with modifications to insure that regulated truckers would not be asked to carry low-grade commodities beyond short distances. Third, when the railroads in the 1950s sought aggressively to reduce many high discriminating rates because they had lost the predominant share of the high-value and profitable traffic to the truckers and the inland water carriers, the ICC often prevented rail rate reductions sufficient to be effective in returning the traffic to the railroads, usually the low-cost carriers. This happened even when rail rates were above their fully distributed costs and their competitive rates did not have to be justified by mere coverage of out-of-pocket costs. Fourth, the ICC adopted the full-cost standard for minimum rates in many cases in which railroads attempted to compete effectively with motor and water carriers. Frequently, in such cases, the ICC would not permit railroads to base their competitive rates on a showing of coverage of out-of-pocket costs. This was so even under general conditions of excess capacity when rail marginal costs prevailed at levels below average or fully distributed costs. In other words, rates greater than marginal costs but less than average or fully distributed costs by railroad were found to involve destructive competition by the railroads.

The net effects of those ICC fair-sharing minimum rate policies were to prevent high rail value-of-service rates from moving downward toward the relevant unit costs and to bring about diversion of traffic and revenues from the railroads. Whether or not the actual result was intended, the ICC actions contributed significantly to misallocation of traffic away from the low-cost mode, to low railroad profitability, to lessened rates of railway modernization, and to inadequate freight car supply. On the other hand, those regulatory actions stimulated rapid, and probably, excessive growth in the role of motor and water carriers.

To an extent, the shippers also played a role toward continuance of the rail value-of-service rate structure in its traditional form. Long-distance shippers of agricultural and extractive products heavily dependent on rail service and the traditional low value-of-service rates resisted strongly proposals to raise the low discriminating rates that once had been at least marginally profitable to the railroads in conjunction with their high discriminating rates. Difficulties encountered in raising such rates as they became unprofitable to the railroads under inflationary conditions in the economy increased the resistance of the railroads to lowering their high discriminating rates on high-value goods. Such obstacles also increased the interest of the railroads in regulatory action to shore up those high rates.

OPPOSITION TO USER FEES

The irrational prices for public transport facilities (infrastructural prices such as the absence of waterway user charges and inadequate user fees for highways, airways, and airports) cannot be blamed on the railroads. The rail carriers have long been ardent supporters of universal user fees, of higher user charges on large and heavy trucks and on airlines for public facility services, and of including property tax equivalents as components in user fees to assure that the same burden for the general support of government rests on both the railroads and their competitors operating over public facilities. In recent years, the railroads, along with many economists, have called for assessment of the social costs of noise and air pollution to air and highway carriers, to be charged out in their rates. Notwithstanding, the opposition of the inland water carriers to waterway tolls and that of the truckers and airlines to user fees sufficient to cover the entire relevant costs of public ways and terminals have prevented rational improvements in infrastructural pricing. Opposition of the owners of automobiles and other motor vehicles to high peak-time prices for their use of congested expressways and highways has prevented adjustment of highway user fees to assess anything like the full peak costs of highway use to users at the peak hours. Shipper groups, particularly in the case of waterways and highways, have not always supported tolls for waterways or more rational user fees for highway services. In fixing minimum rates, the ICC early took the position that it cannot include the costs of public facilities in finding the low-cost mode unless those costs have been charged to the waterway and highway carriers by the authorities operating those facilities.

Clearly, then, for society to enjoy the full benefits of rational or economic pricing in transport, changes will have to be made in the pricing policies of the carrier groups, especially in the case of the railways, and in regulatory decisions as they fix the final rates in rate cases and influence the pricing methods of individual carriers or groups of carriers. In addition, the federal and state governments will have to take several measures to price the services of airways and airports, highways, and inland waterways more completely, and with more attention to the relevant costs of such public transport services and their effects on the privately-owned modes and on overall economy in the provision of transport services.

Rational Transport Pricing under Competition

In view of the irrationality of the pricing of carrier services under regulated conditions since 1935 and the huge costs to shippers and consumers of the misallocations of traffic that have occurred, the question naturally arises whether transport service prices would be more rational and economic if deregulation occurred and rates were determined under conditions of free or freer competition. Would carriers adjust rates more in accordance with efficient costs of service and relative unit costs under such market conditions? Would transport prices better perform the functions of prices, such as dividing traffic efficiently among the modes, calling forth capital for efficient relative investments in the modes, encouraging rapid technological change, and discouraging inefficient operations and maintenance of capital facilities no longer needed? These are highly significant questions in the formulation of public transport policy.

A point to be made at the outset is that allowing competition between the modes to be free or to operate with fewer regulatory restrictions would not in itself make the pricing of public transport facilities wholly rational. It will take state and federal legislative action to close the gaps in user fees and to adjust them more in accordance with the costs of infrastructural services, including the full public and social costs and the peak-use costs of highway, airway and airport, and waterway services. However, if the final rates for the alternative *carrier* services were made to conform more fully to economic standards, then the public investments in highways, airways and airports, and in the inland waterways would be more limited and would conform more closely to efficient investments. Efficient prices for the services of alternative carriers would substantially correct the misallocations of traffic by increasing the market demands for the services of the low-cost modes and by reducing the demands for the services of the high-cost modes. Hence, better market signals would be given to the public authorities of the true investment needs for public transport facilities, and also to the privately-owned carriers not using public facilities, with the result that their investments would rise relatively to investments in public transport facilities.

Competition in transport markets is so potentially pervasive today that competitively-determined prices would generally result from deregulation or from removal of barriers preventing full competitive conditions from prevailing in those markets. Competitively-determined prices in the naturally competitive modes would yield rates that would equal marginal costs and also average costs except in back-haul situations of true joint costs. Discriminating prices, except in true-joint cost situations of back-haul movements and peak-off peak demands, would wholly or largely be eliminated by the pressures of competition. Thus, rates of naturally competitive modes would be rational and economic, since they would be closely related to *efficient* unit costs; would eliminate price above marginal cost or monopoly price increments; and would fluctuate more easily with changing conditions of demand and supply. Such competitive prices would eliminate inefficient carrier firms or compel them to improve their services and lower their unit costs. They would yield price differentials that reflect accurately the relative levels of the costs of service by the several alternative modes. Hence, competitive prices would condition shippers' choices to be rational both from the shippers' own points of view and that of society. The end result would be a far more efficient division of traffic among the modes than exists today; that is, a substantial correction would take place through the market of one of the greatest sources of economic waste in modern transport, the misallocation of traffic to high-cost carriers and modes.

RAILROADS

In the case of the railroads, competition from other railroads and other modes would not eliminate discriminating pricing so long as the roads operated with significant excess capacity. However, free or freer intermodal competition would limit value-of-service pricing by railroads by reducing high rates on high-value goods where such competition impacts vigorously and by exerting increased pressures on the railroads to raise those rates that are lower than the relevant marginal costs or barely above the short-run marginal costs. Thus, railroad rates would become less discriminating than in past periods, and they would move toward levels indicated by the relevant costs of efficient services. In short, they would become cost-based rates to a considerably greater extent, although discriminating rates would continue to the extent economically justified by the presence of significant excess capacity and also as required by the true joint-cost situations that exist in transport.

Discriminating rates for the railroads, to the extent justified by their excess capacity and complex cost structure, would continue to stimulate fuller utilization of fixed railway facilities that are already in place. Thus, such rates would continue to reduce rail unit cost under a given general price level and to yield lower rate levels for both shippers assessed relatively high rates and those charged relatively low, but profitable, rates. But rate discrimination would not hold rates on high-value goods at such high levels that high-cost modes could compete for the traffic and even attain large shares of the markets for medium- and long-distance shipments as has occurred in many instances under the present regulated conditions. In a word, the rail rates that would result under full competitive conditions would avoid the huge costs of traffic misallocations away from the low-cost mode because those rates would no longer hold an umbrella over the high-cost mode. Rate parity policies of modes having different cost levels would end. And even if the high-cost mode's services were of better quality, its rates would be higher than those of the low-cost mode so that shippers could make more rational choices between quality services costing more to produce and priced higher and standard or low-quality services costing less to produce and priced lower.

Competitively-determined freight rates would also perform another function of prices better than the regulated rates of today. That function is to attract capital into transport modes to supply adequate capacity, improved services, lower unit costs, and to stimulate dynamic technical change. Regulated prices in the period after World War II have attracted vast capital inputs into air, pipe-line, truck, and inland water transport, but not sufficient capital to the railroads to provide adequate freight car supply, more efficient railroad operations, and a rapid rate of technological change. As the decade of the 1970s began, large railroads experienced serious shortages of working capital and significant bankruptcies occurred at high levels of traffic, the most important of which was the Penn Central case. The shortage of capital available to the railroads in a growing economy and in a period of growing demands for rail carriage of freight has threatened nationalization of some railroads or general nationalization of the industry.

Competitively-determined freight rates would eventually correct this capital-deficiency problem. Such rail prices would shift high-value freight and the large revenues associated with such traffic to the railroads in large amounts, particularly in medium-distance markets where a very large part of the competitive high-value traffic exists. Shifts to the railroads would also occur in the long-distance markets. Fundamentally, the main reason for this is that the unit costs for rail service are between one and two cents per ton-mile while those for the regulated truckers range from three up to six or seven cents per ton-mile. Although truck service in the past has been worth more to shippers and receivers because of greater speed in delivery, more frequent and adjustable schedules, and better protection from physical damage to the lading, differentials in truck rates over rail rates of the magnitude of the relative cost differentials between those closely competitive modes would frequently offset the greater worth of more flexible truck service, and shippers would more often opt for the savings in rates by choosing rail service. Another consideration is that rail services, especially container, piggyback and forwarder services, are no longer at drastic speed-in-delivery disadvantages as compared with truck transcontinental or other long-distance services. Trains carrying high-value traffic have shortened their time schedules, the Super C service of the Santa Fe Railway to less than 40 hours from Chicago to Los Angeles. With greater capital investment in way modernization and equipment, the railroads could further narrow the gap in the quality of their services compared with truck services. The development of a network of high-speed intermodal freight trains as visualized in the Overmyer Plan for intermodal container terminals in the United States could so improve service as to shift vast amounts of high-grade freight from the highways to the rails.

Though lower rail rates would come about under fully competitive conditions and would be essential to bring about shifts in traffic and revenues to the low-cost mode, railroad revenues would nevertheless rise and their unit costs would fall from greater utilization of fixed plant. Hence, railway profitability would rise, a condition that would attract larger flows of capital to the railroads for provision of adequate freight car supply, improvements in way to permit lower operating costs and increased speed of trains, and for other modernization of rail plant and equipment.

The traditional fear of the industry and the regulators that greater competition would lead to capital shortages and to unprofitable railway operations without general governmental subsidies to the railroads from taxpayer sources overlooks several changed conditions. First, at existing levels of traffic, railroads are no longer as greatly underutilized as in the last century. Hence, rail-rail competition is far less likely to be ruinous by driving the level of rates to unprofitable levels. Second, the principal competitors to the railroads, the motor carriers, operate with distinctly higher unit costs than the railroads, so that the reduction in rail rates to become truly competitive would not necessitate rates on high-value commodities so low that subsidies would be required. Third, the railroads have lost such large shares of specific markets to the trucks in medium-distance situations that the gain in traffic volume would more than offset the price reductions essential to capture the traffic. Fourth, rates on some types of goods and lengths of haul would necessarily rise as marginal costs rose from better traffic utilization of the railways; but as very long hauls are frequently associated with the low-rated traffic, the railroads would not be greatly limited by the competition of other modes in making such upward adjustments as might become necessary. The result could be that traffic paying less than its relevant marginal cost would now at least have to cover the relevant out-of-pocket cost, with a reduction in losses presently sustained by the railroads on some low-rated traffic. Finally, those who fear lessened industry profitability and capital formation from competitive pricing overlook the very serious revenue margin, low profitability, and bankruptcy conditions that have already arisen under regulated prices that "fair-share" the high-value, profitable traffic away from the low-cost mode. They also neglect the traffic and revenue diversion from the railroads that is influenced by carrier and ICC attempts to deal with inflationary costs with general increases in all rates rather than with selective adjustments in rates that reflect the impact of inflation and of intermodal competition.

Of course, competitively-determined rates would lessen the profitability of some regulated trucking operations and the flow of capital into some areas of trucking, especially into the long-distance hauling of high-value goods moving in considerable volumes and in large loadings per shipment. The monopoly elements in the high profitability of regulated trucking of general commodities in the past would be lessened by greater intermodal competition, and reduced still more if intramodal competition within trucking were increased by relaxing control of entry and the certificate restrictions on operating authority.

However, the high rates of return earned in the past by the regulated truckers of general commodities from high regulated rates and rate parity with the railroads on high-value freight have induced greater flows of capital to, and investment in, truck transport than would have been the case had full competitive conditions prevailed. Hence, the lower returns to the long-distance truck carriers that would result from competitively-determined prices and traffic allocations would be economically desirable to discourage excessive investment in truck facilities and in the strength features of primary and other highways. Transport prices, then, would encourage greater investment in the low-cost mode and less investment in the high-cost mode.

In addition, fully competitive prices for rail services would stimulate withdrawal of much trucking from long-distance routes except to the extent that a demand for service continued to exist at rates high enough to cover truck costs. Under competitive prices, the profit incentives in trucking would stimulate greater concentration in serving short-haul markets in which trucking often has a cost advantage and in supplying gathering and distribution services to the railroads, the airlines, the forwarders, and the inland water carriers. An example of such extension of trucking into comparatively short-haul gathering and distribution service is afforded by the discontinuance of transcontinental and other long hauls of new automobiles by truck after the railroads introduced tri-level cars greatly lowering the cost of rail shipment relative to the cost of truck shipment over medium and long distances. Competitively-determined rail and truck rates would bring about many shifts of similar kind, thereby combining the cost advantages of the railroads over long distances with those of the trucks over short distances and over low-density routes.

AIRLINES

Competitively-determined rail freight rates would affect air and inland water carriers less. Air transport today largely attracts very high-value, emergency, perishable, and style goods in which speed in delivery and ease of handling are extremely important, bringing economies or profit advantages to shippers that offset the higher air costs and rates. Lower rail rates on high-value goods under competitive conditions would continue to leave most of this special-needs traffic to the airlines.

BARGE LINES

On the other hand, fully competitive rail rates on bulk commodities would divert some traffic from the barge lines whose services are slower and less flexible than rail service. In particular, such diversion would occur on marginal waterways over which barge costs might be relatively high even without tolls for waterway use. However, in the best and most heavily-utilized waterways, such as the Mississippi River below St. Louis, barge ton-mile costs are sufficiently low compared with rail ton-mile costs that it is unlikely that diversion to rail carriers would be large. And this might still be true if economic tolls were assessed on such waterways, although tolls to cover at least the annual maintenance and operation costs of waterways in combination with fully competitive rail rates would have harsh effects on barge traffic on the marginal waterways. Some such waterways might have to be closed from disuse, and the justifiable annual operation and maintenance costs on other waterways might have to be reduced. Nevertheless, such diversion as might occur to the railroads would likely be economic so long as the railroads covered their relevant marginal costs.

CONCLUSIONS

Accordingly, when the tests of rational and economic pricing of transport services under competitive conditions are applied and the probable results are compared with those evident under regulated transport prices, it can be concluded that the fully competitive prices under total or substantial deregulation would serve society more efficiently than regulated prices have in the past. With traffic misallocations lessened, the total cost of freight transport would fall and this would be passed on in lower prices for goods. Inefficient carriers and modes would be pressed out of certain markets or would be forced to become more efficient. Capital and other inputs would flow more into the low-cost modes and less into the high-cost modes. Greater economic coordination would occur between the modes, with more intermodal shipments combining the line-haul cost advantages of the railroads with the terminal and short-haul cost advantages of the trucks and the inflexibility of railway operations on fixed tracks with the great flexibility of truck operations on the public highways. The lower long-haul rates on high-value goods of the railroads under fully competitive conditions would discourage industrial locations at or near the huge urban centers and encourage them to be located away from already congested areas.

Theoretically, regulated prices could accomplish virtually the same economic gains for society except for the large added costs of the regulatory process to the state and federal governments, the regulated carriers, and the shippers. George W. Wilson has conservatively estimated those administrative costs related solely to the ICC at $54 million per year, or more; and in view of the high costs to the parties in railway merger and general rate level cases, they may be far higher. However that may be, the evidence accumulated in several decades of regulated prices by the ICC under the present concepts of public regulation gives little promise that regulated rates will be adjusted so as to accomplish the economic functions of prices as well as competitive rates would do. Under the type of regulation of competition that has existed since 1935, the process is protective of all modes and of the existing certificated carriers. Minimum rates are fixed in terms of fully distributed costs instead of the relevant marginal costs. This greatly limits intermodal competition by the railroads, often the low-cost mode. Even in the naturally competitive trucking industry, intramodal competition is also greatly restricted by entry control limiting entrance and expansion of firms and by minimum rate and rate bureau processes limiting price competition by the most efficient carriers. Additionally, the unregulated barge carriers are protected from full rail competition in the markets for hauling grain and other bulk commodities, again by ICC employment of the fully distributed cost standard to determine the low-cost mode rather than the economic standard of the lowest incremental or marginal cost. The wording of the National Transportation Policy in the Interstate Commerce Act is such as to suggest or require protective policies of those types, although the ICC might have interpreted the policy guidelines in that policy declaration more in accordance with economic reasoning and the entire public interest. Unless those regulatory policies can be changed, making any large strides toward rational and economic pricing in surface transport requires either substantial or total deregulation, or, at the very least, new policy guidelines from the Congress that would require substantial modifications in present minimum rate and entry control policies.

Transport Markets Not Subject to the Restraints of Competitive Pricing

Granting that competitively-determined prices would be more rational and economic than regulated prices have been or are likely to be, does it follow that all goods movements of importance take place in markets that could be workably competitive if regulatory restraints on pricing were totally removed or relaxed? If not, then some regulated prices would seem to be essential even if many markets would be sufficiently subject to competition to permit them to be unregulated as in the case of exempt carriage of bulk commodities by water or exempt hauling of agricultural products by truck.

OIL PIPE LINES

The carriage of crude oil and refined oil products by large-diameter pipe lines comprises one area of the freight transport market in which the firms are either monopolistically organized or there are not enough firms in each market to result in effectively competitive conditions. Because of the extremely low ton-mile costs of oil pipe lines, neither rail nor truck transport can compete with large-diameter pipe lines. Only barge lines on the most efficient inland waterways and coastal tankers can experience unit costs sufficiently low to compete actively with large-diameter pipe lines. Some market competition does exist between oil pipe lines originating oil at different origins but delivering it to common markets. Notwithstanding market competition and some competition from barge carriers, the pipe lines have effective competition only where coastal tankers of large size can be utilized. Hence, pipe line rates under free markets could be expected to be monopolistically high and discriminating against the smaller outside shippers. Consequently, regulated prices under maximum rate and discrimination controls by the ICC will continue to be necessary for rational and economic pricing of oil pipe line services.

RAILROADS

Railroads present a somewhat mixed situation with respect to the restraints of intermodal and intramodal competitive forces on their pricing policies. With respect to high-value goods moving beyond quite short distances and in carload quantities, the railroads are subject to pervasive competition from both regulated and unregulated motor carriers. And so long as the traditional rail value-of-service rate structure continues in effect and continues to hold a rate umbrella over higher ton-mile cost trucking service, this intermodal competition will exist for all ranges of distances between markets. Where developed inland waterways exist, and especially in the Mississippi River Valley and the Ohio River Valley, the railroads experience severe competition from barge and barge-truck carriers for bulk commodities and for heavy manufactures such as iron and steel articles and steel pipe. Although rail-rail price competition was suppressed after the rate wars of the 1870s and the 1880s by carrier agreements on rates in bureaus and under tacit and explicit exemption from the antitrust laws, sophisticated forms of price competition between the railroads actually do take place from time to time in the present era and service competition of close interest and advantage to shippers has long been a feature of the railroad industry. Accordingly, almost all of the high-value freight and a considerable part of the low-grade traffic of the railroads have been subject to the disciplines of intermodal competition and often to some intramodal price competition within the rail industry. For those important flows of traffic, it seems likely that allowing full competitive conditions would restrain the railroads from charging excessive rates or discriminating in uneconomic ways.

Nevertheless, testimony in railroad merger cases and data from the United States Census of Transportation have revealed that the railroads still carry very high shares of transcontinental and other long-distance traffic in eastbound fruits and vegetables, lumber, and canned goods and in westbound movements of some of those products and in manufactured commodities such as iron and steel and motor vehicle parts. Accordingly, intermodal competition might not be sufficiently strong to limit the level of rates on long-distance movements of such products or to prevent uneconomic discrimination in rates as between long-haul and short-haul markets. However, strong market competition has long existed between producers located in different regions of the United States for the large markets from Chicago to the Atlantic seaboard. Also, much market competition takes place between alternative eastern and southern sources of manufactured products for the growing markets along the West Coast. Moreover, rail-rail competition increasingly has arisen in those long-haul markets, especially competition shortening time schedules, providing improved freight cars, and even competition in rates through the threat of independent action by aggressive railroads in rate bureau meetings or actual independent filings. Nevertheless, those sources of competition in the important transcontinental flows of agricultural, extractive, and manufactured goods might not be sufficient to protect shippers fully against excessive rates and uneconomic discrimination in rates. For those large and long-haul traffic flows, regulated prices under maximum rate and discrimination controls might be essential for rational and fully economic rail rates.

AIRLINES, TRUCKING, AND BARGE LINES

In the other freight modes, air, highway and inland water, there would be no real problems concerning whether the forces of competition under deregulation or relaxed regulation would provide sufficient market restraints to yield fully competitive prices. These are easy-entry fields as investments in fixed way, channel, and terminal facilities ordinarily do not have to be made by the carrier firm. A very large proportion of capital investment per firm is in divisible equipment, and often planes, truck combinations, and towboats can be obtained under leasing arrangements. Hence, wherever traffic flows between markets are dense, there will be several to many firms under free or easy regulatory entry conditions, especially as the economies of scale in size of firm are distinctly limited in those modes. Only over country routes in the case of trucking or over the new or marginal waterways not having dense traffic flows will the number of carriers be so few as to result in monopoly or sluggish small-numbers oligopoly.

Hence, as revealed by the strong intramodal competition among barge carriers transporting exempt bulk commodities on the Mississippi River system and among the exempt trucks of agricultural products over many routes, barge rates would be market-determined under competitive conditions and would fluctuate around efficient cost of service in accordance with demand and supply conditions. On the waterways having traffic sufficient to support only two or three barge lines, as on the Columbia-Snake River system, greater freedom for competitive pricing by the railroads would eliminate most monopoly rates and profits of the barge lines. This was demonstrated by the Pacific Northwest Grain Case in the period after 1958 when the railroads were allowed to cut their grain rates as much as 50 percent and to make effective multiple-car rates and lower single-car rates for shipments in large grain hopper cars with reduced transit privileges. These competitive forces greatly lowered the barge and truck-barge rates, thereby limiting the monopoly gains earlier evidenced by profitable rentals paid by the barge lines to family corporations for leasing towboats.

Railroad price competition would also limit truck rates if rate-bureau practices in trucking should linger on after deregulation or relaxation of restrictive regulation occurred. And the rate levels for air cargo service would continue to be limited by intramodal competition within the airline industry and by long-distance truck service at lower costs and rates. With full competition between motor carriers and between rail carriers and the truckers, intermodal price competition with the air cargo lines would become more intense. This would be true at least until air ton-mile costs could be greatly reduced by employment of very large planes and containerized shipments.

Furthermore, discrimination in rates in the naturally competitive modes would not be a problem. The strong elements of intramodal competition to which carriers in those modes would be subject would eliminate discrimination in rates except in true-joint cost cases of back hauls. In those market situations, discriminating pricing is rational and essential to efficient utilization in the back-haul directions.

Rational Freight Rates under Regulation

MAXIMUM RATES

As indicated, some amount of maximum rate regulation and discrimination control probably will continue to be needed for the oil pipe lines and the railroads even under a policy moving toward substantial deregulation of the railroads and total deregulation of the naturally competitive surface modes. Notwithstanding, Great Britain has abandoned maximum price and discrimination controls for the British railways, and the only regulation of the railroads in the Netherlands is the control of maximum prices applying to all goods. And under the National Transportation Act, 1967, Canada has eliminated control over the general rate level for railways and has limited maximum rate control to specific cases where shippers can show that they are still subject to monopoly conditions in the supply of transport service. In the United States, the standards for limiting general-level rate increases for railroads could be relaxed to permit quicker adjustments to inflationary conditions in the economy.

MINIMUM RATES

It is highly doubtful that regulatory restraints on minimum rates of the kind exercised under the present concepts of protective regulation are needed to maintain the economic health of the regulated carriers in terms of adequate revenues and earnings. Certainly, the minimum rates widely controlled by the ICC in competitive intermodal rate cases have not in the past assured the railroads, the mode carrying two-fifths of the intercity ton-miles, of healthy financial conditions and high enough rates of return to attract capital for full modernization and an adequate supply of freight cars. It seems wholly clear that the railroads would have done better trafficwise, in revenue growth, and in profit rates had they been entirely free or far freer to compete for the high-value traffic over medium and long distances for which they have distinctly lower ton-mile costs than the regulated truckers.

On the other hand, the minimum rate restraints exercised to limit intermodal competition by the railroads and price competition within regulated trucking and the entry and operating-authority restrictions that fragment and monopolize numerous regulated trucking markets have been conducive to high monopoly rates of return for the less restricted truckers. Those conditions have also greatly limited the number of trucking firms, increased their size far beyond any size justified by clear evidence of economies of scale, and stimulated costly service competition. Abandonment of minimum rate control, with or without relaxation of entry controls, would reduce the rates of return for many regulated truckers to the extent that they have been earning monopoly returns. Although some overextended trucking firms might go bankrupt under full competitive conditions as some regulated truckers have done even under protective regulation, there is no reason to expect that the financial soundness of trucking firms would be threatened in a tolerably full-employment economy except in cases of inefficiency in size of firm, in management, or in situations of incapability in making route and other adjustments required under competitive conditions. Competitive rates of return would be earned in short-haul markets, in gathering and distribution services, and even in the long-haul markets in which shipper demand continues for trucking service at costs and rates higher than rail rates.

The barge lines have long operated largely in unregulated markets, for the most part without noticeable injury to their financial situation. As in exempt trucking, their profit rates have been sufficient to maintain good equipment, to register strong growth in traffic, and to stay in business for long periods. Air cargo carriers probably have benefited little from minimum rate regulation of surface carriers.

Under free or freer competitive transport markets, the efficient carriers and modes will be rewarded with relatively high rates of return. But the inefficient carriers and modes, unlike under regulated conditions, would not be so rewarded and many firms would not be able to stay in business. Accordingly, competitive markets would distribute the revenues and returns among the carriers and modes better than has been accomplished under regulated markets. Almost certainly, the efficient railroads, generally the low-cost carriers beyond short distances over land routes, would be compensated better than they have been under regulated conditions, while other types of efficient carriers, protected from competition by the present protective regulation, would lose only their monopoly gains and temporarily some returns while making the essential route and service adjustments to competitive conditions.

Very little regulatory restraint, if any, would be required under full competitive conditions to insure efficient choice by shippers and consignees among the modes. This is because shippers are rational buyers of for-hire carrier services and rational providers of private carrier services to themselves. The only reasons shipper choice does not yield efficient traffic divisions today are first that freight rates, particularly on high-value goods, are not closely related to cost of service or relative modal cost of service; and secondly that infrastructural prices for public transport facilities are wholly lacking or are inefficiently set by the public authorities. But under free or freer competitive conditions, the first reason for socially inefficient modal choice by shippers would be removed. Rates for the different commodities would move toward their respective costs of service as value-of-service pricing became less prominent and as the relative rates for the services of the different modes came to reflect their relevant unit cost differences far more closely than under present regulated conditions. However, the second reason cited for inefficient modal choice by shippers could not be removed without legislative action with respect to user fees for public transport facilities.

CHANGES IN ICC REGULATORY POLICIES

If the existing structure of regulation by the ICC is retained in terms of the present kit of tools in the Interstate Commerce Act, considerable change in ICC regulatory policies would have to take place, together with some change in statutory policy or guidelines for economic regulation, before substantially rational and economic pricing for surface freight could come about. Most of the necessary changes would involve the cost standards for minimum rate regulation and the policy guidelines in the National Transportation Policy enacted by the Transportation Act of 1940. However, some changes in entry control would also be required, especially in the case of interstate motor carriers.

To obtain rational and economic freight prices under regulation, transport rates would have to resemble closely what they would be under free or freer competition. Thus, the rates of the low-cost carrier would have to be permitted to fall below those of high-cost carriers in other modes, and this would especially be true in the cases in which the low-cost carrier had inferior service, high fixed costs, and substantial and continuing excess capacity. For this to happen under regulation, the regulatory body would have to abandon its fully distributed cost standard for determining the low-cost mode and for setting the minimum rates of the high-cost mode where the latter has lower marginal costs than the mode considered to be the low-cost mode. The cost standard that would be required for minimum rates in intermodal competitive cases, then, would be the relevant marginal, incremental or variable costs giving consideration to the particular circumstances of the longevity of the traffic demands being priced, the extent of excess capacity, the new plant or replacements required, and any special services required. Such a standard would not mean that minimum competitive prices would always be established at short-run marginal costs, but usually that they would be set at long-run marginal costs which, at times, might closely approximate average costs. Where demand exceeds supply of transport facilities, rates would temporarily be allowed to rise to equate with short-run marginal costs above average costs.

Nor would rational and economic rates under regulation mean that there would be no discriminating rates. For all regulated modes as well as for unregulated sectors of transport, discriminating rates would be the correct pattern of economic rates for return-haul situations and for peak-offpeak prices, cases of true joint costs. As in such cost situations there are no separate costs for each of the true joint services, only demand considerations can determine the measure of the rates on each of the joint products. However, under competitive conditions the revenues from the two or more joint services would be limited to the total costs for producing the joint services, and only normal competitive earnings would be returned to the carriers.

In addition, the railroads would continue a general discriminating price pattern so long as they operated under conditions of excess capacity, with marginal costs less than average costs. Such discrimination would be the best second-best solution for optimal prices in view of the existence of substantial fixed costs and excess capacity. But the discriminating pattern of rates under rational and economic regulated pricing would be considerably different than under the present regulated conditions. Thus, the high discriminating rates on high-value manufactures and some agricultural commodities would be lower as under free or freer competition, and the discriminatingly low rates that are less than relevant marginal costs would be raised to eliminate losses to the carriers. Moreover, as railroads better utilized their capacity, their marginal costs would rise and the spread between the high and low rates would have to be reduced to limit the discriminating carrier's returns to normal competitive earnings. In other words, the regulatory body, in those circumstances, would have to provide regulatory incentives for lessening the extent to which discriminating pricing would be used. However, except for true joint-cost situations, there would be little or no justification for value-of-service rates for the naturally competitive modes. Rational rate regulation would bring that practice to an economic end.

CHANGES IN STATUTORY POLICIES

To obtain more rational transport prices for freight as outlined under continuing regulation of present structural type, changes in the National Transportation Policy would be essential to assure rapid progress toward economic pricing and only a rational exercise of the minimum rate power. Generally, the ICC has based its protective entry control and minimum rate policies, including its fully distributed cost standard in minimum rate cases involving regulated carriers, on two guidelines in that Policy statement. Those guidelines, which the Congress made substantive law according to which all provisions of the Interstate Commerce Act must be administered, are the "unfair or destructive competitive practices" clause and the "sound economic conditions in transportation and among the several carriers" standard in the National Transportation Policy. As a minimum regulatory relaxation, those statutory standards directing the ICC to protect all modes in the market and to prevent competition from putting inefficient carriers out of business would have to be abandoned. While the ICC probably could have interpreted those clauses more in line with the reasoning of economic theory and have avoided some of the worst effects of protecting the regulated carriers from competition, less legal difficulty would be encountered in making regulated prices rational for surface transport if those guidelines were entirely deleted. An alternative would be for the Congress to adopt an entirely new declaration of policy that would emphasize that the ICC should maintain workable competition within and between the modes. President Eisenhower's Cabinet Committee Report in 1955 outlined such a revision, but it was not enacted by the Congress in the following years.

Price Policies under the Canadian Plan of Regulation

In their search for more rational pricing for transport, Western European countries and Canada have reduced regulatory controls to free transport competition to a far greater extent than the United States. Great Britain and the Netherlands now have almost no special economic regulation of the railroads and the motor carriers. Generally in Europe, the state-owned railroads are given a fairly high degree of commercial freedom in competing with road and water carriers and are allowed to use marginal costs as a floor to competitive rates. European authorities recognize that growing intermodal competition lessens the range for discriminating rates for rail services and that under competition rail rates tend to become more cost-based. However, continued but modified discrimination in rail rates is supported as the best second-best solution for optimal pricing of competitive railroad services. These European pricing policies are similar to rational pricing policies under competition, or under a scheme of regulation that would attempt to simulate competition in the manner outlined above.

FREER TRANSPORT MARKETS

Canada has recently followed the lead of Great Britain and the Netherlands in moving toward substantial deregulation of the railroads and toward greater freedom in transport markets for competitive pricing. In enacting the National Transportation Act, 1967, the Canadian Parliament recognized that control of maximum rates is appropriate only in the case of monopoly markets. Accordingly, no provision was made for any control to be exercised over the general rate level for railways and for motor carriers, except for the requirement that all rates must be filed and published. Only where railroads are found to possess specific monopoly power over captive shippers will maximum rates be selectively fixed. In such cases, selective maximum rates are limited to 150 percent above the variable cost of the movement, a standard which permits a fairly wide range for rate discrimination by the railroads between variable costs and that upper limit.

The standard for maximum rates and Canada's variable cost standard for minimum competitive rates give strong regulatory assurance that competitive pricing in transport will be permitted a very wide scope in Canada. Unlike the ICC, Canadian authorities rejected employment of fully distributed costs as a standard for any regulatory interference that may be justified with respect to rail competitive rates against motor and water carriers. Canada's new regulatory act recognizes that true predatory pricing by railroads should be disallowed as a threat to the maintenance of competition. However, to limit regulation of minimum rates only to those cases in which such rates are truly uneconomic or predatory, Canada adopted the standard that all competitive freight rates must be compensatory. Section 53 of the 1967 Act states that a freight rate "shall be deemed to be compensatory when it exceeds the variable cost of the movement of the traffic as determined by the Commission." Thus, Canada has adopted the economists' standard of coverage of the relevant marginal cost as the evidence of an economic competitive rate. This represents a vast improvement over the cost standards typically employed by the ICC in minimum rate cases.

Under the Canadian variable cost standard for minimum competitive rates, an arbitrary regulatory allocation of traffic to the high-cost mode could not take place as frequently as has been the case under the fair-sharing minimum rate decisions of the ICC. Under the Canadian standard, rail competitive rates below average cost but above relevant marginal cost could not be ruled out in situations where railroads have excess capacity. Thus, if the Canadian railroads are aggressive in meeting their competition from motor carriers, the high-value traffic beyond short distances will more frequently move by the low-cost railroads than in the United States. Although truck transport has grown in Canada with improved highways, this competitive rate standard, in conjunction with the maximum rate standard 150 percent above variable costs, will allow the Canadian railroads to engage in full competitive pricing against intermodal competition and still to continue discriminating rates to the extent required to encourage maximum utilization of fixed plant and a low general level or rates.

APPLICATION OF CANADIAN POLICIES TO THE UNITED STATES

Clearly, if the Canadian standard for minimum competitive rates were to be adopted by the Congress for the Interstate Commerce Act or by the ICC under a revised interpretation of the policy guidelines in the National Transportation Policy, such action would considerably or largely remove the restrictions upon intermodal rate competition that have prevented the railroads from engaging in full competitive pricing against the motor and water carriers. Such a regulatory policy would enable the transport markets to lessen or eliminate the regulatory misallocations of traffic that now cost the shippers and consumers at least $5 billion more for essential transport services each year than would be necessary under rational competitive pricing. If the present structure of regulation of surface carriers in the United States is to be maintained rather than to adopt total or substantial deregulation in order to bring about rational and economic pricing of freight services, then the Canadian variable cost standard for minimum competitive rates, or some refinement of it, should be adopted to assure that minimum rate regulation only rules out predatory and truly noneconomic competition rather than competition itself.

The ICC has an excellent opportunity to adopt the variable cost standard, or the relevant marginal cost, as the standard for minimum competitive price in its current case, Docket No. 34013 (Sub. No. 1), *Cost Standards in Intermodal Rate Proceedings.* If it does not or legally cannot under the present regulatory statute, then the Congress should amend the Interstate Commerce Act to specify that this cost standard must be used in competitive rate cases if the Congress decides not to deregulate surface transport entirely or substantially as recommended by the Nixon administration and leading transportation economists.

The Question of the Application of the Antitrust Policies to Transport

If the alternative of fully competitive pricing under total or substantial deregulation is adopted to obtain the benefits of rational and economic pricing of the freight services of the surface carriers, then the antitrust laws that would be essential to maintenance of workable competition in transport should be applied to the transport industries with the possible, but unlikely, complete exception of the railroads.

AIR, MOTOR, AND INLAND WATER CARRIERS

Certainly, there would be little reason not to apply the relevant antitrust law policies to the naturally competitive modes, the air, motor and inland water carriers, to prevent them from attempting to agree on rates among themselves within each mode, to divide the markets, or to agree with the railroads on the basis of rate competition between the modes. There would be many carriers in the dense-traffic markets in the naturally competitive modes, with the possible exception of the airline industry. If entry or operating authority restrictions did not bar new entries or extensions of service by existing carriers, single-line carriers would principally provide the demanded services over short-distance, medium-distance, and long-distance routes as in the exempt trucking industry today. Hence, there would be less need than in the railroad industry for agreements on joint rates and through routes to be made internal to each of the naturally competitive modes. Although under free or easy regulatory entry conditions there would be less incentive for motor and water carriers to merge into large firms because of limited economies of scale in size of firm, the watchful eyes of the antitrust agencies over mergers and action by them to prevent mergers that would impair competition, including intermodal mergers, would be essential.

RAILROADS

A principal question relating to the application of the antitrust laws concerns the railroads which as presently organized must interchange the bulk of their traffic between or among railroads to serve shippers with efficient through services and joint rates. Even were there truly transcontinental railroads, all points enjoying rail service would not be serviced by competitive rail carriers. Thus, joint rates and through route agreements would continue to be essential, and they would require continuance of the present arrangements allowing particular railroads to meet together, without interference from the antitrust authorities, to discuss and execute the contracts for joint rates and through services and to fix the joint rates and the divisions of the joint rates among the participating railroads.

However, the necessity to allow rail carriers to meet on joint rate and through route issues does not necessarily make a case for exemptions from the antitrust laws as broad as they are under the Reed-Bulwinkle Act of 1948. If rates other than joint rates were subject to the antitrust laws, it might, indeed, be difficult to prevent railroad pricing personnel meeting to decide joint rates and through service matters from also agreeing on other rates as regularly occurs today in rate bureaus. Nevertheless, it would seem desirable to amend the Reed-Bulwinkle Act (section 5a of the Interstate Commerce Act) to make the relevant antitrust laws applicable to all rail rates other than joint rates for through services. If this proposal appears radical for the railroads, it should be recalled that the antitrust laws legally applied to the railroads before the Reed-Bulwinkle Act was passed in 1948. Moreover, the antitrust laws still apply to any attempts by common carriers in different modes to organize intermodally for meeting together to discuss and agree on rates or on policies to divide the markets between different modal groups of carriers. Furthermore, whenever the ICC removes its specific approval of the organization and procedures of a common carrier rate bureau, the antitrust laws again apply fully as in unregulated industries.

MAINTENANCE OF COMPETITION

If it takes competitively-determined transport prices and free or freer transport markets to bring about rational and economic prices for surface freight modes and to reduce or eliminate the great total costs of misallocated traffic and resources, it would not make sense to authorize the common carriers in a mode or between modes to agree on rates or to divide the markets. If such actions were to be permitted and should actually happen, the result might be continuation of parity prices on value-of-service bases by rail and motor carriers even without the restrictive influences of regulatory action on minimum rates and carrier rate policies. Should that type of pricing continue, and its continuation would be likely unless entry control and certificate restrictions were abandoned for the naturally competitive modes, actions freeing the transport markets from regulation would not necessarily yield rational and economic prices. Hence, if the road of deregulation and competitively determined prices is taken to obtain rational transport pricing, application of those antitrust laws that are relevant to maintenance of competition in transport would be as necessary for the transport industries as application of most antitrust legislation has been to preservation of competition in the unregulated industries.

A question of significance is whether the Robinson-Patman Act should apply. Under that legislation, full costs have been used as a standard in determining whether discrimination is involved in geographical or other price competition. There is considerable criticism of the standards applied by antitrust authorities and the courts in cases under that Act involving firms in the nontransport industries. Whatever the outcome of those issues may be, it would not be desirable to apply this particular antitrust law to the railroads. If the Robinson-Patman full-cost standard were to be applied with surface transport deregulated, the railroads would again be restrained uneconomically from engaging in price competition with the inland water carriers and the motor carriers. The full-cost standard under that legislation would be similar to the fully distributed cost standard used by the ICC in minimum rate cases, and its employment would prevent the railroads from competing at rates below their average costs but exceeding the relevant marginal costs by as much as demand would warrant. Furthermore, if the railroads had to reduce all rates on a commodity or on substitute commodities over noncompetitive rail routes in order to be permitted to meet their intermodal water competition on a competitive route or on competitive routes, the revenue losses involved would stop the railroads from trying to compete. Thus, their revenue and profitability situations might become poorer than under current restrictive minimum rate standards. Moreover, misallocations of traffic would continue and could be as great as in the past. Finally, maintenance of essential rail facilities and services would continue to be threatened.

If the avenue to be attempted for obtaining rational and economic pricing for surface freight transport is through retention of the present regulatory structure with liberal and economic standards of minimum rate regulation and entry control instead of the present restrictive policies of the ICC, there would be less reason for application of the relevant antitrust law policies to transport as indicated above. On balance, however, it would still be desirable to utilize the antitrust laws that are *truly relevant* to maintenance of workable competition as an additional tool for obtaining rational pricing simulating competitively-determined prices under regulation.

Such a policy would make a clean break with the recent past. It would place the common carriers in each regulated mode on notice that except for joint rates and through routes the individual firm must make its own rates and be guided by the incentives and restraints of competitive markets to a far greater extent than in the past. With the greater utilization ratios that the railroads enjoy today as compared with the last century, there is much less danger that ruinous rate wars would break out again from independent pricing by each carrier. And with the decades of delay by the railroads and the regulatory authorities in taking decisive action to adjust the railroad rate structure and specific rates as required even under regulated competition, an urgent need exists for the railroads, in their own interest and in the public interest, to compete more widely and aggressively for the traffic for which the railroad technique is the low-cost mode. This competition would mainly be directed against other modes; but in view of the strong tradition of relying on past pricing policies in the railroad industry, more intramodal competition is also needed within that industry, with far more experimentation to test the price-elasticity of demand for rail services, the effects of new techniques, equipment, services and greater utilization on unit costs, and to determine precisely what the effects of raising unprofitable or marginally profitable rates would be on the volume of that traffic and on revenues.

In transport, today, the great need is to recognize that *transport markets are much like those in many nonregulated industries.* Hence, competition is an incentive to efficiency and progress in many ways rather than something destructive to restrain artificially. If competition continues to be restrained as in the past, the railroads will be the industry that will suffer the harshest consequences. On the other hand, if competition is freed to make rational pricing possible or if regulation can be made to simulate such pricing standards, the railroads will have the most to gain among the transport modes. Moreover, the consumers of transport services and other goods will gain lower prices and greater real income and thus the overall public interest will be promoted by enhanced economic efficiency in the economy.

The Question of Through Routes and Efficient Interchange Arrangements

Before rate and entry regulation is relaxed or total deregulation is legislated, the effects of such a policy on through routes and interchange relationships should be faced. This is a complex question, partly unsolved in several fields, including the container field, even with a large amount of regulation by the ICC, the Civil Aeronautics Board, and the Federal Maritime Commission. Even today, the ICC lacks power to compel motor freight carriers to enter into through routes and to make joint rates, though the Commission can compel the railroads to do so and to make such arrangements with inland water carriers.

Entry control has limited the number of regulated motor carriers greatly since 1935, increased the size of the carriers that transport the greatest share of the intercity traffic by regulated truckers, and has increased the profitability and financial standing of many interstate motor freight carriers. However, these conditions have not solved the through route and interchange problems in the regulated trucking industry. Regulated truckers still oppose being compelled by the ICC to enter into through route agreements. And there have been many shipper complaints against the interchange arrangements between certificated truckers, the cost-multiplying effects of combination rates, and the service-deteriorating effects of the lack of through routes and joint rates. Apparently, many truckers would prefer to merge or acquire additional operating authority so as to be able to give single-line service over long-distance routes rather than to enter into joint-rate and through route arrangements with other motor carriers. Hence, it is doubtful that regulation is an answer to the problems of shippers in interchanging shipments between motor carriers. With free entry or relaxed entry and expansion restrictions, the problem might well be taken care of by extensions of service by the originating carriers to the destinations of the shipper's goods. After all, with the pervasive highway system, there are no large investment barriers involved in extending single-line service in the trucking industry.

Inland water carriers would like the railroads to accept the short hauls to the ports and to interchange with barges or ships for the long hauls to the domestic or export markets of the goods transported. But the railroads often demur to the loss of the long haul, usually the most profitable part of their services; to the shipment delays and the circuitous mileage involved in transfer at ports; and to the loss of contact with the consignees where there is no rail haul beyond the destination port. In addition, they believe their own line-haul costs are competitive with the barge costs, when the cost-reducing effects of train-load and volume shipments are taken into account along with the savings from avoidance of circuitous miles. Clearly, this is a highly complicated question, not one for a simple answer. Even regulation of through routes and joint rates by the ICC for many years has not produced a solution agreeable to both the rail and water modes.

An important need for through routes and joint rates arises in connection with container movements, including those moving part way by ocean ships from international origins and to international destinations. Likewise, for domestic piggyback, container movements on flat cars, and coordinated carriage of commodities such as new automobiles on tri-level cars, there is a definite role for interchange between modes as well as between railroads. It would seem hardly more difficult to solve the problems connected with such interchange and joint rates under conditions of competition than under conditions of regulation. The most feasible solutions will be those that are in the best profit interest of the cooperating carriers—all others will naturally be resisted by rational managements, even under regulation. Hence, releasing the competitive forces necessary to obtain rational and economic pricing by surface freight carriers need not destroy desirable interchange and joint rate arrangements, nor would seeking to obtain those conditions under regulation simulating competitive standards of pricing have that effect.

Rational Pricing of the Services of Public Transport Facilities

As noted above, fully rational and economic final prices for transport services that will divide the traffic and revenues efficiently among the modes and perform the other economic functions of prices cannot be brought about unless the services of the infrastructure provided by state and federal governments to the airlines, motor carriers, and inland water carriers are assessed prices that reflect the true and relevant costs of providing such airway and airport, highway, and inland waterway services. For action by government agencies to invest in public transport facilities, to maintain them for use by carriers, and to operate them (including activities to promote safety in their use, to prevent undue wear or breakdown of public ways, channels and terminals, and to promote the maximum and efficient use of such facilities) recurrently requires the employment of scarce resources, including labor, materials, capital, and land. Hence, government provision of infrastructural services can no more be free of resource costs than the supply of the final transport services by the privately-owned or publicly-owned carriers. Accordingly, prices or tolls are essential to assure efficient use of public transport facilities; to limit the flow of capital and other resources into such facilities by ruling out inefficient investments; and to make it possible for shippers and travelers to choose which mode to utilize efficiently for themselves and also for society.

The need for rational infrastructural prices is particularly great in the provision of the services of the primary highway system, of the airways and the large airports serving long-distance air travel, and of the services of the inland waterways to the barge lines. This is because the carriers using those systems of public transport facilities are in direct competition with the privately-owned railroads and the oil pipe lines. However, as the services of urban highways are in competition with rail rapid transit and suburban railways in urban areas, a similar need exists for rational pricing of expressway use and of parking facilities, including peak-time and off-peak pricing.

CONGRESSIONAL ACTION NEEDED

A first step toward more rational pricing of the infrastructural services of public transport systems is for the Congress to act quickly to close the gaps in user charging for those services. Primarily, this means enactment of suitable and sufficient user fees or tolls for the inland waterways to recover at least all annual maintenance and operating costs of keeping individual waterways navigable and open and all annual costs, including capital costs, of new waterways not yet constructed. A number of federal studies have been made of the economic case for and against user charging for waterways and to ascertain the user fee structure best designed for that mode. Hence, the intelligence essential for this final step in bringing about uniform application of user fees for public transport facilities is clearly available. Only the strong opposition of the barge lines, the large corporate users of their services at uneconomically low rates or private barge costs, and the nearby communities benefiting from subsidized transport, often at the expense of the nation as a whole, prevent this return to the toll-pricing policies practiced for inland waterways, such as the Erie Canal, in the last century. Inland waterways are not free goods, even after they have been constructed, as they continue to utilize scarce resources for operation and maintenance. Hence, the myth should be ended that inland waterways are free goods to their users and that their services need not be priced as are other transport services, including highway services, airport services, airway services, and the services of international canals such as the Panama Canal and the St. Lawrence Seaway.

HIGHWAY USER CHARGES FOR HEAVY VEHICLES

A second step toward rational user fee pricing would be to adjust existing state and federal user fees for highway services to increase the payments from the large and heavy vehicles, especially the diesel-powered vehicles, to closer equality with the long-run marginal construction, maintenance, and operation costs occasioned by those vehicles. Although finding the differential costs of highway services for each class of motor vehicles is complicated by the existence of fixed and common costs in the highway function, a great deal of federal-state test-road and other research has been done on that problem. Sufficient differential cost and user payment information is available, and has been reported to the state legislatures and the Congress in numerous state studies and in recent studies by the Highway Research Board and the Bureau of Public Roads, to enable immediate action to be taken by the state and federal legislators that would go far toward eliminating the underpayments of large and heavy vehicles.

By enacting state and federal diesel motor fuel fees approximately 50 percent above the fee levels for gasoline used for motor fuel (because diesel-powered vehicles obtain about 50 percent more miles per gallon), the states and the federal government could approximately exact the amounts required to raise the payments of the large and heavy over-the-road combinations to substantial coverage of their differential highway costs. This step has been recommended in many state and federal highway user fee studies on both equity and economic grounds and by several presidents of the United States. But the opposition of highway and highway carrier interests has prevented enactment of diesel differentials except in a few states. As most of the truck combinations in medium- and long-distance carriage are powered with diesel fuel and are often engaged in carrying high-value goods that have uneconomically been misallocated away from the railroads by regulatory action, parity pricing on value-of-service concepts, and unbalanced promotional policy with respect to public transport investments, enactment of the diesel differential would to an extent lessen the wastes of traffic misallocations and indirectly tend to lower rail freight rates.

SOCIAL COSTS OF HIGHWAY USE

A third step toward rational user pricing for public highway services requires giving much more consideration than in the past to the social costs of highway use, including the differential costs of highway use by the large and heavy vehicles. Because of the social costs of air and noise pollution, displacement of residences and business units, displacement of alternative forms of travel without substituting entirely and efficiently for the displaced modes, and the lack of adequate user prices for highway use, the social marginal cost of highway use often rises above the highway-service (or private) marginal cost. Hence, user fees should be higher than levels just sufficient to cover the long-run marginal costs of rendering highway services whenever the social costs are tangible and significant, and especially when they can at least be roughly measured. Moreover, when congestion exists on urban streets and on intercity highways, the social marginal cost of highway use rises steeply above the levels during uncongested periods of highway use (and above private marginal costs). Peak charges should be high in congested traffic periods to equate with the high social marginal costs occasioned by congestion, with lower off-peak prices when there is no congestion to raise the private marginal vehicular cost of all users or to lower highway capacity. Such pricing policies for street and highway use would reduce expressway and highway investments needed to accommodate the traffic that moves most efficiently by highway carriers and would reallocate intercity traffic to the low-cost railroads which contribute little to the social costs of modern transport. In addition, by raising the cost of automobile use for driving to and from work, most of which travel occurs in peak periods, specific expressway user charges in urban areas to assess the social and peaking costs attributable to that use of automobiles would enlarge the effective demand for ordinary bus services, express bus services, suburban rail services, and for rail rapid transit services. Thus, such peak pricing would make it easier to finance much needed mass transit systems from revenue from users collected through the fare box.

User prices for the services of airports and the federal airways have also been insufficient generally to cover the long-run marginal costs of their use by airlines and other aviation users. The Airport and Airway Development Act of 1970 and the Airport and Airway Revenue Act of 1970 increased some of those user fees, and the Department of Transportation engaged in a study to determine the adequacy of user charges for air transport. As the airlines now represent an established industry and have registered rapid growth, the time is ripe for imposition of fully rational and economic user charges for the use of both the civil airways and the commercial airports. As with urban highways, congestion has arisen in the airline operations at some large airports. Rational pricing in congested airport situations requires the use of congestion peak prices to encourage more efficient use of airport facilities by scheduling airline departures and arrivals more over the entire day and by giving preference to runways and other facilities to the large aircraft carrying many times the number of travelers or the tons of freight carried in small planes.

PROPERTY-TAX EQUIVALENTS

A fourth step in rational pricing for public transport facilities, as mentioned earlier, would be to add property-tax equivalents to the user fees for airways and airports and for highways and to include such assessments of the general costs of government in waterway tolls when user prices are enacted for waterways. The carriers using public transport facilities are recipients of many benefits of general government services just as are the railroads, the oil pipe lines, and other privately-owned transportation units. Hence, equivalent charges for the benefits of government services and the general costs of government should be imposed on the carriers using public transport facilities in spite of the tradition that publicly-owned land and capital goods are not subjected to property taxes. Another alternative would be to relieve the railroads and oil pipe lines from having to pay property taxes on their fixed facilities in way, terminals and pumping stations, utilizing general tax sources to replace such levies for the support of state, municipal, and county functions such as public schools, residential streets, and country roads.

The effects of enacting universal user charges for public transport facilities and adjusting the existing user fees better to reflect the long-run marginal costs of provision of public transport services to the carriers, including assessment of social costs, property-tax equivalents and peak-time prices, would be to make the final prices for alternative carrier services fully economic. Then, the shippers and travelers could rationally choose between or among the modes, with the result that socially efficient divisions of traffic would result, more efficient investments among the modes would come about, and transport costs and rates could be lowered for the shippers and the general public.

Ernest W. Williams, Jr.

6
The Urban-Intercity Interface

Intercity and urban transport have long been dealt with as though they were separate and unrelated areas of study, investment and operation. The development of both promotional and regulatory policies that relate to intercity transport has gone forward with only the slightest recognition of the impact of such policy upon urban areas or, alternatively, of the degree to which urban transport capability might aid or frustrate intercity development. Only recently have relationships come to be recognized in principle. Policy has scarcely caught up with that recognition.

Although data on traffic flow, whether passenger or freight, are grossly inadequate in the United States—particularly data which permit origins and destinations to be joined—certain general features are clear. Most raw materials, agricultural and forest products and fuels, find their origins outside the urban areas but, sometimes after intermediate processing, they are overwhelmingly destined for industrial concentrations which coincide with major urban centers. The dispersion of manufacturing activity which has been going forward at least since 1920 has not been a dispersion into rural areas, but a spreading toward the periphery of established manufacturing centers, into cities formerly of predominant commercial character, and into newly-grown concentrations. Hence most movement of manufactured products is out of urban areas—the largest proportion destined for other urban centers. Freight traffic flows, accordingly, are predominantly rural to urban and urban to urban and they tend to occupy well-defined channels.

Passenger traffic exhibits similar concentration around the urban nodes, a result unavoidable with so large and growing a concentration of urban population. The airline network is built around a limited number of city pairs—service to smaller communities having proved costly and difficult to sustain with the result that numerous small points have been eliminated from the network in recent years. Remaining rail intercity passenger service as well as the principal intercity bus services also cater predominantly to traffic moving between the principal city centers. The limited network proposed for Railpax has a clear urban orientation. While rural passenger movement is principally by automobile, the Interstate Highway System concept clearly recognizes the predominant urban orientation of most automobile traffic.

URBAN CAPABILITY VS. SYSTEM PERFORMANCE

With some 50 percent of the nation's intercity freight transport (measured by value) unregulated, statistics embrace large elements of estimation and are of dubious accuracy. If coastwise and intercoastal water transport are included, intercity freight volume now exceeds two trillion ton-miles annually and generates revenues of the order of $60 billion. Estimated local truck transportation, not included in these figures and performed principally in urban areas, adds $30 billion to the freight bill. All intercity modes encounter significant costs in the performance of terminal services, again largely in urban areas. It is not unreasonable to suppose that the proportion of total freight service costs encountered in urban terminal areas is approaching 40 percent of the whole and it is plain that the proportion has been steadily growing, probably at an accelerating rate.

Transport policies directed toward the intercity system inevitably impinge upon urban transport conditions. Federal investment programs, with enormous funding, have concentrated upon the intercity links on the assumption that terminal facilities and urban networks were local responsibilities. Thus federal highway policy has expanded intercity capacity with too little regard for the fate of traffic once it is delivered into the urban networks. Waterway improvements have been confined to the navigable channels leaving other levels of government and private organizations to finance necessary terminal facilities. Airport assistance has been moderate and largely confined to land acquisition and runway construction. Even regulatory policies have sometimes operated to exacerbate the problems encountered in urban areas. Undue certification of competitive airline services between principal city pairs, for example, has resulted in reduced load factors and excessive aircraft movements at major airports. Certification of undue numbers of motor carriers to serve new industrial plants or areas, likewise, has led to dispersion of traffic among numerous carriers with reduced load factors and unnecessary vehicle movements. The reluctance of the regulatory authorities to permit reduced rates for multiple pick-ups deprives shippers of the incentive to concentrate their freight and thus limit the number of trucks required to call at their docks. Such impacts have only recently been recognized and the policy directives under which the promotional and regulatory agencies operate characteristically fail to require any consideration of urban impact.

The relative neglect of urban transport capability began when the federal government moved to foster nonrail forms of transport in intercity operation, i.e., during the early 1920s. It has, thus, existed for a long period of time during which the weight of federal investment lavished upon the intercity facilities has greatly increased, while the sources of funding in urban areas have become steadily less adequate. The growing gap between intercity traffic flows and the capacity to handle those flows in the urban terminals has increasingly sapped the vitality of the intercity modes and undermined the efficiency of the transport system as a whole.

State policies have been at fault in the same direction. Both federal and state programs have tended to allocate excessive proportions of available funds for facilities construction, whether as direct investment or grants in aid, to the less populous states and the rural areas. This is a reflection, of course, of the long-term dominance by rural interests in the Congress and the state legislatures. It is a tendency that has compelled the more populous states and the urban areas to contend with increasing congestion of their highway and airport facilities. It is a tendency confirmed as recently as the adoption of the Interstate Highway System, during the execution of which major overbuilding has occurred in many of the sparsely populated areas. But if the more populous states have suffered, major urban areas have suffered even more severely, federal and state funding for city street systems and all other urban transport requirements having been minimal.

The impact of urban congestion upon freight transport performance has been felt primarily through the impedance of movement of vehicles performing pick-up, delivery, and transfer services via the city street systems. Those systems are, indeed, great terminal systems for the intercity network. While more than 90 percent of rail carload traffic is siding-to-siding movement with the complete operation performed on the rails, the rapidly growing piggyback services require highway movement to and from ramps which are sited to serve as concentration points or load centers, hence are located predominantly in the larger cities. The airlines, air freight forwarders, domestic freight forwarders, REA, UPS, and the motor common carriers of general commodities all perform door-to-door services and deal predominantly with small shipments that must be platformed at a terminal and handled in pick-up and delivery services by city vehicles.

Motor carriers, members of the Middle Atlantic Conference, for example, handled 56.9 percent of their tonnage in 1967 as truckload (over ten thousand pounds) shipments, but 93.7 percent of the shipments were less truckload, including 57.5 percent that were minimum charge or under three-hundred-pound shipments. Many "truckload" shipments required topping off at terminals or a second pick-up to fill out the load. The Middle Atlantic pattern is not unrepresentative of motor carrier experience in the more heavily populated areas of the United States. And, as the New York truck survey shows, there is a strong concentration of traffic in the more congested sections of the cities.[1] Manhattan, with 7 percent of the City's land area, accounts for one-third of the truck tonnage. So great has been the decline in productivity of pick-up units in such areas that rate arbitraries are often assessed. In other instances linehaul carriers have turned over the pick-up and delivery function to local cartage operators. Surcharges for waiting time have become common and, where they are assessed, the total freight bill is unpredictable.

A prime example of the want of coordinated development of facilities designed to cope with intercity traffic and the urban gathering and distributing capacities needed to serve them is the large city airport. These have become major nodes of activity including, in addition to passenger service, the handling of air cargo, aircraft maintenance, light manufacturing, and office and hotel facilities. Characteristically the personnel movements of employees substantially exceed those of passengers utilizing the airport. Cargo movements are minor in relation to total traffic, yet the handling of pick-up and delivery directly at the airport results in light vehicle loads and concentration of freight move-

[1] The survey was conducted by the Tri-State Transportation Authority and was designed to record the movement of tonnage as well as vehicle trips.

ment at the most congested periods of the day. Here, as in the general case of imbalance between intercity and urban facilities provision, divided authority, disparate sources of financing, and the want of broad planning jurisdiction within the metropolitan area must share responsibility for ground congestion which seriously reduces the point-to-point capability of air transport.

INTERCITY TRANSPORT INTERFACES IN URBAN AREAS

The rail-highway interface, represented increasingly by piggyback and auto-rack rather than team-track operations, most commonly occurs in urban areas. The same is true of the air-ground interface whether of freight or passengers. Since rail, highway, and air networks center upon the cities, substantial traffic by each of these modes funnels through them as "bridge" traffic. Only the highway portion of such traffic contributes materially to congestion of the urban street system. It has been little studied and its importance doubtless varies greatly from one city to another. Although New York undoubtedly has a lower proportion of such traffic than many inland points, the truck survey showed 28 percent as much truck traffic bridging through New York as terminated there.

Of more importance is the fact that a large proportion of the interchange between carriers of the same mode occurs in the urban centers. The railway system was built up with the break between carriers occurring chiefly in the large cities, especially at major river crossings. Thus Chicago, St. Louis, Kansas City, Memphis, New Orleans, and similarly located points became primary gateways between lines. Upward of 30 percent of the cars handled in the Chicago Switching District are interchanged between connections—larger proportions are encountered at some other points. The concentration of rail terminal activity was earlier criticized principally because of its heavy use of valuable urban property for terminal yards and attendant facilities, the tendency of yards and running lines to impede street traffic flow, and the blight cast upon adjacent areas. With the passage of time rail facilities have become obsolescent, frequently inadequate, and hemmed in by surrounding urban development. More than any other factor, the complexity and congestion of these great urban terminals create the slow and irregular movement which is the principal deficiency of rail point-to-point freight service. Only in the last decade and upon a limited scale has an effort been made to bypass some major terminals with pre-blocked interline trains and pooled power.

The great bulk of motor carrier freight interchange also occurs in the cities. Some 30 percent of all Middle Atlantic general commodity traffic is interchanged, although very little is handled by three or more carriers. A number of the largest motor carriers have broader service areas than any railroad, and the merger movement in the industry, relatively unimpeded by the regulatory authorities, has gone in the direction of expanding system territorial coverage. Yet the vast majority of motor carriers have limited service territories and, perforce, interline considerable freight at their major terminals. Little interline business is handled by the interchange of loaded trailers. Most such traffic is platformed by the inbound carrier, transferred to the terminal of the on-carrier by a city rig, and platformed a second time. Although motor carrier terminals tend to locate toward the urban periphery, a large amount of transfer movement via the city streets is an unavoidable incident of interchange. Federal and state regulatory controls of entry have emphasized fixed route patterns and limited expansion largely to acquisition of existing certificates. The notion of single-line service between major city pairs, which has been an important criterion of CAB certificate issuance, appears to have no counterpart in motor carrier operating rights proceedings.

The carriers that are faced with the necessity of doing so much of their interline and intermodal business within urban areas have little control over the conditions under which such business is done. Apart from determining the location of their terminals when expansion or relocation appears to be in order, they are virtually without influence in respect of the development of the facilities over which they must operate. When congestion develops to impede their operations, the bulk of it is generated by vehicle movements over which they have no control. Hence the growing cost of interlining leads them to seek to curtail such traffic by closing through routes or by refusing to accept shipments tendered to them, either of which steps incurs the wrath of the regulatory authorities.

TERMINAL PRODUCTIVITY LOW AND DECLINING

The productivity of American freight transportation, taken as a whole, has more than kept pace with the productivity of the economy at large. Technological improvements in all forms of transport, however, have made little impact on terminal efficiencies. The principal exception is the containerization of marine freight which has made possible substantial reductions in per-ton handling costs for general cargo in ports where investment has been made in suitable container-handling facilities. All transport modes have tended to concentrate managerial attention upon the line haul to the neglect of the terminals. This reflects, in part, the difficulties of measurement and of control in terminals, in other part, preoccupation with the leading edge of technology in the line-haul performance, e.g., the aircraft. Nonetheless, terminal deficiencies are seldom recognized and faced up to until line-haul performance has been adversely affected by terminal disability.

The thrust of technological development comes largely from the improvement of the power unit, often accompanied by increases in the size and capacity of freight carrying units. Thus railroads have been able to increase both the tonnage and speed of freight trains. The composite measure, net ton miles per train hour, grew 28 percent from 1960–1969. Barge operators, similarly, by the increase of towboat horsepower more than doubled the weight of maximum tows in two decades. The jet transition not only increased airline capacity, but reduced break-even load factors by some twelve percentage points. The phasing-in of jumbo jets will produce analogous results. Motor carriers, by contrast, have been limited in their ability to improve line-haul performance by size and weight restrictions. Nonetheless improved vehicle design and some permitted increase in vehicle size have contributed to improved line-haul efficiency.

The benefits which improved power, equipment, and signalling have contributed in the line haul have no counterpart in rail terminal operations. Cars handled per engine-hour in yards have shown little improvement in consequence of the shift to diesel power. Work rules impose inflexibility in the conduct of terminal services and enhance their cost. A limited number of major automated yards show substantial improvement in productivity, but the hundreds of industrial and support yards operate essentially as they always have. The performance of transfer and industrial crews is governed principally by volume of traffic, size of cuts to be handled, and standard of service rendered. Similarly, while the line towboat in the barge business shows enormous increase of productivity, the harbor tug is limited by the nature of its work of cutting barges in and out of tows. Only limited horsepower can be employed.

The decline of terminal productivity is perhaps most notable in the motor carrier business which, more than other transport modes, must contend with vast volumes of small shipments to be picked up and

TABLE I. *Class I and II Motor Common Carrier Out-of-Pocket Costs of General Commodities, Middlewest Region*

	1960	1968
Line-Haul Cost, average, all weight brackets 200–299 mile block	.15910	.15289
Terminal Cost per 300 lb. shipment, cents:		
Pick-up and Delivery	108.7	180.1
Platform Handling	48.9	74.1
Billing and Collecting	53.8	90.0
Total Terminal	211.4	344.2

delivered in congested urban areas. As an example, Table I shows the out-of-pocket costs for Class I and II motor common carriers[2] of general commodities, Middlewest Region. Despite inflation, line-haul costs have shown a modest decline. Terminal costs, however, for a fairly typical small shipment have increased by 63 percent. Such an increase, applied to the whole of the nation's less truckload traffic, would imply an average annual increase in the cost of terminal operation of the order of $150 million, or about two and a half times as much as the recorded profit of the regulated intercity motor carrier industry last year. Pick-up and delivery costs, affected by growing urban congestion over which the carriers have no control, have increased by 67 percent. The costs of physical handling over the platform have been held better in check than other elements of terminal expense. These are, of course, average territorial figures which doubtless understate the increase of unit costs in the larger urban areas. Present prospects are for continuing productivity declines in the more congested areas as the number of stops per truck continues to fall. Pilferage and hijacking have grown rapidly, also, especially in some of the urban areas which require service, and driver protection has become an issue in some areas.

IMPROVEMENT REQUIRES URBAN TRANSPORT REFORM

The improvement of terminal productivity of intercity transport which serves the urban areas is not separable from the improvement of urban transport as a whole. Despite the burden which these operations place upon the nation's intercity service, they represent only a minor portion of the use of the street and highway systems within

[2] Class I are those with annual gross revenues exceeding $1 million, and Class II are those with annual gross revenues between $300,000 and $1 million.

metropolitan areas. The Chicago Area Transportation Study found weekday vehicle trips within the survey area to include 4.8 million by private automobiles, 802,000 by trucks, and 171,000 by taxicabs. In addition 337,000 vehicle trips of all kinds entered or left the survey area or passed through it. Traffic was, moreover, heavily concentrated on a relatively small portion of the total street mileage—83 percent of vehicle miles on the 28 percent of streets which were of arterial or expressway type. A good portion of truck delay, however, occurs on ordinary streets at and close to the commercial premises which are being served and is incident to the pick-up or delivery called for.

Truck movements are inextricably mixed with those of other vehicle types and, while much truck traffic can be handled between commuter peaks, a substantial portion of over-the-road movement must coincide with them if intercity schedules are to be maintained. Improved productivity in local service will, therefore, be generated concomitantly with improvement in the general traffic flow, a matter which is discussed in chapter 7. A problem peculiar to the older commercial and manufacturing areas of some of our largest cities, is, however, the general want of off-street loading and unloading space, the lack of dock areas, and the inadequate capacity of elevators and other internal handling devices in the buildings served. Pick-ups and deliveries are made in the face of incredible obstacles while the use of the street as a substitute for dock space grossly inhibits traffic flow.

The obvious solution is the reconstruction or replacement of existing business premises in order to provide ample off-street working areas. Rarely, however, can the businesses concerned sustain such costs, nor will they make any improvement save under intense pressure. The common failure to insist upon such provision in new construction is, of course, open to correction. But a more promising solution is likely to be found in the consolidation of pick-ups and deliveries to reduce materially the number of truck stops required and, of course, the number of vehicle movements through the often narrow streets serving the type of area in question. This possibility will be examined below.

Despite long-standing concern about the impact of rail terminal facilities, predominantly located a half century or more ago, upon urban development, little has been accomplished in the relocation of, consolidation of, or development of the air rights over such facilities. The rapid decline of passenger service, especially in the last decade, has made it possible to discontinue passenger stations and attendant facilities in some large cities and has enabled partial consolidation of pas-

senger terminal operations in Chicago, an object long sought. Little
has been done, however, to improve freight terminal facilities. Rail
carriers, dependent upon their own ability to generate internal funds
for such improvements, have been compelled largely to utilize available space adjacent to existing terminal yards for the development of
piggyback and container facilities. Nothing has impeded the development of joint intermodal rail-motor transport more than the inability
to provide adequate well-located facilities of this type. Congestion of
the terminals rapidly destroys both the cost and service advantages
of the intermodal form of transport.

Freight terminal unification, thought in earlier times to be a pan-
acea for the high costs and delays of conventional terminal services
operated by the line-haul carriers, now appears as an obstacle to controlled terminal performance and interchange movement. The Terminal Railroad Association of St. Louis is a prime example, but Chicago and other major junctions produce analogous results. The factor
most clearly responsible is the change in the character of rail traffic
in the period since the facilities were designed and installed, but the
joint control and management of such facilities also mitigates against
effective control of operations. For the present little recourse seems
available to the line-haul carriers other than an expansion of pre-
blocked movement of through traffic *via* direct interchanges between
them. In the longer run, however, it would appear that readjustment
and improvement of rail terminal facilities must be incorporated into
urban planning. The benefits to the community may well justify a
substantial measure of public finance. Should railroads be merged,
ultimately, into regional systems, a simpler and more effective rail
organization would develop in the major urban terminal areas, presenting a better climate for the consideration of desirable improvements.

URBAN GOODS MOVEMENT—A NEGLECTED SUBJECT

Examination and discussion of urban transport has focussed heavily
upon passenger movement. Undue emphasis has, no doubt, been
placed upon the journey to work to the neglect of other problems of
people movement. These aspects of the urban problem will be explored in the next chapter. Here, it may be noted that goods transport
within urban areas has been accorded minimal study and has only
recently become an object of attention by researchers. Urban transport

planning processes, of course, provide for the survey of goods vehicle movement and extrapolate the observed volumes in projecting required highway capacities. But the characteristics of goods transport and the factors which generate goods movement are not customarily explored. Trends in purchasing practices, related inventory policies, and physical distribution practices are not reflected, although it is plain that major changes have been underway.

In the 1920s, general commodity freight in and out of urban areas was handled almost exclusively by rail, except for package movements by water at Great Lakes and ocean ports. Most urban centers were serviced by a limited number of rail carriers: Los Angeles, 3; San Francisco, 4; Philadelphia, 3; Baltimore, 3; New York, 11. The midwest gateway cities were exceptions, with 28 line-haul and terminal carriers serving Chicago. Rail carriers generally provided a number of freight stations and team-track facilities along their lines, located as strategically as possible in relation to areas of heavy receipt and dispatch of goods. Trucking distances were thus minimized, each shipper did business with only a small number of line-haul carriers, hence could consolidate freight in cartage services to and from stations. Large shippers having rail sidings frequently used trap cars so that their less carlot traffic was handled to station or transfer by rail and kept off the streets. Even under these circumstances, a complex pattern of trucking to and from stations developed as early studies by the Port of New York Authority demonstrated. Congestion in the wholesale and light-manufacturing and waterfront areas of cities was by no means unknown.

In the period since, however, the product mix handled in the economic system has exploded. Household appliances are almost wholly new in the distribution pattern. Product lives tend to be shorter. Bulk has grown in relation to weight, unit values have climbed greatly. Enterprises at all levels in the distribution chain, from retailers to manufacturers, have been compelled to tighten inventory policies and operate as nearly on a hand-to-mouth basis as possible. In consequence small shipments, less than the truckload or carload of line-haul movement, have been increasing both absolutely and as a percentage of total freight traffic. Total freight traffic has about tripled since the early 1920s—small shipments tonnage has multiplied about nine times and the average individual shipment has become lighter in weight. At the same time business is far more dependent than formerly upon speedy and reliable small shipment service, tight control of inventory without undue risk of stockouts being otherwise impossible. The systems approach to physical distribution management has spread rapidly in some industries and the computer has been called upon to facilitate control of distribution operations. Hence shippers, more than in former times, appraise the trade-offs between speedy and reliable transportation services and the freight charges assessed therefor. Private trucking operations are often instituted because of the lack of service quality offered by commercial carriers.

The move to the five-day week soon after World War II adversely affected the utilization of the domestic transportation plant of all modes, other than the pipe lines which operate with continuous flow. The change is estimated to have cost the railroads 15 percent of the capacity of their car fleet. The effect upon motor carriers must have been similar. The same volume of business had now to be handled within a shorter period of time and the normal build-up of volume late in the week was augmented. The impact was felt most severely in pick-up and delivery and industrial switching operations, for the traffic brought to the terminals on Fridays could be spread over the weekend in line-haul dispatchment. The weekly peaks in freight operations, like other periodicities in transport, have never been taken account of in the pricing structure. Hence shippers are neither deterred from peaking their freight offerings, nor are carriers compensated for the standby facility costs and the congestion costs generated in peak periods.

The relatively compact rail system for the handling of less carlot traffic has given way to a highly dispersed service rendered by a multitude of motor carriers, freight forwarders, shippers' associations, and other agencies. Railroads, with few exceptions, are out of the small shipments business except as they may accommodate some such business in their Plan II piggyback services.[3] Motor carriers of general commodities handle nearly all of that class of traffic. Hundreds of carriers now share, in any major urban area, the class of traffic which used to move in a few concentrated rail flows. The carriers' customers, too, now exhibit a more dispersed pattern. Goods density may not have declined in the older commercial and industrial sections, but newer industrial and warehouse location has cut loose from the restricted rail pattern and dispersed along arterial highways and express-

---

[3] Service in which traffic moves in motor pick-up and delivery service provided by railroads under rail billing and rates, the rail furnished highway trailers moving in line haul on rail cars.

ways. Much of the movement has been outward, in search of lower land values that permit single-story construction.

Few but the largest motor carriers will provide more than one terminal in a metropolitan area. Hence most carriers must serve customers throughout the area from a single terminal location. Average hauls for city trucks are long and become longer as the dispersion of business premises proceeds. Cross hauls by units of different carriers are frequent. And shippers often apportion their traffic among numerous competitive carriers. Productivity of city vehicles is nevertheless high in the outlying areas and in the areas of new industrial development, not only because highways are less congested, but also because better provision is usually made in respect of loading docks. It is in the older and more densely utilized areas that terminal services threaten to pass out of control.

The New York truck study shows 24.8 percent of tonnage handled within the cordon to be in for-hire carriage, 22 percent handled on behalf of retail and wholesale trade, and 16.5 percent for the account of manufacturers. Some 32 percent of the tonnage was handled in peddle trips—trips that make multiple stops for the receipt and discharge of cargo. The average consignment weighed about 600 pounds, but special studies of downtown areas showed much lower weights. One square mile in downtown Brooklyn was visited by four thousand local trucks on the average weekday. The average consignment size was about 165 pounds and stops were made to deliver as little as 25 pounds. Individual blocks were found that were visited by upwards of one hundred trucks per day delivering in the aggregate a volume of freight capable of being handled by one or two large vehicles. Trip and delivery patterns were said to show a great deal of cross hauling and duplication.

It is obvious that pooling of inbound and outbound traffic requiring pick-up and delivery, perhaps with containerization of a substantial part of the traffic, could make a major contribution to reduced congestion and lowered operating costs for city truck units. Higher platform costs incident to inbound consolidation and outbound separation for line haul would represent a trade-off. Past efforts at consolidated freight stations have generated less substantial results than hoped for, both in the inland freight stations provided for rail service in earlier times and in the two Port of New York Authority truck terminals presently in operation. Yet the increasing burden of present duplicated services cries urgently for attention.

CONCLUSION

Concern with urban transport has largely focused, hitherto, on problems of circulation within the urban complex itself. Massive improvement of intercity facilities without comparable upgrading of urban systems has created a major gap that must be bridged. Recognition that one affects the other is growing, but has yet to be translated into effective policy responses.

Nearly all forms of commercial transportation now find some of their most important and baffling problems in the conduct of terminal services within the urban environment. Each finds the alternatives open to be limited unless that environment can be altered. The tendency of recent decades appears to have been a proliferation of duplicative services in goods movement coupled with a change of product mix and an expansion of the areas to be served. It is plain that freight movement within cities warrants far more attention than it has received, that freight traffic requirements must be better integrated into urban transport planning, and that measures for coordination need to be devised and examined. The carriers themselves, whether commercial or private, are hardly in a position to originate such measures nor is there evidence that they may be prepared to mount an initiative.

Lyle C. Fitch

7

Improving Urban Transportation

Transportation Technology and Urban Patterns

The kind and quality of transportation affect the economic efficiency of cities, intra-urban patterns of city development, and the activities and life styles of urban dwellers, as do few other public services. But transportation is one of the many things which nowadays seem to be going wrong or growing no better in large cities (defined as urban regions). This chapter concentrates mainly on intra-urban passenger transportation, its present state, and its longer-run role as an urban-shaping force. (Goods movement, though equally important, is beyond our scope.)

American cities, which originally were closely clustered around ocean or river ports, have been conditioned as to development, shape, and life style by a series of transportation technological developments.

First was the railroad, which freed industry and commerce from exclusive dependence on ports; linked cities with hinterlands and other cities; encouraged suburban towns to develop like pearls along a string; and initiated a peculiar urban phenomenon, the commuter—a term that originated in the "commutation" of railway fares to people

LYLE C. FITCH is president of the Institute of Public Administration, New York. In 1957–61 he was successively first deputy and city administrator of the City of New York. Dr. Fitch has served as consultant on urban transportation planning to federal, state, and city government agencies and has written several books and many articles on urban planning, finance, administration, and transportation, including Urban Transportation and Public Policy (1964).

who rode daily to the city and back. Railroad technology produced several offshoots—the trolley car, interurban railroads, and surface-subway rapid transit.

A second major technological development was the high-speed elevator, which spread cities into the third dimension, made possible great increases in land-use densities, and created problems, not yet solved, of integrating horizontal and vertical movement.

Third was the motor vehicle; it loosened the bonds which historically had tied many activities to the central city and transformed, much more drastically than had the railroad before it, the city-suburban complex and its functions.

Fourth was the airplane; while not a significant intra-urban transportation mode, it has had several important urban-shaping effects: air transportation, for instance, links many urban residents more closely to the outside world in ways that affect their working and living patterns; large-city airports tend to become major subcenters because they are large employers themselves and because they attract many different other types of economic activity.

Intra-urban goods transportation has been taken over almost entirely by trucks, and intra-urban passenger transportation systems in most cities of the United States rely primarily on private automobiles supplemented by taxis and by rags and tags of public transportation. Only New York and Chicago rely mainly on public transportation to bring workers to their major central business districts. New York, Chicago, Philadelphia, Boston, and Cleveland have rail transit whose most distinguishing feature is a separate right of way.[1] Other transit consists almost entirely of buses which must compete with other vehicles for road space.

Most transit is uncomfortable, though some of the new rail transit systems (unfortunately located in other countries) offer a level of amenity which contrasts sharply with the discomfort of, for instance, the New York City subway. With fares in most cities rising to 40 and 50 cents and beyond, transit is no longer cheap.

Forced to compete with the comfort and convenience of the auto, bus transit has declined; passenger volume fell by some 39 percent between 1950 and 1969. United States rail transit hangs on like the whooping crane—passenger volume on the five major systems has

---

[1] Other cities on the North American continent having rail transit are Toronto, Montreal, and Mexico City. The trains of the last two cities use rubber-tired wheels instead of steel.

edged up slightly over the last twenty years—and even manages to proliferate; a new San Francisco Bay Area transit system will begin service in 1972, and construction of a new system for the Washington, D.C., area is underway.

The great expansion in the number and use of automobiles has brought to light basic incompatibilities between high-density urban land use, particularly in central business districts, and the unrestricted use of private autos. (The incompatibility is most evident in larger cities; those under five hundred thousand are suffering less pain.) The manifestations of incompatibility, as they began forcing themselves on the unwilling attention of large-city officials after World War II, were growing street congestion, parking shortages, environmental damage, noise and air pollution, and the loss to other uses and to tax rolls of land preempted for urban roadways.

By 1960 a number of large-city mayors had become sufficiently aroused to launch a considered drive to obtain federal assistance for mass transportation improvement. A bill was finally passed by Congress in 1964 to provide such assistance, but appropriations therefor have been small by transportation-industry standards (some $600 million between 1964 and 1970) and have gone mainly for re-equipping existing transit systems with new buses and rail cars. A fraction of the funds was earmarked for research and demonstration, but though the various projects produced some modest technological improvement and some information on matters such as the response of riders to various forms of improvement, nothing has happened to reverse the general malaise of the transit industry.

Even as the industry has declined, however, the support for doing more about it and about urban transportation in general has risen. Congress, in the Transportation Act of 1970, tentatively pledged to put $10 billion into urban mass transportation improvement over the next dozen years. Thus far there is little agreement on how the money should be spent. Meanwhile, expenditure for construction of arterial highways in urban communities is in the magnitude of $4 billion per year, and urban dwellers are spending about $25 billion annually on new automobiles.

Recent Urban Physical Development

Most urban growth in population, employment, and other activities is occurring outside central cities; the prevailing pattern is one of ever more dispersal. The scatteration of residences and activity centers in "suburban sprawl" development requires random-access transportation which can take different members of households to different places in different directions at different times. The only transportation medium produced thus far to meet these requirements is the private automobile which, along with its cousin the truck, was responsible for the dispersal in the first place.

Central cities have been losing most of their manufacturing and other goods-handling activities for reasons stemming largely from the development of motor vehicle transportation; these activities gravitate to the periphery where land is cheaper, congestion less, and taxes lower. Older central cities which have attained the status of national and regional capitals have continued, until recently, to provide a congenial climate for certain specialized manufacturing activities, cultural, recreational and educational functions and, most notably, corporate and management functions and their attendant services. Office industries are now the predominant economic activity of the large central cities; the towering skyscraper has replaced the factory as the hallmark of high concentration. Central cities which are not management centers have tended to decline relatively, and many older ones have declined absolutely.

The middle-class white-collar workers who man the office industries have been leaving central cities for residences in the suburbs. This does not necessarily lead to corresponding declines in central-city nighttime population, for the middle-class emigrants have been replaced by immigrants from agricultural regions, particularly from the southern United States. Many immigrants are black; most are uneducated, unskilled, and poor. While they have been concentrating in the deteriorating housing of central cities (the only available housing they can afford), the jobs they might fill either have been disappearing or have been moving suburb-wards. These trends in the location of settlement and employment centers have led to what Wilfred Owen refers to as the quaint tribal custom whereby people of light complexions live in the suburbs and commute inward to jobs in the central city, whereas people of dark complexions live in the central city and commute (if they can) outward to jobs in the suburbs. The transportation difficulty of this arrangement is that the in-commuters have service that is at best fair to middling and the out-commuters have service that is poor to nonexistent.

In some cases, what appear in the first instance to be transportation problems can be solved by nontransportation means, simply by making it possible and desirable for people to move closer to their work. For the central-city resident, this means opening up more housing opportunities in the suburbs—a direction which continues to be vigorously opposed by many suburbanites who got there first.

Deficiencies of Urban Transportation Viewed from Three Standpoints

We will look at *existing* deficiencies from two different standpoints: (1) people who are poorly served by existing systems, and (2) the existing systems themselves. Third, we will consider *future* needs having to do with the role of urban transportation systems in complementing and shaping future community development.

PEOPLE NOT WELL SERVED

One of the several indictments of existing systems is that they fail to serve, or serve well, a substantial segment of the population, including the following:

Aged, Youth, Disabled and Poor—Many people do not drive or do not have access to automobiles and cannot afford taxis. About 5 percent of the population is above 70 years of age; another 15 percent is in the 10–17 age bracket. A considerable number in the 17–70 bracket cannot drive because of physical disabilities or for other reasons. Many families still lack automobiles: in 1966 cars were owned by fewer than half of families with income under four thousand dollars, Negro households, and households with heads over 65 years old.

A special case is that of ghetto residents whose housing is widely separated from available jobs. It was estimated in 1965 that the distance gap between segregated residential areas and job centers may have been costing ghetto residents as many as thirty-five thousand jobs in the Chicago area and nine thousand in the Detroit area.

There is some evidence of a recent dramatic increase in the rate of black migration from central cities to suburbs. If such trends are confirmed and if they continue, much recent thinking about the functions of central cities and the central city-suburban relationship may have to be revised.

There is no evidence of much diminution in the separation-of-workshops-and-bedrooms problem, however. The problem was highlighted by the Watts riot of 1965, when the McCone report cited lack of transportation to jobs as one of the contributing factors to the riots.[2]

Much of the travel demand of the nonworking poor, the old, and the disabled could be met by travel in nonpeak hours, which suggests that part of the answer may be in higher utilization of existing transportation during off-hours.

Commuters—Many working commuters in and around large cities are plagued by traffic congestion, or by crowded, uncomfortable mass transportation. In the last four decades, and particularly since the inauguration in 1965 of the Federal Interstate Highway Program, main emphasis in urban transportation has been on building highways (with a large measure of federal assistance) to bring suburban workers to the perimeters of large cities, but street systems in older cities were never designed to handle the volume of traffic funneled into them by the arteries, and in many cities congestion has grown apace. In some cases, even the arteries around cities have run out of capacity.

The fact that employment growth in large central cities has leveled off has led some to the conclusion that there is no need for much concern about improving facilities for traveling to and from the central city. This proposition, however, ignores the changing pattern of transportation demand toward improvements in both quantity and quality growing out of the change in composition of central-city jobs, the middle-class movement to the suburbs, and the growth of central-city poverty ghettos.

Recreation Seekers—Many large-city dwellers can and do travel to out-of-city recreation areas; those who lack transportation cannot reach any recreation centers.

The first and third of these deficiencies are primarily manifestations of low income. Individuals with enough money can ordinarily get around, in nonrush hours, even if they cannot drive; the affluent suburban commuter's problem is primarily one of facilities for peak-hour travel. Whereas suburban commuter problems are concentrated mainly in large cities, the deficiencies associated with low incomes are common to both large and small urban areas, though they are relatively more

[2] John F. Kain, "The Effect of the Ghetto on the Distribution and Level of Non-white Employment in Urban Areas" (RAND Corporation, May 1965, multilith).

National Committee Against Discrimination in Housing, *Jobs and Housing: A Study of Employment and Housing Opportunities for Racial Minorities in Suburban Areas of the New York Metropolitan Region*; interim report (multilith, March 1970).

Governor's Commission on the Los Angeles Riots, *Violence in the City—an End or a Beginning?* (1965).

serious in the large metropolitan centers where average travel distances are greater.

SYSTEMS DEFICIENCIES

The chief ailments for which most large cities are seeking palliatives are peak-hour congestion, discomfort, inconvenience, and slow movement. The underlying factors, for transit and automobiles, include:

Transit—Rapid transit systems are underfinanced, owing in part to political reluctance to raise fares coupled with unwillingness or inability to supply necessary financing from nonfare sources.

Indifference to surface transportation systems has long been a fact. Historically they have been expected not only to pay their own way but also to contribute to general revenues through franchises, street maintenance and snow removal charges, and other levies. Present handicaps include technological backwardness, opposition from nontransit motor vehicle interests, difficulties of moving in congested traffic, poor scheduling and routing, slowness and effort of boarding and exiting, and uneconomic fare systems.

Automobiles—A large proportion of urban space is required for moving and storing more than 62 million cars owned by urban residents; in some areas as much as 60–65 percent of the land is dedicated to roads, parking, and service facilities.

Pollutants engendered by internal combustion engines are estimated to be the source of more than 60 percent of the nation's air pollution. Internal combustion engine fumes have replaced coal smoke as a noxious mark of prosperity.

There are other indirect costs of motor vehicle transportation, such as noise, preemption of land for highways, and so on.

ORGANIZATIONAL CHAOS

Urban transportation is provided by a number of different industries and modes: auto, bus, and truck; rapid transit; airplanes; and various short-haul conveyor systems, such as elevators and escalators. Though the different transportation services may be complementary or competitive, they are nowhere, in this country, subjected to systematic coordinated planning implemented by muscular administration. The disciplinary influence of the price system, which in much of the economy operates to coordinate consumer selection of different goods and services, and to relate the demand for goods to the cost of supplying them, is lost in a crazy-quilt pattern of prices and costs found in various urban transportation modes. The relationship between private and public sectors is complex and differs sharply among the several transportation industries. A maze of subsidy and planning patches overlies the crazy quilt.

The dominant voice in this modal melange has been that of the highway interests, particularly state highway departments. Until recently, a main objective of highway policy has been to move as many vehicles as possible as cheaply as possible, with little regard for the effects of highway construction and alignment on the development patterns, or even traffic patterns, of urban areas. Although this picture is changing, highway planning, construction, and operation still keep their distance from other transportation and from urban development planning in general.

These problems of modal and functional fragmentation have been exacerbated by the familiar problem of metropolitan areas—multiple municipal and special district governments, and in many cases state governments, within metropolitan areas. Few urban areas are organized to undertake the job of planning comprehensive programs of transportation improvement. Fewer have machinery for making considered decisions among alternative regional transportation development programs, even assuming that such alternatives are perceived and analyzed. Administrative machinery for controlling and for regulating metropolitan and regional transportation systems nowhere exists.

DISREGARD FOR ECONOMIC LAW AND ORDER

From the economic viewpoint, much of the trouble with urban transportation arises from the fact that the price-and-subsidy systems employed for private automobiles and other transportation modes have no systematic relationship to cost, to prevailing conditions of demand, or to each other. One result is congestion. In the economic frame of reference, congestion is clear and sufficient evidence of one or both of two things. The first is that the components of the road system are out of balance (see discussion of this and other design deficiencies below). The second is that road space is underpriced—the demand exceeds the supply.

The common response to congestion is to build more highways and freeways rather than to raise charges. But building road space runs into the difficulty that in and around large cities demand for road space is governed by the traffic analogues of two laws: those of Parkinson and Malthus. The analogue to Parkinson's law says that traffic always appears to fill available space. Malthus's analogue says that traffic is limited only by checks corresponding to those which, according to Malthus's doctrine, limit the human population, with congestion, accidents, and other misfortunes taking the place of wars, plagues, and famines.

As things now stand, we accept the proposition that the man whose time is worth least, and the man with the least important reason for driving, have the same right to be in the traffic stream, at the same price, as anybody else, regardless of congestion. As long as we take this ultra-democratic point of view, it will be difficult to abate congestion in the long run without diverting so much space to movement and parking that other activities are seriously curtailed. A more sensible, less socialistic, alternative is to ration scarce road space by a system of differential pricing which imposes special charges for the privilege of driving in congestion-prone areas at congestion-prone times. Since congestion is ordinarily a peak-hour phenomenon, the indicated policy is to charge higher prices during peak hours than at other hours. But the notion of anti-congestion pricing, or special peak-hour charges, has always been anathema to highway user groups even though the principle is used with many other types of service, for example, telephone service.

URBAN DESIGN DEFICIENCIES

Weaknesses in urban transportation per se are compounded by basic deficiencies in city design which, in the United States, has virtually ignored transportation efficiency. Older cities, particularly those designed in pre-automobile days, exhibit such deficiencies as

1. Gross mismatches among capacity of arterials that carry vehicles into central cities, capacity of streets to distribute them, and amounts and locations of offstreet parking space.
2. Failure to separate different kinds of traffic—buses, trucks, trains, autos, and pedestrians.
3. Lack of facilities for moving pedestrians, such as malls, passageways protected from the weather and from vehicular traffic.
4. Lack of facilities for short-haul, high-volume horizontal movement.
5. Failure to integrate vertical and horizontal transportation, notably in the location of high-rise office buildings with no concern for the transportation problems they will generate.

Some Policy Directions for Urban Transportation Improvement

IMPROVING COMMUTATION SYSTEMS

People may be badly served because of system deficiencies, because of bad physical planning, or simply because of low incomes. The first problem can be helped by transportation system improvements; the second requires comprehensive urban planning and design which integrates transportation with land-use planning; the third is a matter for income redistribution policy, which is largely outside the province of the first two areas.

I turn first to issues of improving commuter transportation in congested urban areas.

Concepts of Congestion—To deal with congestion, we first must define it. Despite endless complaints of traffic congestion, there still is no generally accepted definition for purposes of control. Two possible definitions are noted here:

1. Congestion exists in a traffic artery or network when the number of vehicles *trying* to move at the same time is so large that the number of vehicle miles traveled in a given period is substantially less than if traffic flowed freely. (Average speed corresponding to maximum traffic flow depends to some extent upon prevailing driving habits, but in general it is in the range of 35–40 miles per hour.)
2. Congestion exists when the value of time lost because of traffic delay, as the result of having too many vehicles in the traffic system, exceeds the value to marginal travelers of traveling at that particular time. (The marginal travelers are those to whom travel at peak hours is worth the least.)

A traffic control policy based on the first definition would aim at promoting maximum use of a highway-street network (that is, a maximum flow of vehicles in the whole network). A more useful variation of this policy is to maximize the "people-throughput," that is, the number of people moving through the system or any part thereof during a given period of time.

A policy based on the second definition would seek to maximize the value to users of the network by facilitating the movement of those to whom time is worth more while discouraging, temporarily, trips by those to whom time is worth least. This approach involves more systematic use of the price system. Though the notion continues to be politically unpalatable, it has sufficient merit to warrant discussion in a following section. Here I consider measures which aim either to expand the capacity of the existing roadway network or to reduce peak-hour travel.

LARGE IMPROVEMENTS THROUGH SMALL INCREMENTS

In every community there are numerous opportunities for improving transportation by incremental measures, each of which involves outlays that are modest relative to the cost of large new freeways or new rail systems. Many small improvements can add up to large improvements.

One way of implementing a maximum "people-throughput" policy is to improve the attraction of buses as compared to private automobiles. For example, bus travel time can be improved by giving preference to buses at entrances to arterials and to traffic lights. Lanes reserved for buses can considerably expedite such movement in some situations, although these appear to work better on arterials than on city streets. The capacity of and average speed on road networks generally can be improved by a multitude of simple and familiar devices such as one-way streets (although these may reduce the convenience of buses), good traffic management, enforcement of traffic regulations, and so on. Next are a number of devices whose effectiveness has been demonstrated but which are as yet little used. One of the most important of these is traffic-responsive signaling by which traffic signals (equipped with electronic sensors and computers) give proportionately more green-light time to direction of dominant traffic flow. Still more sophisticated are systems which maximize traffic flow on freeways by monitoring access thereto, for example by holding vehicles at entrances until such time as they can be accommodated without causing congestion. (One such system is being used in Queens, New York, with good results.)

A still more sophisticated notion involves a planned balance between capacities of arterials leading into cities, local street systems which distribute traffic, and parking capacity. This has not been systematically attempted in any United States city, to my knowledge. The New York City Planning Commission some years ago attempted to limit the construction of parking garages in midtown Manhattan in order to reduce street congestion; the measure met with hot opposition from merchants who could not understand that more congestion might decrease, rather than increase, the number of shoppers in the central business area.

Cars may be kept off streets by providing parking areas near freeway exits, with mass transportation available into congested areas; a variant is the familiar park-and-ride arrangement which in many cases has been notably effective.

Another technique for reducing street traffic is reported from Godesburg, Germany, which has divided the central city into wedge-shaped segments with barriers to prevent movement between the wedges. Access to wedges is by ring roads. City streets are thereby reserved for local movement.

Unfortunately, there is in most communities no mechanism for searching out, designing, and implementing incremental improvements such as those mentioned above. Federal technical assistance could be valuable; the Urban Mass Transportation Administration in the federal Department of Transportation several years ago launched an experimental program along these lines which was dropped, unfortunately I think, before it had had a fair trial. The Federal Highway Administration has a "corridors" project, useful but only partial, which is now looking for opportunities to improve conditions along corridors into cities.

ANTICONGESTION PRICING

The market-price system has been highly effective with most commodities and services in determining how much should be produced and consumed. But it runs into hot opposition when it comes to the idea of imposing special charges for the use of road space in congestion-prone areas at congestion-prone times, even though motor vehicle users generally do not pay nearly the full cost of peak-hour driving in congested urban centers. There is a disposition to resent the imposition of new charges for services, particularly public services, once they have been provided free of charge. Moreover, public understanding of the matter has been clouded by obfuscation of the facts about the cost of driving. Hence the proposal to put tolls on the East River bridges linking Manhattan to Brooklyn and Queens continues to be staunchly resisted despite heavy peak-hour congestion on the bridges and on the roadways leading thereto, and on the streets of Manhattan.

In spite of the obstacles which continue to suppress experimentation with pricing, the potential advantages are so great that they should not be forgotten altogether. A pricing system could promote the following adjustments in travel habits which would reduce congestion and the need for transportation facilities.

1. *Number and Timing of Trips*—If a price differential between peak and off-peak travel were introduced, some traffic would shift to off-peak and the total number of trips probably would decrease.
2. *Average Length of Trip*—An increase in the amount charged for travel per mile would encourage people to live closer to their jobs and to make other adjustments to shorten the average length of trips; and it might induce employers to locate closer to residential centers. In the long run such adjustments might produce greater compactness of the urban area with greater residential and employment densities than would be obtained with relatively cheaper transportation.
3. *Choice of Mode*—The higher the prices of transportation generally, other things being equal, the greater the use which will be made of the less expensive mode.
4. *Choice of Route*—If price differentials are introduced on high-cost and congestion-prone routes, traffic will tend to shift to lower-cost routes.

In the present system of imperfect pricing, subsidies, hidden costs and indirect benefits, ordinary price-cost considerations play a small role in determining either the volume of travel or the investment in urban transportation facilities. Most cities and metropolitan areas lack data on expenditures and revenues associated with motor vehicle travel, or for that matter transit travel, and therefore have little notion of what various forms of travel are costing per trip.

A technical problem of imposing anti-congestion charges has always been that of administration. Placing toll booths at entrances to congestion-prone areas is practicable only where the entrances are few in number; this situation prevails for Manhattan, which is entirely surrounded by water and can be entered only via bridges and tunnels, but not in most downtown areas, which can be entered by dozens of highways and local streets.

Probably the most feasible means of imposing charges is through use of automatic vehicle monitoring systems (AVM), which are now in an advanced stage of development. Such systems, which link electronic sensors and computers, can identify the location in any given short period of large numbers of vehicles in a given area, such as an urban center. AVM would make it possible to compute the amount of time spent in congestion-prone areas and to bill vehicle-owners therefor. Charges should vary for different periods, according to the demand for travel: they should be high during peak hours and lower (or zero) during periods when travel is light.

The main disadvantage of AVM systems is that they require each vehicle to be equipped with a device which emits electronic signals that identify the vehicle. The devices would be fairly expensive, though mass production might enable their cost to be brought to below $100. In addition, each monitored area would need a number of sensors, or receivers, located throughout the area, a central processing station, and various other equipment. Costs of equipment, exclusive of vehicle equipment, would run to $1 million up, depending on the size of the area.

AVM has many applications—it would be useful to police departments, taxi companies, and any other organization with a fleet of vehicles whose location needs to be frequently known. In addition, AVM can keep track of things like containers, which are likely to be stolen. (Various AVM systems have been described and evaluated in a recent report to the Department of Housing and Urban Development prepared by the Institute of Public Administration and TEKNE-KRON, Inc.)

Transit Issues

We turn now from incremental approaches to large new transit systems as a means of solving central city problems.

The concept of more freeways to carry people to and from the established large central cities appears to be played out. Road space used only in peak hours, for automobiles carrying an average of 1.4 passengers, is likely to be the most expensive transportation solution in terms of direct financial cost; and there are the additional problems of local street and parking capacities, environmental damage from displaced people and firms, costs of traffic management and of auto theft (which accounts for about 16 percent of all reported major crimes).

Rightly or wrongly, planners, businessmen, and political leaders in a number of large cities have become convinced that more and better transit is necessary to preserve and expand the economic vitality of central cities. This raises a number of broader issues of patterns of future urban development, which I will discuss later.

It appears that no dramatic technology which would contribute significantly to intra-urban transportation is likely to emerge for at least another few decades. There are, however, opportunities for improvement in already existing technologies. Various European manufacturers offer bus designs with greater flexibility, convenience, and comfort than are available in the United States. The concept of small automobiles which might be rented at random times and places for intra-city trips or even for commutation has been around for some years; there has been no agency or funds for giving the concept an adequate trial. The principle of continuous-flow service is familiar, through escalators and moving sidewalks, but it has not been adapted to moving around central business districts. The San Francisco Bay Area rapid transit (BART) rail system will feature automation and passenger comfort, both noteworthy innovations in the United States. (Monorails may be dismissed as serious contenders; there is nothing monorails can do which cannot be done better by duo-rail systems.)

An interesting technological possibility is the so-called "dial-a-bus," a computerized version of the jitney. Persons desiring service would telephone, or they could hail vehicles on the streets. A computer, tied in with an automatic vehicle monitoring system, would register origins and destinations of requests, and would work them into the routes of taxi-buses already on the streets, employing a mathematical routing formula or algorithm which would select the most efficient routes for the passengers being carried by each vehicle. "Dial-a-bus" would carry more passengers at a time and would require more time for an average trip than would a taxi, but would be cheaper per trip. (Airport limousines serving certain cities, such as Washington, D.C., employ some of the same principles in picking up and distributing passengers, but without the advantage of an AVM and computerized routing system.)

Otherwise, the most promising technology on the horizon, in my opinion, is electronic guidance and control of highway vehicles, which would increase highway capacity by enabling the operation of vehicles at higher speeds and shorter headways, and could make possible more flexible transportation systems. But electronic systems have still far to go, both in research and development requirements and, thereafter, will require substantial capital expenditures.

Tracked air cushion vehicles now under development, which dispense with wheels and can operate at very high speeds, appear to be more suited for relatively long-distance travel, as in megalopolitan corridors, than for intra-urban travel.

Otherwise, the main alternatives to private automobiles are still rail and bus transit, which in most areas have been caught in the vicious cycle of declining riders and revenues, deteriorating service, and rising fares.

RAIL VERSUS BUS

The main technical difference between conventional rail vehicles and conventional buses is that rail offers automatic guidance and exclusive right-of-way. Rail automation can be carried still further with starting, stopping, speed, acceleration, and braking controls, although these thus far have been used on only a few systems and have not been developed for wide-scale application.

Any high-speed, high-capacity public transportation system must have some of the characteristics of rail in that it must be free from interference by other vehicles and have well-delineated corridors with stations and terminals. Given the possibility of devising efficient and dependable electronic guidance and control systems, it may be possible to achieve high-speed, high-volume service on reserved freeway lanes, using vehicles that could be manually operated on leaving the automatic system. Rail systems, as now conceived, have the disadvantage of relative inflexibility compared with buses, in that they can be used only by special vehicles. (Dual-purpose vehicles, which can operate on either rails or highways, have been tried but thus far have not been impressive.)

Conventional buses are typically slow because of competitive street traffic (as already noted) and are poorly designed and uncomfortable. Better design and more efficient fare collection systems would expedite loading and unloading and help to reduce travel time. Routes and schedules in many areas are poorly adapted to changing travel needs; thus in the Washington, D.C. area, bus routes are designed to bring workers from suburban to downtown jobs, but the comparatively simple task of arranging routes to carry central city workers to suburban jobs on reverse trips is neglected. In many cities, the sheer task of discovering how to get from one point to another can be a major research project for the would-be rider.

The first requirements in improving bus service are more speed and more frequent service. A number of measures have been suggested above for improving speed. Reserved lanes, or even entire streets and highways, can be justified as a means of increasing people throughput and might be a considerably more flexible solution than rail transit if reserve lanes could be used for freight and even private automobile traffic during non-journey-to-work hours. Other simple improvements could greatly improve bus service, for example eliminating the tendency to travel in herds like fearful elephants.

The bane of express bus service into downtown areas is distribution of passengers to destinations, which cannot easily be handled by buses operating on congested city streets. The problem could be solved in part by putting buses into downtown subways. Ultimately these might be equipped with electronic guidance and control systems to give buses essentially the same characteristics as rail.

Because there is frequently confusion on this point, it should be emphasized that the higher cost of rail transit roadways, compared with conventional highway lanes, comes from putting rail underground; where both rail and asphalt are on the same level, there is no great cost difference (other things being equal). A disadvantage of buses, relative to multi-car trains, is the cost of labor—one operator for each vehicle. A study done by the National Capital Transportation Agency comparing costs of operating buses in such a way as to provide the same service as a rapid transit line indicated that the costs are of the same order of magnitude with the proviso that the bus system would have a considerably lower maximum capacity and (with present design and operating characteristics) would offer a somewhat lower level of comfort.[3]

As things now stand, however, it appears that a highway mass transit system may have some advantage over a rail system for several reasons. First, right-of-way may be used in non-peak hours for non-passenger purposes, e.g., hauling freight, thus giving the roadway network greater flexibility overall. Second, buses can be used (as rail vehicles cannot) for charter services and other off-peak special uses.

The possibilities afforded by highway automation constitute a third reason for preferring highway over rail solutions. If and when both public and private vehicles are equipped for automatic operation, automated highway lanes might be shared by both types, making for greater economies of right-of-way use. By itself, this consideration argues against large investments in conventional rail systems and in favor of highway systems designed for later adaptation to automatic guidance and control.

One frequently hears the argument that rail and other transit systems will not relieve traffic congestion. The proposition, however, depends on one or both of two conditions: (1) that transit systems generate a volume of centrally located jobs equal to or greater than the number of transit riders, and (2) that transit patronage is essentially the over-spill driven off the highways by "intolerable" congestion or by the shortage of parking space, or both. Either of the above conditions may obtain, but neither is inevitable.

The Bay Area rapid transit (BART) system was justified on the

---

[3] National Capital Transportation Agency, *A Study of Bus Rapid Transit Operations for the National Capital Region* (July 1963).

grounds that travel into San Francisco would increase substantially and that the cost of carrying the projected volume of traffic by individual automobiles on freeways would be prohibitive; indeed, it would require more freeways than would be practicable from an engineering-design standpoint. Many transportation experts, however, believe that the rail system will never fulfill its intended objectives and that other means, such as express buses operating on freeways, could do the necessary job more cheaply than the $1.5 billion rail system.

TRANSIT LABOR PROBLEMS

One advantage of passenger-driven vehicles over transit is their relative invulnerability to labor disturbances. Heavy dependence on mass transportation under present technologies and labor practices may jeopardize a city's economic life.

Even without service interruptions, however, the fact that much transit is labor intensive makes transit highly sensitive to wage increases and union reluctance to cooperate in raising labor productivity. Of the two factors, productivity has been the more serious problem in recent years. Wages rates and increases therein, although they have compelled repeated fare hikes (and consequent passenger losses), have not been out of line in most communities with wages for comparable work elsewhere. Productivity is another matter. Thus operating costs per revenue mile on the Boston Metropolitan Transportation Authority's (MTA) rapid transit lines are nearly twice those of any other rapid transit system in the country, owing largely to union insistence on obsolete staffing patterns with much redundant labor. (There have been exceptions: New York's Transport Workers' Union [TWU] consented to a reduction in force of some six thousand Transit Authority employees in the middle 1950s as a means of avoiding a fare increase.) Faced with monuting wage demands and operating deficits, transit operators, led by Boston's MTA, have mounted a campaign for federal operating as well as capital subsidies, and Congress in the Urban Transportation Act of 1970 directed that a study be made of the feasibility of operating subsidies.

With bus operations, there is no great latitude for labor saving. On most existing rail systems, the possibilities for automatic guidance and control, and automatic fare collection on commuter railroads, cannot be exploited because of union opposition. (New York's one attempt at automatic control of subway lines was vigorously opposed by the TWU, which required the employment of a standby motorman; the experiment finally ended when the control system was destroyed by a fire of mysterious origin.)

Meeting Transportation Needs of Low-Income Individuals

PUBLIC POLICY MEASURES

There is needed first a definition of a "minimum standard of mobility" to guide public policy. Such a standard should cover access to work, shopping, medical care, churches, social centers, educational facilities for children and adults; to friends and relatives; and to outdoor recreation in the metropolitan area. This implies that lack of mobility should not be allowed to interfere with the realization of a minimum standard of living for all, as it is defined and redefined over the years.

Assuming that lack of mobility due primarily to low incomes is to be attacked head-on, the next question is whether public transportation should be subsidized specifically as a means for providing services to lower-income groups. General subsidies, considered by themselves, encounter the objection that public transportation is used by middle-income as well as lower-income persons, particularly in large cities. In fact, public transportation is being increasingly subsidized, especially in large cities, though frequently with small regard for the special needs of the poor people. The whole urban transportation system is permeated with various kinds of subsidies, most of which have come about more or less accidentally and tend to favor higher-income groups. This is the case, as previously mentioned, with subsidies to automobiles moving in high-density areas, and with present and proposed commuter rail systems whose primary function is to move white-collar workers to and from central business districts.

General subsidies to public transportation may serve the dual purpose of benefiting the poor and reducing the cost of providing road-space and other facilities for private automobiles. If transit is more economical than private automobile, everything considered, it is better to subsidize transit. But in many cases, expensive transit services are kept running to serve only a few people, and in such cases, it may be cheaper to provide subsidies for taxi service for low-income individuals, or (for those able to drive) assistance in acquiring dependable cars (not "jalopies"), which is ordinarily inhibited by such factors as high costs of insurance and financing.

While the idea of facilitating automobile ownership by the poor would doubtless outrage a considerable segment of public opinion (particularly that which fails to distinguish between the worthy poor and the idle and dissolute poor), the idea might be acceptable if applied to the journey-to-work from areas not well served by public transportation. As previously noted, existing transit and rail commutation systems have not been well designed to carry people from residential areas in older core cities to dispersed job locations. Even where public transportation is available, it is frequently costly in time as well as money: a two-hour journey each way may be required from the Watts area of Los Angeles to major employment centers. Proposed new rail systems, such as those under construction in the Washington and San Francisco regions, offer little help; they also are designed primarily to get people into and out of central business districts.

In many instances, car pooling (already widely used) may provide the most economical journey to work. But car pooling requires ownership of a dependable car by at least one person in a pool; special assistance for purchase thereof, and for setting up car pooling arrangements, may be justified. Another possibility is special buses or station wagons, operated by drivers who do other work during the day.

In various other countries, employers themselves provide, or assist in providing, transportation for workers, but the practice has not found much acceptance in the United States, except for high-paid executives, baby sitters, and domestic servants.

For persons who do not drive, most of whom are nonworkers, transportation is a difficult and expensive problem. Many persons are forced to resort to taxis; in some areas, taxis are patronized more by the poor than the nonpoor. Where transportation deficiencies result from archaic transit routes and scheduling, remedies may lie in introduction of new services or modification of existing services. Another possibility for nonworkers is reduction of fares for off-peak daytime service when the incremental cost of providing the service is relatively low. While off-peak reductions are common in prices of other services (including airline and rail transportation, theaters, and restaurants), they are seldom found in transit fare systems, because off-peak fare reduction ordinarily does not attract sufficient additional patronage to offset revenue losses resulting from reductions. This may be due partly to the fact that off-peak services usually are grossly inferior.

Jitney-type services, falling between conventional bus and individual taxi service, might contribute significantly toward meeting transportation needs. They are widely used in many foreign and a few

American cities, but unfortunately have been frozen out by unions and by taxi and transit operators. The above-described "dial-a-bus" concept, a sophisticated and more efficient version of the jitney, is the only technological innovation now in sight which has much potential for meeting the transportation needs of low-income groups.

The long-run solution for the journey-to-work problem, and for other transportation problems of low-income groups, may lie in urban planning and design rather than in transportation facilities. Either jobs should be moved closer to people, or low-income housing should be moved closer to jobs. The location of low-income housing and other activity centers (particularly shopping, recreation, and schools) should be planned to reduce transportation requirements.

Locating large numbers of new jobs in ghetto areas is likely to be costly and impracticable, and moving ghetto residents closer to suburban job opportunities runs into desperate opposition by middle- and working-class suburbanites. Such problems may be solved over time (as in the case of other immigrants) by increasing productivity and rising cultural status of presently "disadvantaged" people. But in the meantime, measures to facilitate the transportation of ghetto residents to jobs, and provide inexpensive transportation for the low-income aged and others not in the labor force, should be regarded as a form of public assistance. Congress, in the Urban Transportation Act of 1970, expressed particular concern about transportation for the elderly, and directed that a study be made of this subject.

This raises the question of whether there should be direct subsidies to poor people, such as the aged, at least to provide access to special services. Direct subsidies have the disadvantage of requiring means tests, which impose both indignities on the poor and administrative burdens on public agencies; but it is not easy to think of practicable alternatives. For groups easily identified without means tests, such as the aged and the crippled, special subsidies are less of a problem.

Transportation Investment and Metropolitan Development Trends

Conventional-type rail systems are designed primarily to haul workers to and from the high-density business districts of large cities. Arguments for improving and extending existing systems, and for building new ones, rest on the assumption that such improvements are necessary for maintaining and expanding managerial and related office functions (the office industries of large cities). Common observation suggests that powerful centripetal forces operate to bring such occupations together. There is, on the other hand, a school of thought which holds that advancing communications technology will diminish the strength of these forces and will produce less, rather than more, centralization.

As yet there is no convincing evidence (though some indications are appearing) that the central-city obsolescence thesis applies to urban areas based in already established central cities with long-standing patterns, traditions, institutions, monuments, and cultural centers, and having vast amounts of capital already sunk in a way of life. In these centers, technology is not a one-way force toward decentralization; indeed, some technological devices—the skyscraper, the high-speed elevator, and mass transportation systems—are agents of centralization. New concepts of design have begun to appear which offer, instead of decentralization, highly concentrated areas containing residential, recreational, shopping, school, and office activities juxtaposed in arrangements which make round-the-clock use of scarce land.

The concept underlying most of the existing and proposed rail transit is the radial-type layout, linking suburbs to the central business district, a concept little changed since the old days of the large-city commuter rail systems of the late nineteenth century. To the extent that such systems have a substantial effect, it will be to encourage centralization of activities which inherently tend to cluster together. Large new urban mass transit systems now under construction, or on the drawing boards, have the specific design objective of preserving and expanding the role of already existing large central cities in metropolitan regions. Thus the San Francisco Bay Area's rapid transit (BART) system, which will begin operating in 1972, represents an attempt to obtain as much regional growth as possible for the central city. This objective of San Francisco's businessmen was not supported by their counterparts in San Mateo County to the south, who had aspirations of capturing for their own area the development which, given the transit system, might locate in the central city. On the other hand, communities on the east side of the Bay, in Contra Costa and Alameda Counties, opted for the system in expectation that it would promote their own area development.

Since the decision was taken, a number of construction projects, mainly office buildings, have gone forward in San Francisco, transforming the famed skyline. We do not know how much of this development would have been initiated in the absence of the decision to build the rail system, but even assuming that BART did promote the new skyline, we still have no basis for judging whether the region will be a better place than it would have been if some of the employment centers had located elsewhere. The office-building boom may be choked off by rising protests from those who believe that the sky-scrapers are desecrating the San Francisco urbanscape and overcongesting the downtown area. The power of such a movement should not be taken lightly in a city which forced the abandonment of freeway construction, leaving several freeway extensions virtually hanging in mid-air, because of the aesthetic damage that (it was felt) freeways were doing to the city.

New rail transit systems nowadays come at costs which seem very high, until one compares their cost with that of additional highways to do the same job. The first phase of the San Francisco BART system will have cost approximately $1.5 billion by the time service begins, and the projected costs of the Washington, D.C., area rail transit system, just getting underway, are now up to $3 billion (from $500 million in 1958). Notwithstanding the high cost, if the federal government would supply matching grants on the scale contemplated by the Mass Transportation Act of 1964 which authorized federal assistance of up to 75 percent of construction costs, at least a half-dozen cities where rail transit has strong support (Seattle, Baltimore, Los Angeles, Atlanta, St. Louis, Pittsburgh) would probably get new systems underway within the next few years. (The San Francisco area was remarkable in that three counties undertook to finance the initial cost of BART with no assurance of federal assistance; the federal government has in fact contributed less than 5 percent of the prospective cost.)

Recent trends, on the other hand, suggest that the preponderance of population growth around large central cities will locate in ever expanding peripheries. Extrapolation of trends, though a hazardous game, indicates that we can look for little further increase in large central-city daytime or nighttime population, even in central cities that remain economically vigorous, and that overall densities of metropolitan areas will continue to decline. Los Angeles and other newer cities of the southwest, it is suggested, are prototypes of new cities of the future—low density, many central nodes instead of one concentrated business district, heavy dependence on private autos, and preservation of a high proportion of space for automobile movement and storage. The decentralization which makes for such heavy dependence on automobiles and which increases the average length of trips has, of course, resulted in these cities being smothered in auto-generated smog. The effects of air pollution, which have only begun to be appreciated in the last decade, are so catastrophic that this fact alone might significantly modify the shape of future cities in the absence of drastic improvement in the power plants of automobiles. If such improvement (now mandated by Congress) materializes, one may expect to see heavy dependence on the traveler-operated automobile for the foreseeable future.

TRADEOFFS

The above discussion suggests that the quality of urban transportation, and the amount of transportation facilities required, are more matters of land-use planning and development and good urban design than they are of transportation technologies and systems. Thus funds which might otherwise be spent on transportation might be spent more economically for locating residential centers close to employment centers. Such tradeoffs could be facilitated by broadening concepts of what constitutes "legitimate" uses of earmarked highway-user revenues. Until recently, the concept has been that they should be used only for building highways as cheaply as possible, meaning that funds could not be applied to such purposes as avoiding damage to existing community and aesthetic values, putting routes underground through high-density areas, or even for traffic signaling and maintenance, and certainly not for housing or recreation. This limited concept, which has little substance either in equity or economics, has begun to crumble and we can expect that concepts of "legitimate uses" will continue to expand over time. The first great break will be when highway user funds are permitted to be used for nonhighway transit, on grounds that the overall costs of meeting travel demands will be decreased thereby. There are already several instances of such "diversion." Thus, the BART tunnel under San Francisco Bay is being financed by tolls from the Bay Bridge, though the California Automobile Association was nearly excommunicated for approving such a heresy. The New York Metropolitan Transportation Authority will be able to draw on revenues from its tunnels and bridges to provide financial assistance to transit.

Other means of improving transportation, or simplifying transportation requirements, include such simple matters of urban design as:

1. Separating vehicular and pedestrian traffic, and facilitating pedestrian circulation. The principle of the enclosed pedestrian mall lined with shops is becoming increasingly popular, and open-air pedestrian malls are common in outlying shopping centers and some downtown shopping areas. Minneapolis reserves Nicollet Avenue for pedestrians and buses, and is developing a system to allow pedestrians to circulate, away from weather and traffic, among major downtown buildings.
2. Requiring offstreet loading facilities in buildings, particularly new buildings, and offstreet parking space for tenants where the existing street system will accommodate the traffic (frequently it will not).
3. Requiring that new buildings be located where they can be adequately served by existing or planned transportation facilities; in other words, providing a workable balance between the capacities of vertical and horizontal transportation systems.
4. Providing parking lots in the periphery of central office districts for private automobiles, with fast convenient public transportation between lots and key points in the central area. Here we badly need devices for moving large volumes of people horizontally—"horizontal elevators." Horizontal transport is still limited to such crude forms as buses on congested streets and the somewhat swifter rail transit systems where routes happen to coincide with travel desire lines. More efficient systems, such as those implying the moving belt principle, are in advanced design stages but have been used only in elementary applications and in small areas (as moving sidewalks in airports).
5. In general, making the transportation system a part of overall urban design in the same way in which elevators are part of a building plan.

The above suggestions represent familiar design principles most of which have been followed, at least to a degree, by various cities in the United States. Other examples might be mentioned: Philadelphia's Penn Center, New York's Radio City and Grand Central Station, Montreal's Ville Ste. Marie—all successful integrations of transportation facilities and building design.

Transportation and Better Urban Development

By the year 2000, the nation's population will have increased by seventy-five to one hundred million persons. The increase will all be living in urban areas, along with another twenty-five million or so which will shift from rural or semi-urban to urban lifestyles. Most of the urban population, it is projected, will be concentrated in several great megalopolitan strips (San Francisco to San Diego, Milwaukee to Buffalo and Pittsburgh, Boston to Norfolk, Jacksonville to Miami, and part of the Gulf Coast) and a dozen or so large metropolitan centers (Kansas City, Denver, St. Louis, the Twin Cities, for example). But the concentrations will be at lower densities than have hitherto prevailed in most urban centers.

As the nation proceeds to build the equivalent of perhaps 150 more cities the size of Cleveland, and with rebuilding much of the cities which already exist, it is faced with the problems of how to build better, to achieve economic efficiency and aesthetic quality within the confines of the market system, where much of the planning and most of the construction will be done by private firms.

Transportation and Orderly Urban Development

There will be enormous sums spent on highways in and around cities over the next decade—this much is assured by the amount of earmarked highway-user tax proceeds that will be available—and action taken by Congress in the Transportation Act of 1970 indicates that something more than crumbs will be tossed to the perennial Cinderella, mass transit. To date there has been little thought given to how such funds might be used to improve the economic efficiency and aesthetic quality of urban development.

A decade ago, many planners held that transportation systems are a principal determinant of urban configuration. Today it is recognized that transportation is only one of several tools which, to be effective, must be implements of a larger planning process predicated in turn on a clear notion of what kinds of cities the nation wants. Thus far we have been getting mainly unpatterned development—urban sprawl —which tends to be both inefficient and ugly and which, incidentally, maximizes transportation requirements because of the poor relationship in space of various activity centers.

The underlying principle of planned urban development has been stated by a noted American planner, Catherine Bauer Wurster, as follows:

> Instead of scattering houses, factories, shops, offices and services all over the landscape, we should pull them together into compact cities, with adjacent open space saved for recreation, agriculture and general amenity. There would be disagreement as to ideal city size, but suitable housing for a cross-section population should be provided, with more emphasis on row houses and garden apartments. A variety of employment opportuni-

ties should be encouraged, as well as a bona fide urban center. The cities would be readily accessible to each other and to the central city; indeed, such a pattern would favor a mass transit system if it is needed. The central city would normally provide certain region-wide services, and its population should also become better balanced.[4]

The principle has been widely applied in some European countries, and in a few new towns in the United States, notably Columbia, Maryland, which is being financed, planned, and constructed by private enterprise. Columbia employs many important design principles, such as a balance between employment and resident workers; a system of villages each of which provides school, shopping, recreation and other facilities in a larger urban hierarchy which reduces the average length of trips required to reach major activity centers; and an internal circulation system which separates local roads from arterials and pedestrian from vehicular traffic.

Unfortunately, no urban region in the nation yet possesses the planning and administrative machinery, let alone public backing, needed to implement visions of development like that exemplified by Columbia, or a metropolitan development plan such as the Year-2000 Plan proposed for the Washington, D.C., region a decade ago by the National Capital Planning Commission. Little recognition has been given to the possibilities of implementing such principles by the two federal agencies most concerned, the Departments of Transportation and of Housing and Urban Development. A few states, notably New York with its Urban Development Corporation, are beginning to take tentative steps toward improving tomorrow's new cities.

Postscript

To recognize that institutional obstacles to better urban planning and development are formidable is not to conclude that they will continue blocking improvement.

Urban transportation is not an end in itself, it is a means of promoting other objectives such as linking urban families to work, schools, shopping centers, friends, and recreation. The greatest improvements in urban transportation can come from urban design rather than from constructing more roads and rails and highways to run on. The savings potential is enormous—in the course of building

[4] Catherine Bauer Wurster, "Form and Structure of the Future Urban Complex," in Lowdon Wingo, ed., *Cities and Space* (Johns Hopkins Press, 1963).

new cities and rebuilding old ones in the next three decades, something in the magnitude of $3 trillion will be spent for public facilities, of which 30 to 40 percent will be for transportation. But the better design, which can reduce transportation requirements and free more funds for activities served by transportation, requires understanding by all—bankers, real estate developers, industrialists, governmental officials, the public—of the principles involved.

Because transportation is essential to most other urban activities, it has important social benefits along with social costs which frequently are not taken into account. These warrant an economic approach to prices and subsidies of a far more systematic nature than that provided by the present hodgepodge.

Because the price system gives inadequate help in evaluating consumer demand, and hence in investment decisions, the role of planning is central. But information for adequate planning is not now available, and in any event there are many uncertainties—uncertainty respecting the impact of transportation on urban development, difficulties of projecting transportation demands, and uncertainty about future technological developments in transportation and communications.

Transportation planning, therefore, must rely heavily on strategies to cope with uncertainty. The first strategy is to reduce risk by proceeding incrementally and experimentally. Specifics include methods of increasing highway capacity by increasing throughput of people. An appropriate pricing policy could help all highway users even though it is difficult to persuade users of this beforehand. There are many methods of improving bus service, among them experimenting with demand-activated taxi-buses and expediting bus movement.

But incrementalism pursued too far is, in effect, a policy of letting transportation be guided by development. If transportation is to help *shape* development, large capital outlays will be required in specific situations, and these necessitate taking high risks, but this is sensible if the potential gains are commensurately high. In some cities, rapid transit development is an example of high-risk, potentially high-gain, projects. But more important, this level of transportation planning must be integrated with other aspects of urban development planning in order to increase the potential yield of each major investment input and reduce the risk of failure.

Ernest W. Williams, Jr.

Editor's Postscript

Our survey has been confined to domestic transportation, intercity and urban. It has focused principally upon public policy as it affects the commercial transportation industries, the facilities which they employ, and their relationship to private operations both in the transport of freight and the movement of passengers. It is in public policy that changes can conceivably be made, presuming that a consensus can be developed in respect of the direction and major features of such change. Our authors have sought to identify what objectives should guide transport policy in the national interest, to identify problems that have arisen under recent policy, to trace the consequences (especially the costs) of present policy, and to suggest directions for change. Their examination of the horizon of technology suggests only limited impact from those developments which may begin to come to bear in the decade of the seventies.

THE THRUST OF THE ARGUMENT

The authors are not unanimous either in their diagnosis of problems or their prescriptions for improvement. A larger group of analysts would display even greater diversity. Yet there is substantial consensus that improved efficiency is a major goal to be sought in intercity freight transport, that present regulatory policy as it has been administered is a major source of inefficiency, and that uncoordinated government investment in transport infrastructure contributes to the same end. The two are not unrelated and a revised regulatory policy, by its effects upon traffic allocation, is expected to influence investment policies in the appropriate direction. User charges, upon a basis more fully compensatory to the governments and more equitable in their impact upon classes of user, should reinforce that tendency.

National goals in intercity passenger transport are seen in a somewhat different light, the continued maintenance of a wide range of alternatives for the passenger appearing to have primacy over simple efficiency. Safety and environmental factors clearly require high priority. Apart from the need to move rapidly in the development of new alternatives in the congested corridors, regulatory policy appears to require reform, especially in air transport. There regulation appears to have restricted service and price alternatives open to the passenger, to have confined the service to a limited clientele, and to have prevented price from operating effectively upon the development of capacity and the shaping of the route structures. Financial crisis is impending in air transport as in a segment of the rail industry. In both instances regulatory policy is seen as one of the causes and as a bar to alleviation.

The problem of urban transport is of greater complexity than that of intercity transport, since its nature differs from one city to another and transport development must be intimately tied to comprehensive urban planning. Aesthetic and environmental factors are of far greater importance. And the fragmented governmental structure stands in the way of effective policy development and implementation. The long-term neglect of public transit, the concentration of investment on arteries feeding in and out to the neglect of those of internal circulation, and the undisciplined scattering in land-use development together led inevitably to the present dependence upon the automobile, to congestion, and to the immobilization of large sectors of the population.

No pending change in transport technology will provide a magical solution. Rail mass transit will rarely contribute to alleviation of the more pressing problems. Economic pricing of the use of city streets, particularly peak-period pricing in the more congested areas, might well contribute more than any other single measure to the relief of present problems. It may be a necessary prerequisite to the revival of effective public transit which, most often, will utilize the bus upon established routes and such variants as the dial-a-bus concept. But longer-range solutions are probably not transport solutions, but a restructuring of major urban complexes to bring residences closer to work and recreation and to facilitate the coordination of urban freight movements which today grossly burden the freight carriers.

PUBLIC INVESTMENT AND USER CHARGES

Massive public investment has characterized transport development. That investment has been out of balance, overemphasizing highway development, indulging in marginal waterway facilities construction, failing to keep airports and air traffic control abreast of requirements, and almost wholly neglecting the rail industry despite growing obsolescence and long-standing inadequacies in the freight car supply. Urban transport requirements, too, have been largely neglected. Only recently has some redressment of priorities begun to appear. The Department of Transportation, by design of the enabling legislation, lacks authority in respect of inland and coastal waterway development and merchant marine policy. Limited progress has been made in reducing the imbalance in programs that are within its jurisdiction. Cost-benefit analysis needs improvement, especially to take account of environmental issues and to enable valid appraisal of alternatives, e.g., rail *versus* highway development. The greatly weakened condition of a large portion of the railroad industry presents critical issues for the Congress, since additional public financial support in some form appears essential.

Those of our authors who advocate reduced regulation and increased reliance upon competitive forces in transport recognize that inadequacies in the user-charge structure upset competitive balance and encourage the misallocation of traffic. While progress has been made, except in respect of inland waterways which remain free of user charges, inequities are still found in highway user charges. There is disagreement about the importance of such inequities, but agreement in principle that they should be eliminated. It is plain that both this problem and that of achieving balanced public investment require legislative action by Congress and the state legislatures.

THE ROUTE TO REGULATORY REFORM

Regulatory reform is seen as essential and, perhaps, as entitled to primacy of consideration. This is especially true, because at no time since the passage of the Act to Regulate Commerce in 1887 has criticism of the regulatory agencies, and especially of the Interstate Commerce Commission, been so sharp and indiscriminate. The solution of our problems in this area will not be found in repeal of the statutes and abolition of the administrative agencies. Transport is an industry that has peculiar characteristics that distinguish it from manufacturing, other production industries, and even most service industries. Separate statutory and administrative treatment are necessary.

Common carrier service, contemplating regular operations held out to the general public at published rates, is an essential. This requires continued statutory provision for uniform bills of lading incorporating carriers' service obligations and minimum liability. If we are to have nationwide service, carriers must join in through routes, make joint rates, agree upon the divisions thereof, and use rate-publishing agencies to avoid undue tariff complexity. All of these require a specific statutory plan. Though the present plan may be capable of improvement, it provides a sound foundation. Common-law jurisdiction in the United States is vested in the state courts and could provide no adequate substitute for a uniform federal statute applicable to interstate commerce.

REGULATION OF ENTRY, ABANDONMENT, AND MERGER

While a separate statute and administrative jurisdiction appear essential, it does not follow that the substance of economic regulation should remain unchanged. The principal thrust of deregulation proposals has concerned rate regulation and control of entry. Both ought, clearly, to be reexamined.

There is no entry control for pipe lines; that for railroads was not enacted until 1920 when the rail system had reached the height of its development. In the period 1935–40, however, entry control was extended to motor, air, and water carriers. In the motor carrier business it has been restrictively applied both as respects commodity authority and route flexibility. A larger case load is generated in this area than in any other, but control of entry appears to serve no public purpose. Instead it fractionates the industry, generates unnecessary cost, creates endless and expensive dispute on the borders between regulated and exempt transportation, compels severe restriction of private carrier operations, and protects inefficient carriers from the advent of new competitors. Hence it has come under attack by economists as a major source of inefficiency in transport.

Merger or acquisition of control among regulated carriers also requires application and prior approval. Nothing in the economic characteristics of motor or water transportation appears to require such control. Any undue concentration of market power which new entries failed to check if present entry controls were removed could be amply policed under the antitrust statutes. Nor is there any persuasive reason why common carriers of any type should be confined to that area to the exclusion of contract operation.

The railroad case is substantially different. Control of entry is now of little consequence, since the likelihood of any major line construction is minimal. The restraint that has been exercised upon abandonment, however, and the limited willingness of rail management to propose significant trimming of line mileage have been serious obstructions to desirable disinvestment in an industry that has large excess line capacity. An affirmative program designed to secure substantial disinvestment through abandonment seems essential, but the present statute lacks any expression of such a policy. The railroad merger program is in serious disarray. The cost of a major merger proceeding in time and money is grossly excessive. The case-by-case approach of the Commission leads to decisions that foreclose desirable alternatives. Penn Central was an almost inevitable result of two prior decisions in each of which the Commission refused to broaden the record and take a look at the entire picture in the northeast.

It is not at all clear how far rail merger should proceed or according to what pattern. The natural monopoly characteristic inherent in the rail technology strongly suggests regional monopolies, but it is unclear what size and complexity of rail system can be effectively managed. It is equally unclear what advantages can be secured from merger in the face of the inflexible labor arrangements that have attended most recent mergers. The right to merge has been bought in part by concessions to labor and in part by deferral of desirable coordinations and abandonments. In the circumstances a moratorium appears appropriate while disinvestment is pushed, price-making restraints are relaxed, and an optimum scheme of merger is studied. In any event, jurisdiction should remain with the Interstate Commerce Commission and the statute should ultimately be amended to provide an affirmative and comprehensive policy.

REGULATION OF RATES

Greater latitude in rate-making is sought by the railroads and by a number of the airlines. It is opposed by the regulated motor common carriers and by the water carriers. It is not looked upon with great favor by the organized community of shippers. The line-up of carrier interests is explained by the fact that the pattern of rate regulation in force since 1935 has worked generally to the advantage of motor and water carriers while it has deprived the railroads of the opportunity to reflect their cost advantage in rates. Twelve years of litigation concerning the meaning of the 1958 amendment to the rule of rate making has left the position essentially where it was prior to that date. Serious misallocation of traffic among modes has occurred and the shipping public has been denied the advantage of service at cost-based rates upon a wide spectrum of traffic. The value-of-service rate structure has retreated slowly in the face of competitive pressure, buttressed by wont and custom and the admonition of the statute to preserve the rate structure. Regulated carriers have been protected in considerable measure against their regulated competitors, but the whole regulated industry has suffered attrition from the sallies of the 50 percent of transport that is unregulated.

Except in the rail and pipe-line industries there appears to be no necessity to retain the power to fix maximum rates. The other forms are capable of competitive organization and, with rare exception, alternatives open to shippers will protect against carrier exactions. Even in the rail industry the competition from other modes as well as widespread commercial competition afford significant protection. The power to suspend increased rates and to control large segments of the rate structure through outstanding maximum rate orders compel irrational across-the-board general rate increases during inflation. The difficulty of agreeing upon such a step and the inevitable prolonged regulatory proceeding greatly defer the time when significant revenue relief can be secured. The carriers have been seriously weakened by regulatory lag and the rate level is higher than it might have been given a more prompt and selective adjustment to inflationary circumstances. A return to the posture of 1906 might be desirable—no suspension of increases, but a right of the shipper to complain in respect of rates thought to be unlawfully high after they are in effect and a power to prescribe maximum rates in the stead of any found unlawful.

No minimum-rate control exists with respect to pipe lines, but it has been applied to all other regulated forms of transport. The suspension of reduced rates is the principal means by which a sharing of traffic and the protection of competitors have been secured. Motor and water carriers rarely have the economic strength to indulge in prolonged predatory price-cutting, and the use of suspension to discipline the more efficient, progressive, or specialized carriers is economically undesirable. If suspension is retained for reduced rail rates, a step not clearly necessary, it ought to be strictly limited to rates whose level gives evidence of being, on average, below variable cost. A rule similar to the Canadian which regards rates below variable cost as unlawful might be provided across the board but, in the ordinary circumstance, to be applied only upon complaint in respect of rates already in effect. Under no other circumstances ought the minimum-rate power come to bear.

Under these more circumscribed powers of rate regulation, protection would remain for shippers in the rare instances where monopoly powers may still exist and for carriers who might be faced with overt predatory attack or irrational behavior by competitors. Rate litigation would be vastly reduced and, accordingly, expedited. Carriers could be expected to exercise initiative to raise the large body of rates presently at a noncompensatory level and to protect their profitable traffic by appropriate competitive adjustments.

Discrimination is open principally to the rail carriers as long as excess line capacity exists in the industry and marginal costs lie below average costs. Freedom to raise noncompensatory rates and to adjust high rates to a more competitive level should reduce the range of discrimination. Nevertheless it would appear desirable to retain the present statutory rules with respect to discrimination both in rates and service, corrective power to be exercised upon a finding of unlawfulness following complaint. These rules have been devised to deal with the peculiar conditions of transportation; to repeal them would open the industries to the risk of Robinson-Patman application, a step that would be destructive of competitive behavior in transport and productive of litigation far exceeding anything encountered under the present statutory plan.

TRANSPORT AND ANTITRUST

Apart from mergers, already discussed, the principal issues of antitrust arise in the area of rate making. Group rate making under section 5a of the Interstate Commerce Act is the pattern of the regulated domestic transport industries, other than air. There is little doubt that the practice has greatly circumscribed competitive rate-making activity, with the help of the suspension power to frustrate independent actions. It has helped to preserve the traditional rate structure, enhanced the exposure of regulated carriers to unregulated competition, and greatly slowed the process of rate adjustment to changing circumstances. Yet the practice is supported not only by the carriers, but by the organized shippers. The latter find the docketing and hearing procedures of the rate bureaus advantageous in providing notice of rate changes in contemplation which might affect them or their competitors. They value the opportunity to influence the outcome at the level of the rate bureau prior to publication, where a rate change may be pending longer than before the Commission if suspended.

It is plain that carriers must agree upon joint rates, probably on a group basis. Similarly the statute must provide for publication of prospective rates, an action which would apparently be barred without antitrust exemption. Finally the use of publishing agents must be authorized. Some of our authors would attempt to draw a line at this point, repealing the Reed-Bulwinkle Amendment and eliminating antitrust exemption for group consideration of rates that are local to the lines proposing them.

STATUTORY AMENDMENT

While it appears that little modification of present law, other than a revision of the declaration of policy in the Interstate Commerce Act, would be necessary to permit application of appropriate economic tests in the regulation of rates, the long administrative history of contrary behavior counsels need for amendment of the statute in respect of its suspension provisions and the area of discretion for exercise of the minimum and maximum rate powers. Likewise if merger and entry controls are to be shaped in the direction suggested above, the statutes must be revised. Most of the states also regulate transportation more or less comprehensively and the continuance of their present plans of regulation would, in some measure, defeat the objectives stated for federal reform. What appears of largest importance is to move in the indicated direction as rapidly as acceptance can be secured for such a course. Any change will affect vested interests which derive from traditional policy and will be vigorously opposed.

If the analysis offered is correct, substantial advantage has accrued to various carrier groups which are founded not entirely on their economic characteristics but partly on artificial circumstances created by regulatory policy. Similarly location decisions in the industrial and commercial sectors of the economy have been influenced by long-standing practices which, if not created by regulation, at least had the sanction of regulatory policy. Whether and how fast to alter the structure will depend not only upon expectation of beneficial effects to the nation, but also upon an appraisal of the burden and cost of adjustments which any such change will induce.

The present state of the transportation industries has been substantially shaped by government policies. Their future character will, in major degree, be determined by what is done to improve, augment, and revise those policies. The health of the commercial transportation industries, in general, has been deteriorating and there is little to suggest early fundamental improvement. The time is ripe for reappraisal.

Index

Abandonments, rail service, 71, 96
Act to Regulate Commerce (1887), 63, 199
Airline industry, 32, 61, 74, 75, 80, 81, 144
  cargo operations, 54
  earnings and income, 85, 86, 87
  investments in, 93
  rates, 32, 48, 131
  safety, 31
  transportation technology, 30, 56, 64
  user charges, 89, 90
Ames brothers, 95
Antitrust policies, application to transport, 144–48
Association of American Railroads, 102, 111
Auto and bus transportation, 46
Auto–highway system, 51
Automated vehicle systems, 52
Automatic vehicle monitoring systems (AVM), 181–82, 183
Automobiles, 96
  and pollution, 51
  and urban development, 38, 39

Barge lines, 131, 133, 134, 135, 136, 138, 161
Board of Transportation Investigation and Research, 7, 94

Boston Metropolitan Transportation Authority (MTA), 186
Bretey, Pierre R., 97
Bureau of Public Roads, 151

California Automobiles Association, 192
Canada, 55
  plan of regulation, 141–44
Car pools, 188
Carriers, 4, 5, 125, 126
Chicago Area Transportation Study, 163
Civil Aeronautics Act of 1938, 64
Civil Aeronautics Board (CAB), 33, 70, 86, 87, 106, 148, 160
Clayton Antitrust Act (1914), 73, 74
Commerce, Department of, 49n
Common carriers, 17, 18, 27, 28, 63, 64, 65, 66, 67, 68, 69, 71, 96, 200, 201
Commuters, 174, 178–79, 188
Competitive market forces, 26
Computers, 54
Congestion, 46, 47, 177, 178
  and pricing, 180–82
Conglomerate form of business organization, 77, 78
Congress, 7, 15, 20, 31, 72, 79, 88, 90, 94, 97, 106, 133, 141, 143, 150, 151, 157, 171, 186, 189, 194, 199 (see also Act to Regulate Commerce of 1887; Clayton Antitrust Act of 1914; Interstate

Congress (*cont.*)
 Commerce Act of 1887; Interstate
 Commerce Commission; Mass Trans-
 portation Act of 1964; Motor Carrier
 Act of 1935; National Transportation
 Act of 1967; Public Utility Holding
 Company Act of 1935; Rail Passen-
 ger Service Act of 1970; Railway
 Labor Act of 1934; Reed–Bulwinkle
 Act of 1948; Robinson–Patman Act
 of 1936; Sherman Antitrust Act of
 1890; Tax Reform Act of 1969;
 Transportation Acts of 1920, 1940,
 1958, 1970; Urban Transportation
 Act of 1970)
Conventional takeoff and landing
 (CTOL), 49
Cost–benefit analysis, 81
Cross-Florida Canal, 34

Darmstadter, 61, 72, 73
Demand-activated transit, 51
Demand–supply equation, 45
Dial-a-bus, 183, 189
Dial-a-Ride Service, 53
Dividend policies, rail, 100–102
Doyle Committee, 85, 88, 90
Durant, Thomas C., 95

"Effect of the Ghetto on the Distribution
 and Level of Nonwhite Employment
 in Urban Areas, The" (Kain), 174n
Eisenhower cabinet committee report
 (1955), 141
Entry control, 68, 70, 71, 200, 204
Environmental damage (*see* Pollution)

Federal Highway Administration, 180
Federal Interstate Highway Program, 174
Federal Maritime Commission, 148
Federal Trade Commission, 60
Fishy-back service, 22
Freight rates, 12, 17, 18, 22, 26
Freight transportation, 6, 12, 13, 14, 25,
 27, 32, 112
 dilemma of, 57n
Friedlaender, Ann E., 57n

Gould, Jay, 95
Great Britain, 50, 141
Great Depression, 64, 96
Gross National Product (GNP), 42, 43n,
 44n

Hennis motor common carrier, 1
Highway Research Board, 151
Hilton, Harbison, Friedlaender, and
 Wilson, 115
Hines, Walker D., 7
Holding companies, 78, 99
Housing and Urban Development, De-
 partment of, 182, 195
Housing discrimination, 38
Huntington, Collis P., 95

Infrastructure, 79, 80, 81, 82
Inland water traffic, 98 (*see also* Rail-
 roads)
Institute of Public Administration, 182
Intercity transportation, 29, 33, 35, 39,
 41, 56, 64, 91–93, 96, 155–68 *passim*
 freight, 29, 36, 39, 41, 42, 53, 56, 65, 66,
 115, 155
 passenger, 30, 36, 42, 49, 65
Intercity travel, 31
Intercity travel market, 42
Interface, urban and intercity, 155–68
 passim
Intermodal competition, 25, 60, 80, 134,
 137, 141, 143, 146
Intermodal ownership, 76
Intermodal service, 54
Interstate Commerce Act (1887), 4, 99,
 119, 120, 132, 141, 143, 145, 203, 204
Interstate Commerce Commission (ICC),
 6, 15, 20, 23, 28, 31, 61, 65, 69, 70, 72,
 73, 78, 87, 88, 92–96, 98, 101, 106,
 116, 118, 119–25, 130, 132–34, 137,
 142, 143–44, 145, 146, 147, 148, 149,
 199–201, 204
 regulatory policies, 139–40
 statutory policies, 140–41
Interstate highway system, 54, 156, 157
Intramodal competition, 62, 134, 147

Japanese National Railways, 50

Job discrimination, 38

Jobs and Housing: A Study of Employment and Housing Opportunities for Racial Minorities in Surburban Areas of the New York Metropolitan Region (National Committee against Discrimination in Housing), 174n

Johnson, Lyndon B., 7

Justice, Department of, 5, 59

Kain, John F., 174n

Kennedy, John F., 7, 28

Kennedy Airport, 32

London–Manchester Service (*see* Great Britain)

Los Angeles Riots, Governor's Commission on the, 174n

McCone report (*see* Watts, riots [1965])

McGinnis, Patrick B., 100

Malthus's law, traffic analogue to, 176–77

Marine container operations, 54

Mass Transportation Act of 1964, 191

Mergers, 61, 72, 73, 132, 200, 201, 204

Chicago, Milwaukee, and North Western, 61, 72

Metroliner rail service, 50

Metropolitan development, trends in, 189–96

Metropolitan Transportation Authority, New York, 192

Meyer and Associates, 115

Miller, Rene, 49n

Monopoly, aspects of in domestic transportation, 64, 68, 69, 71, 73, 76, 92, 136, 137, 138

Monopoly theory, 62

Motor Carrier Act of 1935, 64, 118

Motor carriers, 2, 3, 61, 69, 71, 73, 74, 75, 80, 86, 87, 93, 120, 144, 148, 158, 161, 167, 202

Motor transport, 6, 64, 79

Nathan, Robert R., 93

National Capital Planning Commission, 195

National Capital Transportation Agency, 185

National Committee Against Discrimination in Housing, 174n

National Economic Projection Series, 84

National Planning Association, 84

National Resources Planning Board, 7

National Transportation Act of 1967, 136–37, 142

National transportation policy, 85, 90, 132, 139, 140–41, 143

Nelson, James C., 115

Netherlands, 141

New Haven Railroad, 100, 101

New Tokaido Line, 50

New York Central Railroad, 100

New York City Planning Commission, 178

Nixon, Richard M., 7, 144

Nonfreight trucking, 45

Nontransportation pollutants, 35

Northern Securities case (1904), 72

O'Hare Airport, 32

Overmyer Plan, 128–29

Owen, Wilfred, 35, 172

Ownership, government, 107–13

Pacific Northwest Grain case (1958), 136

Pacific Southwest Airways, 70

Panama Canal, 117, 151

Pan American Airways, 70

Parkinson's law, traffic analogue to, 176–77

Passenger transport, 12, 56, 75

Penn Central, 1, 3, 7, 20, 73, 76, 78, 79, 98, 100, 101, 103, 128, 201

Piggyback service, 22, 53, 54, 99, 128, 149, 158, 159, 164, 166

Pipelines, 61, 70, 79, 80, 81, 91, 92, 116, 120, 133–34, 153, 200, 202

Plumb Plan, 7

Pollution, 2, 11, 34, 35, 46, 51, 105, 117, 124, 152, 171, 175, 192
Port of New York Authority, 165, 167
Price policies, on domestic transportation, 115–54
Private ownership, 80, 91, 119, 126
Public facilities, 39, 105, 116
Public policy, 61, 63, 64, 71, 103–4
Public transit, 38, 125, 126, 153
Public transportation, 51, 139, 150
  and low-income needs, 187–89
Public utilities, 6, 70, 72, 74, 78, 81
Public Utility Holding Company Act of 1935, 79
Public Works Administration (PWA), 94

Rail freight service, 53
Rail Passenger Service Act of 1970, 109
Railpax, 20, 71, 156
Railroads, 2, 3, 6, 61, 64, 79, 80, 81, 85, 87, 91, 92–96, 98, 116, 120, 122, 127–30, 134–36, 144–45, 148, 153, 200
  and consolidation, 72, 75, 76
  and mergers, 5, 18, 28
  and safety, 31
  and stockholders, 78
  and technology, 96
Railroads, Class I, 88, 89, 94, 100, 101, 102, 116
Rail tonnage, 98
Rail transit, 37, 54, 72
Rail unions, 7
Railway Express Agency (REA), 158
Railway Guide, 96
Railway Labor Act (1934), 3
Rates, rail, 25, 98, 99
  after World War II, 128–29
  and income tax, 102
  value-of-service, 117–19, 122–24, 127, 134, 140, 145, 202
Reconstruction Finance Corporation, 94
Reed–Bulwinkle Act (1948), 145, 204
Robinson–Patman Act (1936), 146, 203

St. Lawrence Seaway, 117, 151
San Francisco Bay Area Rapid Transit (BART), 183, 185–86, 190–91, 192

Santa Fe Railway, 128
Sawyer Report, 7
Scott, Thomas, 95
Senate Commerce Committee, 85
Sherman Antitrust Act (1890), 72
"Short Haul Inter-Urban Air Systems" (MITRE), 49n
Simpson, Robert, 49n
Smith, Adam, 23
Social costs, of domestic transportation, 117
STOL Aircraft (Short Takeoff and Landing), 48, 49
Subsidies, government, 111, 129
Subsonic aircraft, 48
Subway, New York City, 170
Supreme Court, 5, 15

Taxi system, 38
Tax policies, 115–16
Tax Reform Act (1969), 95
Technology, 50, 51, 53, 55
  and terminals, 160–61
  in urban patterns, 169–71
  (*see also* Railroads; Transportation)
TEKNEKRON, Inc., 182
Terminal Railroad Association of St. Louis, 164
Terminals, productivity decline of, 160–64
Tolls, 117, 125, 131, 150, 151, 153, 180, 181, 192
Tracked Air-Cushion Vehicles (TACV), 50
Traffic congestion, 51
Transportation Act (1920), 61, 64, 72, 95
Transportation Act (1940), 62, 64, 139
Transportation Act (1958), 95
Transportation Act (1970), 171, 194
Transportation companies, 75, 76
Transportation, Department of, 27, 42, 48, 88, 97, 106, 112, 180, 195
Transportation facilities, 25, 90
Transportation industries, 26
Transportation Investment Review Board, 27
Transportation markets, 16

Transportation policy, 32, 39, 40
Transportation safety, 32
Transportation technology, 43, 56
Transport economics, 72
Transport firms, 26
Transport industries, 3
Transport policy, 8, 9, 13, 21
Transport regulation, 4
Transport services, 72
Transport systems, 2, 17, 59, 60
Transport Workers' Union, New York (TWU), 186
Travel patterns, 39
Tri-State Transportation Authority, 158*n*
Truck costs, 25
Trucking company right-of-way costs, 89, 90
Trucking survey, New York, 158, 167
Trucks, 54
Truck transportation, 46, 122, 130–31

United Parcel Service (UPS), 158
Union Passenger Depot (Los Angeles), 69
United States, 55, 84, 90, 92, 95, 141
United States Census of Transportation, 134
Urban design:
  deficiencies of, 177
  directions for improvement, 178–82, 192–93
Urban goods movement, 164–68
Urban Mass Transportation Administration, 180
Urban transportation, 2, 29, 39, 47, 51, 92, 155–68 *passim*
  deficiencies of, 173–77
  freight, 41, 55, 56, 57

Urban Transportation (*cont.*)
  improvements in, 169–73
  and labor disturbances, 186–87
  and new transit systems, 182–86
  and organizational chaos, 175–77
  passengers, 41
  planning, 13
  policy, 36, 38
Urban Transportation Act (1970), 186, 189
User fees, 104, 110, 112, 116, 124–25, 150, 151, 152, 153

Vietnam war, 85, 86,
Violence in the City—An End or a Beginning? (1965), (Governor's Commission on the Los Angeles Riots), 174*n*
VTOL Aircraft (Vertical takeoff and landing), 48, 49, 50, 56

Wage settlements, 4
Water carriers, 6, 54, 61, 70, 71, 73, 74, 75, 80, 93, 121, 130–32, 144, 148, 202
Watts riots (1965), 173
Week's Report of 1955, 7
Williams and Bluestone, 115
Wilson, George W., 132
World War I, 92
World War II, 15, 28, 35, 84, 93
Wurster, Catherine Bauer, 194–95

Year-2000 Plan (*see* National Capital Planning Commission)
Young, Robert R., 100

About The American Assembly

The American Assembly was established by Dwight D. Eisenhower at Columbia University in 1950. It holds nonpartisan meetings and publishes authoritative books to illuminate issues of United States policy.

An affiliate of Columbia, with offices in the Graduate School of Business, the Assembly is a national educational institution incorporated in the State of New York.

The Assembly seeks to provide information, stimulate discussion, and evoke independent conclusions in matters of vital public interest.

AMERICAN ASSEMBLY SESSIONS

At least two national programs are initiated each year. Authorities are retained to write background papers presenting essential data and defining the main issues in each subject.

About sixty men and women representing a broad range of experience, competence, and American leadership meet for several days to discuss the Assembly topic and consider alternatives for national policy.

All Assemblies follow the same procedure. The background papers are sent to participants in advance of the Assembly. The Assembly meets in small groups for four or five lengthy periods. All groups use the same agenda. At the close of these informal sessions, participants adopt in plenary session a final report of findings and recommendations.

Regional, state, and local Assemblies are held following the national session at Arden House. Assemblies have also been held in England, Switzerland, Malaysia, Canada, the Caribbean, South America, Central America, the Philippines, and Japan. Over one hundred institutions have co-sponsored one or more Assemblies.

ARDEN HOUSE

Home of The American Assembly and scene of the national sessions is Arden House, which was given to Columbia University in 1950 by W. Averell Harriman. E. Roland Harriman joined his brother in contributing toward adaptation of the property for conference purposes. The buildings surrounding the land, known as the Harriman Campus of Columbia University, are fifty miles north of New York City.

Arden House is a distinguished conference center. It is self-supporting and operates throughout the year for use by organizations with educational objectives.

AMERICAN ASSEMBLY BOOKS

The background papers for each Assembly program are published in cloth and paperbound editions for use by individuals, libraries, businesses, public agencies, nongovernmental organizations, educational institutions, discussion and service groups. In this way the deliberations of Assembly sessions are continued and extended.

The subjects of Assembly programs to date are:

1951——United States–Western Europe Relationships
1952——Inflation
1953——Economic Security for Americans
1954——The United States' Stake in the United Nations
——The Federal Government Service
1955——United States Agriculture
——The Forty-Eight States
1956——The Representation of the United States Abroad
——The United States and the Far East
1957——International Stability and Progress
——Atoms for Power
1958——The United States and Africa
——United States Monetary Policy
1959——Wages, Prices, Profits, and Productivity
——The United States and Latin America
1960——The Federal Government and Higher Education
——The Secretary of State
——Goals for Americans
1961——Arms Control: Issues for the Public
——Outer Space: Prospects for Man and Society
1962——Automation and Technological Change
——Cultural Affairs and Foreign Relations
1963——The Population Dilemma
——The United States and the Middle East
1964——The United States and Canada
——The Congress and America's Future
1965——The Courts, the Public, and the Law Explosion
——The United States and Japan
1966——State Legislatures in American Politics
——A World of Nuclear Powers?
——The United States and the Philippines
——Challenges to Collective Bargaining
1967——The United States and Eastern Europe
——Ombudsmen for American Government?
1968——Uses of the Seas
——Law in a Changing America
——Overcoming World Hunger

1969——Black Economic Development
——The States and the Urban Crisis
1970——The Health of Americans
——The United States and the Caribbean
1971——The Future of American Transportation
——Collective Bargaining in American Government

Second Editions, Revised:

1962——The United States and the Far East
1963——The United States and Latin America
——The United States and Africa
1964——United States Monetary Policy
1965——The Federal Government Service
——The Representation of the United States Abroad
1968——Cultural Affairs and Foreign Relations
——Outer Space: Prospects for Man and Society
1969——The Population Dilemma